D0434895

BULLY MARKET

My Story of Money and Misogyny at Goldman Sachs

JAMIE FIORE HIGGINS

Simon & Schuster

NEW YORK • LONDON • TORONTO • SYDNEY • NEW DELHI

Simon & Schuster
1230 Avenue of the Americas
New York, NY 10020

Copyright © 2022 by Jamie Fiore Higgins

All rights reserved, including the right to reproduce this book
or portions thereof in any form whatsoever. For information,
address Simon & Schuster Subsidiary Rights Department,
1230 Avenue of the Americas, New York, NY 10020.

First Simon & Schuster hardcover edition August 2022

SIMON & SCHUSTER and colophon are registered
trademarks of Simon & Schuster, Inc.

For information about special discounts for bulk purchases,
please contact Simon & Schuster Special Sales at 1-866-506-1949 or
business@simonandschuster.com.

The Simon & Schuster Speakers Bureau can bring authors to your
live event. For more information or to book an event, contact
the Simon & Schuster Speakers Bureau at 1-866-248-3049
or visit our website at www.simonspeakers.com.

Interior design by Hope Herr-Cardillo

Manufactured in the United States of America

1   3   5   7   9   10   8   6   4   2

Library of Congress Cataloging-in-Publication Data has been applied for.

ISBN 978-1-6680-0102-8
ISBN 978-1-6680-0104-2 (ebook)

For Dan, for everything, forever.

AUTHOR'S NOTE

This book is about my perceptions and experiences as a high-ranking woman in finance. It represents my present recollections and opinions of these experiences over time. I have used journal entries, other written correspondence, and conversations with friends and family to inform the content. I've changed the names and identifying details of the characters outside of my family. Many of the Goldman Sachs individuals referenced are composite characters, no clients are identified, and no business deals or other nonpublic matters are discussed. While all of this did happen to me, the timing of some events has been compressed. Where dialogue appears, my intention was to re-create the essence of the conversations rather than provide verbatim quotes.

INTRODUCTION

2016

"The money hit," I said, pointing to the credit in the online ledger. My husband, Dan, stood over my shoulder as I sat at the kitchen table. This early in the morning, the room was quiet, the kids still asleep. I felt his warm breath on my neck and smelled the coffee brewing on the counter.

"Congratulations," he said. "You ready to leave?" I looked at the new balance in my account. Even though it was late January, it was Christmas morning at Goldman Sachs. Our yearly bonuses had been paid overnight.

This was a huge windfall, a sinful excess. I knew I worked hard, but so did many others. I felt guilty making so much—forty times more than my cleaning person, twenty times more than my kids' teachers, and ten times more than my doctor. My income covered me with a mix of satisfaction and shame.

I also knew my bonus wasn't without strings. Goldman wanted even more from me. The bonus was a carrot and my managing director (MD) title, although I'd earned it years before, was an IOU. Only the top 8 percent of Goldman employees achieved this rank, and the firm expected more from me than ever. I owed them my days, nights, and life. If I chose to stay, today started another year. Another 365 days of hardly seeing my family, another 365 days of working in a culture where those in power created a racist, sexist, and intolerant environment, another 365 days where the Goldman gods would dangle the next bonus over my head. No amount of money was worth it. I'd almost lost my family in the process of getting to where I was, and I very nearly lost myself.

"Today's the day," I declared.

"They'll be shocked," Dan observed as the ice-covered branches of the sycamore outside tapped against our kitchen window.

"Maybe," I said, "but there'll be a dozen guys chomping at the bit for my job." I couldn't blame them, Goldman was a kill-or-be-killed world, and my departure would be someone's golden opportunity. One would take my place, but none would resemble me in the slightest, except for probably being white. My replacement would inevitably be single, male, childless. As a woman—a mom of four, no less—I had never fit their mold.

"Let's just review the sheet one last time," I tried to reassure myself. Dan sat next to me at the table as I pulled up the financial planning spreadsheet we dubbed the "Spreadsheet of Freedom." I'd calculated everything we'd need to supplement Dan's income as he built his business. I was hard-wired to imagine catastrophe, something my husband of twelve years knew well. He patiently read out our expenses, line by line, and went over our Plan B and Plan C, in case we were hit with something unexpected. The spreadsheet was bulletproof. I had my freedom, if only I had the guts to take it. *You can only leave Goldman once* echoed in my head, the refrain I'd heard countless times during my eighteen-year career there.

With a little distance, I would come to realize that I was just the candidate to fall for this warped world. Starting my career at Goldman without any connections, I felt pressure to be financially successful for my entire immigrant family, for my grandfather who took his life when he couldn't make ends meet, for my parents who'd sacrificed. And with the cloak of defectiveness stemming from childhood health issues, I was determined to refute any "you'll never" doubts that I confronted, to prove that I was just as whole as the next person. Not only would I show that I could fit into this foreign land of high finance and privileged access I had never experienced before, much less the many types of discrimination I witnessed and then became a part of, I would prove to Goldman and myself that I could climb the ranks to claim one of Wall Street's most elusive and exclusive titles.

But now I finally had clarity to break this abusive cycle, and knew what I had to do.

After years of looking at my life through Goldman's warped lens, after years of tolerating and perpetuating harassment and abuse, after years of complying with its sexist and outdated culture, after years of questioning who I was and what I deserved, I was ready to quit it all. I was ready to stop being complicit in a broken system and instead reclaim myself and my family.

I couldn't rewind the clock and choose a different first job. I couldn't go back and launch a career that fulfilled me and reflected my values. Or start with a role that had more purpose and balance, so I might have been able to see the first steps of my twins, Abby and Beth, or hear my son Luke's first words. But I could enjoy my life and my family now. I could find a new career path where I could make a difference in the world and help and support others, instead of making rich people richer.

I could experience the firsts of my baby, Hannah, help the girls with their homework, and pick Luke up from preschool. I was lucky enough to be able to take a sabbatical from work to reflect on what I had just been a part of and have the opportunity to think about what I'd want to do next with my life. I closed the laptop and grabbed my workbag.

"Okay," I said. "It's time."

CHAPTER ONE

July 1998

T he elevator opened to a large lobby, where dozens of people mingled in a sea of black and blue business suits. Bright light shone through the floor-to-ceiling windows overlooking the glistening harbor and the Statue of Liberty. I approached the reception table and looked for my nametag with shaking hands. There it was: *Jamie Fiore,* printed in bold black lettering that announced that I had a right to be here. I'd made it to Wall Street.

I followed the crowd into the pantry where breakfast was served. I scanned the room for other women and noticed only a few, with flawless makeup and hair, like they'd just come from a salon. I put a hand to my hair and felt, to my frustration, that the curl had started to frizz from the humidity. My face, with nothing on it but Cherry ChapStick, felt pasty and dry like pizza dough.

With a bagel and coffee in hand, I went into a meeting room the size of a movie theater, with stadium seating and capacity for more than a hundred people. An empty podium sat at the front, and behind it a large screen displayed the Goldman logo. I chose one of the few seats left at the end of an aisle, next to a tall blond guy with a chiseled jawline and bright blue eyes. He looked like an Abercrombie model.

"Taylor Hughes," he said. "Wharton, Economics." He sounded so stern and proper, like a soldier, but then again, the Goldman Sachs' training program was described as a boot camp.

"Jamie Fiore. Bryn Mawr, Mathematics," I reciprocated. It sounded weird coming out of my mouth. His large white hand shook mine with such a tight grasp that my knuckles rolled against each other. Introductions done, he returned to his *Wall Street Journal*.

"Good morning," boomed a stern voice. I looked up to see a tall man wearing a black fitted suit and red tie stride into the room. He pulled the double doors closed behind him and locked them, then tugged hard on the handle to make sure it was secure.

A flutter of panic bounced around my stomach. I glanced at Taylor for his reaction, but his eyes remained steady, locked on the man. The room fell silent, the trainees still as stone, as the man walked to the podium and put his hands on his hips, his face expressionless.

"Welcome to the Goldman Sachs Global training program," he said. His voice bounced off the walls of the auditorium, the screen behind him now a projection of his face. "I'm Tom White, the head of this program. Getting a job at Goldman Sachs is harder than getting into Harvard, so you must've done something right because you're here with me, lucky enough to get this once in a lifetime opportunity. Keep in mind though, that for the next six weeks, I own you." He laughed, pleased with that fact. He was in his forties, with black curly hair that showed whispers of gray.

"Expectations are high here," he said, "because expectations at your real job, on your real desk, are even higher. The program starts at 7 a.m. sharp, not 7:01. At 7 a.m. the doors will be locked, just like today." I craned my neck to survey the room. "If you're late, I only let you in with a letter of apology signed by your department's partner."

Silence fell over the room. That's when we heard the knocking, pounding so hard that the closed doors shook. "Like these guys," Tom said. He chuckled and gestured over his shoulder with his thumb at the door. I took a sip of my hot coffee as the back of my neck dampened. The knocking stopped. The day had officially begun.

The first day of training was filled with classes like Intro to Financial Accounting and Stock Pitching 101. My hand was tight and cramped, half of my new notebook was filled by noon. It was like getting a whole new degree in finance—I knew nothing and had to catch up.

At 4 p.m. we got an email that our first Open Meeting was at 4:15 p.m. I had no idea what an Open Meeting was, but I noticed the looks pass between a few fellow trainees. I overheard someone saying, "Are you ready for this?" and someone else mutter, "God help me."

At 4:15 p.m., Tom locked the door with one hand and carried a clipboard and pen with the other. He announced, "I'm looking for a John Tate." Everyone's faces swept around the room and searched for John. A redhead right in front of me popped out of his seat.

"John Tate, sir," he said. "Amherst, Economics."

"John, today a Goldman analyst published a report on the Yuan," Tom said. "What were his predictions for next quarter?" The back of John's ears flushed bright red, they looked too hot to touch. A dead silence hung in the room. My stomach was shredded to bits as I watched John Tate stew, realizing I didn't know the answer either. What the hell was the Yuan? That wasn't something that had been covered in today's classes. "I don't know, sir," John admitted with a cracked voice. The crowd let out a hushed moan.

"No, you idiot!" Tom said. He smacked his clipboard on the podium. "No!" Everyone froze except for John's shaking hands. My pulse throbbed in my ears. "That's never the answer," Tom yelled. "The answer is, 'I don't know, sir, but I'll find out.'" I looked at Tom's face on the projection screen and noticed the edges of his mouth were lined with white foam.

"I don't know, sir, but I'll find out," John corrected himself. I could hear him push cries down his throat.

"Good," Tom said. "Now leave, and report back to us tomorrow at 7 a.m." John stumbled over the people sitting in his row as he rushed out, running once he hit the aisle, his messenger bag flopping against his shoulder.

"Welcome to Goldman," Tom declared. "Home to the most paranoid and insecure people in the world. That's what it takes to put up with this environment."

What the hell did I sign up for? My body shook as I wrapped my arms around my waist to try to stop the trembling. This was the last place I wanted to be. Nothing about it felt right, none of it resonated with who I was. And yet I knew exactly why I'd ended up here.

⭒

"What's that?" Almost exactly a year before this first day as a trainee, my mom was chopping watermelon when she noticed the wide manila envelope. My dad sat next to me at the kitchen table, reading the newspaper, while my grandma, my mom's mother, crocheted nearby.

"Oh, I took a personality test through the career center at school," I said. I'd just finished my junior year at Bryn Mawr and it was time to start thinking about what came next. "These are the results. It's supposed to help you figure out what career would be a good match."

My dad's burning cigarette rested in the black plastic ashtray between us. I scanned the results first and then read the report. I couldn't believe how accurate it was. I thought I knew what I wanted to do with my life, but I was surprised by just how affirming the test results were.

"I know what I want to do after graduation," I announced.

My mom stopped cutting and looked up. "What?"

"Social work," my smile grew wide as I said it. Social work was noble, the kind of job that changed lives for the better. And it felt like a continuation of the path I was already on. I'd struggled with severe scoliosis as a kid, and the endless back braces, treatments, surgeries, and bullying always left me feeling like an outsider. I always noticed other outsiders and felt drawn to bringing them in, to helping them however I could.

My mom's face scrunched like she smelled a rotten egg. My dad put down his newspaper. "No way," she said. "We didn't take out loans to pay $35,000 a year for you to get a $20,000 job."

The smile melted off my face and I warmed with shame. "You'll be miserable making so little," she said. "You need to suck it up and get a good paying job. Save your money, and then you can do what you want down the road."

I held the report tight in my hands. "But social workers make good money if they have a private practice," I countered. "They don't all make $20,000 a year."

My dad leaned toward me and his newspaper crinkled. "Listen," he said softly, almost gently. "We made a huge investment in you, from your medical bills to your college tuition. We didn't mind doing it," he assured me, touching my hand, "but now we need to see a return on that investment, so you need to do something better with your life and make decent money."

I thought back to applying to colleges four years before. Several schools offered me full rides, but my first choice was Bryn Mawr and my parents supported me. It was the highest ranked school I'd gotten into, and my parents felt that a Bryn Mawr degree was worth the expensive price tag. They had to scrimp and save to pay for the tuition, but they were convinced that a degree from a Seven Sister school, the women's college equivalent of the Ivy League, would open doors for me.

"Don't you get it, honey?" my mom said. "I grew up with nothing. My house didn't have plumbing. Our parents were lucky to leave the farms and villages of Italy. Your grandparents weren't educated, they didn't have a childhood like you did, they went to work in the factories after they finished grade school. Your father and I were the only ones in the family who got to go to the local college and look at what we've built. Everything we've given you and your brother and sister. We can't go backward, so now you all must do better. Every generation must do better. Not just for you, but for our entire family, for those who came before us. Tony is a lawyer. If it had been up to him, he'd be an artist. Janine is a pharmacist and she wanted to be a writer. They're thanking me now. Being a social worker is moving the family backward, not forward." I looked out the sliding glass door into the backyard, not a cloud in the sky. I heard the final chop of the watermelon cut to pieces.

All that talk at the career center at school, about finding your passion and purpose in your work, it hit me in that moment that that path wasn't meant for me. I was expected to get a job that would make the rest of my life financially stable, so the sacrifices of my ancestors weren't for nothing—so I wouldn't become destitute if my kid needed expensive spinal surgery as I had. My life was part of a larger narrative, not just living for myself, but for my family spanning back generations. My future career wasn't about passion, but about security and pulling my entire family forward.

"Our job is to cover tuition," my dad had said when he dropped me off at college. "Your job is to make the most of it."

At the time, my parents paying for my college tuition and being debt free seemed like a gift. But now I realized that I wasn't debt free at all—it was time to show my parents that their college investment was well spent, time for me to pay them some dividends, time for me to find the best paying job in the most lucrative industry.

A few hours later I walked into the family room, where my mom sat on the brown fabric couch, knowing what I needed to do. "I'll go to the career office at school and start applying for jobs this fall," I said. The evening news played from the TV and the room hummed from the AC unit in the window.

"Good," my mom replied. "You'll need an interview suit. Let's go to TJ Maxx tomorrow."

❧※❧

My TJ Maxx suit was sweaty and restrictive by 5 p.m. that first day as a trainee, but I'd have to make it work for the evening, as Goldman had planned a social event. At least three nights a week we were expected at networking events, so I made a note to bring extra blouses, since I soaked through my first one by lunchtime. The large budget for entertaining the Goldman newbies covered everything from booze cruises to exclusive $1000 spa days. It seemed so excessive and unnecessary, but I'd go where I was told.

Our first event was at a steak house in Midtown. I arrived with Sofia and Michelle, two other trainees I'd met earlier, and sat in the main dining room. Dark wood paneled the walls and thick red drapes covered the windows. The walls boasted framed pictures of Frank Sinatra and Dean Martin. Servers poured wine freely and topped off glasses with each sip. I was grateful I didn't have to order a drink, not sure what the right choice would be. I looked at my watch; it was already 7 p.m. I made a mental note not to drink too much since I'd have to get up at 3:30 a.m. to get to work on time.

At a table with other trainees, we went around and introduced ourselves. A guy named Rob, who went to Yale, said his dad was a partner at the firm. He talked about his apartment in SoHo and the neighborhood restaurants he'd tried. Michelle sat next to him and hung on his every word; her body leaned into him as he spoke. She spoke next about her place in the Village, and how she discovered a boutique nearby that she loved. My stomach knotted as my turn grew closer; I wished I could disappear.

"So, Jamie," Rob said. "Where are you living?" I didn't want to share my story, I didn't want to say where I lived, I didn't want to explain myself, that I was commuting from home to save as much money as I could. But everyone was watching me. An awkward silence hovered. "I commute from New Jersey," I said.

"Hoboken!" Rob exclaimed. "That's a great scene."

"No, I commute from the suburbs," I clarified. "I live with my parents."

"Seriously?" he said, his blue eyes wide.

"Yes."

"Okay, then." He chuckled uncomfortably, because what else was there to say? My insides got hot and I grabbed my glass to take a swig of wine. Its acidity burned as it went down.

The meal lasted for hours, as the drinks and food kept coming. Gigantic seafood towers arrived first—six tiers of chilled silver dishes piled with oysters, shrimp cocktail, lobster tails, and king crab legs. Michelle said that each one cost $200, the same price of a nonstop flight to Los Angeles. Then the meat came. Filet mignon, New York strips, and double Porterhouses so big they hung off the sizzling plates. Then the sides, truffle mac and cheese, creamed spinach, and hand-cut potato fries. For dessert, plate after plate of New York cheesecake and molten lava chocolate soufflé. From the rich food to the excessive prices, it was pure decadence. The only steak house I'd been to prior was an Outback on Route 22 in New Jersey. I thought about my dad, who loved Saturday steak dinners at home, and how blown away he'd be by this spread.

With each hour, everyone got more and more drunk. Instead of coffee at dessert, Rob ordered a dozen tequila shots. Everyone's hands reached for the waiter's tray before he could put the drinks on the table, and two shots knocked over. The table roared in laughter; the waiter rolled his eyes. I felt embarrassed that I was part of this crew. I didn't take a shot, but everyone was too drunk to notice. Rob's arm was around Michelle—her head rested on his shoulder, her eyes were glassy. Sofia focused on the guy next to her, Tim, who'd been on the crew team at Duke. She stared wide-eyed at him and smiled and nodded at his slurred anecdotes about frat parties and summers on the Cape.

The final plates were cleared, and another set of shots ordered. Out of the corner of my eye, I saw Tom White leave the restaurant. He'd made it clear that nobody could leave before he did. I took a deep breath and looked at my watch again: 10 p.m. In less than six hours, I'd have to leave my house to get to work. At this point, I wouldn't crawl into my bed until midnight, but at least with Tom gone, I could start making my way.

I didn't bother saying goodbye since nobody would notice anyway. I was grateful that Goldman had a fleet of Lincoln Town Cars waiting outside for us to shorten our commutes home. But first, I popped into the ladies' room on my way out. Laughter bounced off the tiled bathroom floor. Inside the oversize handicap stall, with the door open, three women clustered over an open compact mirror. One woman's face was over the mirror, her nose pressed against it as she inhaled. I slowed down and stared, never having seen anyone snort drugs in real life. One of them turned toward me.

"Hey," she said. Her blonde hair was stringy and fell in her eyes. Her name tag said she was Megan from Columbia. "You want in?"

I froze and smiled widely. I shook my head. "No, thank you."

I went into the next stall. I knew I was a prude; I'd never done anything other than smoke pot a few times in college, but snorting coke at a work event, on the first day on the job? At least I thought it was coke. I didn't know what else you could snort. We'd just had drug tests and signed contracts that morning pledging to be drug free. I didn't think twice about it as I handed over a cup with a urine sample. With the money Goldman was paying us, I felt like they could ask whatever they wanted.

But these women, didn't they worry about getting in trouble? Or fired? Their audaciousness stupefied me. I washed my hands as the women came out of the stall. They giggled and held on to one another as they teetered on their heels. Echoes of their cackling laughter lingered after they left. And so did a great sense of loneliness. Here we were, the same age, all recent college graduates. I thought we'd have so much in common. I'd hoped I'd have a good time with them, make friends with them, be a part of a group together. But in just one day, it had become clear to me I wasn't one of them.

※

I rubbed my eyes and looked over my presentation for the millionth time. Well past 10 p.m., I was the only one left in the Goldman cafeteria. The fluorescent lights buzzed overhead and empty coffee cups and Diet Mountain Dew bottles covered my table. I'd set up shop there hours ago to put the final touches on my stock pitch. I was so tired that when I looked at my talking points, scribbled in the margins, they started to blur.

Every trainee was assigned a company's stock to analyze and then present a stock pitch to Tom. I would have twenty minutes to convince Tom that my stock was a good investment. The last week I'd put in several fifteen-plus hour days to finish it. First,

I devoured several basic stock market books because before I could pitch a stock, I had to figure out what one was. I'd been reading *Understanding Wall Street* during lunch one day when a trainee named Aaron helpfully pointed out that he'd read that book during middle school, when he started managing his own stock portfolio. "If you're reading that basic book," he'd said, "you don't have a chance of nailing your pitch. You're so behind, you'll never catch up and make it here." I'd been sitting in the corner of the room, my chair against the window, my back against the proverbial wall. "Thanks for your feedback," I'd said, and looked back at the book.

"You'll never" was a statement I was familiar with. After spinal surgery at age twelve, I went to physical therapy for months, where I started hearing it more and more.

"I can help you get stronger," the physical therapist had said, "but you need to be reasonable about your future. You'll be active of course, but you'll never be an athlete. You'll be able to run of course, but you'll never be a track star." Those two words were a challenge to me—I wanted nothing more than to prove her wrong.

The next year, I was cleared for non-contact sports, so I signed up for my school's cross-country team. Every practice I went to, every mile I ran, every weight I lifted, I thought of that physical therapist. Her low expectations of my potential became fuel for improving my performance. All I ever wanted to do was break out of the boxes of limitations that others put me in to. With my medical issues, I always felt like a defect, that I was born wrong and that my potential was stunted from the start. I wanted to prove to others, and myself, that I was just as whole as the next person and could handle anything. Nobody could tell me what my body and mind were capable of, only I had that power. I ended up running varsity track and cross-country all four years of high school.

So, after Aaron's obnoxious comments, I wanted to nail this presentation. I wanted to show him, Tom White, and anyone else who didn't think I could hack it, that I had what it took to succeed.

My stock pitch was complete, all I had left to do was head to the computer lab to print a final copy. When I got there, all was quiet. Long tables lined the space, with individual workstations containing a computer, monitor, and telephone staggered every few feet. The room was empty, save for Rob, who leaned against a desk at the far end of the room. His head was back, his eyes closed, and his face slack. The rest of his body was blocked by the row of desks in front of him. The door closed behind me with a loud thud. When Rob saw me, his eyes opened wide and his mouth fell open.

"Stop," he said. I saw his mouth form the words more than I heard them. I stood motionless in front of the door, a row of empty workstations and chairs in front of me, screen savers bouncing around monitors. Rob wore a white dress shirt with a blue tie, but it was loose around his neck. His mussed hair stuck straight up in parts. Rob looked down toward his feet and mouthed words, and I heard ruffled sounds and muted whispers but couldn't make out a thing. Then, like a plant sprouted from the office tile floor, Michelle emerged.

Rob zipped up his pants, while Michelle yanked down her black pencil skirt and then used her fingers to smooth her fly-away hairs. Staring at their feet, they walked past me and out of the room. I was surprised by the flush of anger I felt about how these two didn't seem to have a care in the world. They were able to literally dick around while their country club parents held their safety nets. Here I was cramming for my pitch and they were having sex. And Michelle, well she and Sofia had joked on the way to the steakhouse that maybe their real goal shouldn't be a career at Goldman, but rather nabbing a Goldman man.

I realized that night that I could study the Dow Jones to my heart's content. I could read research reports, investing textbooks, and *The Wall Street Journal*. I could nail a stock pitch. For a moment, I could be in their world, but then it would be over, because although I could study their lifestyle and eventually earn a salary to mildly afford it, I didn't think I could live it, and I wasn't sure I wanted to. The country clubs, the fancy restaurants, the Broadway shows, the laissez-faire attitude, the casual sex with each other, the cocaine, this strange world that seemed to operate with different rules but rule so much more of society. I couldn't give myself a blue blood transfusion. It was a chasm I didn't think I could cross.

❧

Training lasted eight weeks, with the same rigorous schedule as the first day: classes and projects by day and mixers by night. The final week, we prepared for the licensing exam, the Series 7, required by the U.S. Securities and Exchange Commission— the SEC—for anyone who worked with stocks and bonds. It's a pass/fail test that required a 70 percent to pass. I'd heard horror stories of trainees who failed the tests after training, and instead of going to work on the desk that hired them, they were shown the door.

On the second to last day of training, I went to a midtown testing center for the exam. A proctor registered me at a computer, and I began the four-hour test. We got an hour break for lunch halfway through the test, so I went outside and the thick air of the hot August day hit me. My stomach felt like a rock and I couldn't eat a thing. The exam seemed to be going okay, but I wasn't sure. I couldn't get the image of a big FAIL screaming at me on the computer screen out of my mind. It ate up all the real estate in my brain. When I returned to the exam, my head throbbed. If I didn't pass, my career on Wall Street would be over before it even began.

When I answered the last question, I hit "calculate," held my breath, closed my eyes, and counted to twenty. When I opened my eyes, "Congratulations!" displayed across the screen. I put my head down on the desk. The relief hit me with a wave of exhaustion.

That last night of the training program, Goldman hosted an event—a graduation party of sorts. Goldman closed Barneys department store on Madison Avenue for a fashion show that featured the fall's business wear collections. We'd been wined and dined and lavished with excess all these weeks, and this was the grand finale. Everything for the working professional was displayed: suits, shirts, ties, scarves, shoes, jewelry, and handbags. We ate from a buffet dinner, drank from an open bar, and watched the models, who marched down the catwalk to the heavy bass beat of techno runway music, strobe lights dancing around them. At the end we were offered appointments with Barneys' personal shoppers to create our new analyst wardrobes. Judging from the length of the line, most of the trainees scheduled time with one.

After the show, I walked around the store with Michelle and Sofia, whom I'd become friendly with after all the weeks of training.

"I love this one," Michelle commented as she picked up a black suit off the display.

"You should totally get it," Sofia said. "It's only a grand."

I froze in my spot. There weren't price tags on anything. How did she even know the price? And who would ever drop a grand on a suit? But I didn't say a word, just smiled, nodded, and acted as though I was considering buying one.

Instead I sheepishly glanced at my suit in the mirror. I had used my graduation gift money to buy a work wardrobe at Marshalls and TJ Maxx, buying shoes, blouses, pants, skirts, jackets, and a workbag for $800 total. I looked at a suit on a hanger and wondered if it looked that different. Maybe the Barneys one was nicer, but twenty times nicer?

My grandma had taught me better than to fall for brands. Six years before, when I was sixteen, she'd come into my room on the day after Christmas, put out her hand, and smiled. "Hand it over," she'd said. She wanted my Christmas gift money so she could put it in my bank account, like she did every year. I'd hoped she'd forgotten. "Grandma," I said, "this year I wanted to use it to buy a sweater from the Gap." Everyone had *something* from the Gap, it seemed, and I wanted something too.

My grandma scrunched up her face. Her lips were framed with deep wrinkles. "You have a closet full of sweaters," she said. "Why is this one so important? Because of a label? I taught you better than that. Save your money. You never know when you'll need it, for something more important than a sweater."

I grudgingly handed over the money. I didn't need it, I wanted it. And in my family, wanting just wasn't enough.

❯❮

"I have one final thing to discuss," Tom said. We were in our last meeting of training. "Your licensing exam." The room fell silent.

"It's a pass/fail test," he said, "but at Goldman, we are competitive with our counterparts and with one another. Take a look." He gestured to the large screen next to him, where everyone's names and scores suddenly appeared in descending order. "See how you did," he instructed, "and note who your competition is." When I saw my results, I almost cried out. I was in the top ten of all scores. I couldn't believe it. *How do you like me now, Aaron,* I thought.

As the room emptied, I grabbed my bag and headed home. I walked straight and tall down the crowded sidewalks of Broad Street, alongside the other Wall Streeters in their blue and black suits, with their canvas workbags embroidered with their company logos slung over their shoulders. I'd survived the long weeks of training, I'd pushed through, and I'd proven I could do it.

I thought back to my second-to-last interview for the position, six months before, when I thought for sure I'd blown my chance at Goldman. Mike, the partner who had interviewed me, brought an analyst named Joyce into our meeting. "Joyce saw you're a math major," Mike said as he leaned back in his chair, his thick arms folded against his round midsection. "And she thought it'd be fun to give you a brain teaser." With black rimmed glasses and brown hair in a short bob, she read a piece of paper in her hand. "Let's say you're on a game show, and you're given the choice of three doors," she'd said. "Behind one is a car; behind the others, goats. You pick door number one, and the host, who knows what's behind the doors, opens door number three, which has a goat. If you switch to door number two, what's your chance of getting the car?"

My body softened. My senior seminar that semester was in probability. This was the first proof we reviewed. "If I switch," I said, "my chance of getting the car increases to two out of three, or 66 percent." Mike and Joyce had looked at each other and smiled, then looked back at me. "Sorry, you're wrong," Joyce said. "It's 50 percent, or one out of two."

"I'm sorry," I said, "but I am positive it is two out of three, or 66 percent."

Mike picked up his phone. He asked someone to join us and suddenly a woman introduced to me as Vicki stood in the doorway.

"Vicki, you were a math major at Dartmouth," he said. "I need you to weigh in on this." Joyce read her the problem. Vicki stood there for a moment, her eyes closed. Her eyelids fluttered and her mouth twitched as she calculated in her head. "One out of two, or 50 percent," she said.

"So we're three against one," Mike said. He leaned forward in his chair. My face flushed. I wasn't sure how to choose words that were respectful and truthful at the same time.

"I guess we have to agree to disagree, then," I said. It sounded like a question more than a statement. I wanted to lie and make him pleased with me. Disagreeing with a Goldman partner couldn't be the way to land a job, but I had to. It was *math*, for God's sake, and the part of math I respected the most was the fundamental truth it held. Whether you were at the top of the world, or the bottom, two plus two always equaled four and I loved that power or influence couldn't change that fact.

Vicki walked me out after my interview and said, "You should be careful what you say to senior people at Goldman. You were an idiot." Tears burned my eyes. "Come back at 6 a.m. tomorrow for the last of the interviews," she sighed, though part of me wondered what the point was.

That night I wrote up a math proof for the gameshow problem, and I even faxed it to my math professor to make sure I was right. I left the house at 4 a.m. the next morning to get to the Goldman office on time. I placed a photocopy of the proof on the desks of all the people who had said I was wrong. Nobody ever acknowledged it, but I was offered a job the next day.

Now, all those months later and with training boot camp under my belt, I felt a bit wiser. *This is just how it's going to be at Goldman*, I thought. I'd be discounted, I'd fight, I'd pull through, and no one would acknowledge they'd underestimated me. *I* would know they had. I could live with that. Plus, I'd hit the lottery with this job. I'd be making $55,000 a year and a $40,000 bonus. $95,000 as a twenty-two-year-old in 1998 was nothing to sneeze at. But in my relief and pride, it was easy to forget one basic fact: I hadn't yet started my real job.

CHAPTER TWO

The halls of Goldman really weren't that different from the halls of high school. The cast of characters were the same, they just went to jobs instead of class. The researchers and strategists were the "nerds"; they loved to pore over spreadsheets and reports, trying to predict the future of the markets. The bankers were the "preps" or "preppies." They were dressed to perfection and well-spoken, ever at-the-ready to advise a Fortune 500 CEO on an acquisition. These two groups even had favored "locker" locations, or offices next to the executives. Not that the C-suite team was ever there; they were busy traveling the world, spreading the Goldman word to our clients. Those guys were so busy that their assistants had assistants. The Sales and Trading team were the "jocks," and it was little wonder the trading desk was often called the locker room. That's where I found my desk—in a space that later, when we moved buildings, was affectionately dubbed the Casino. The trading desks sat in a space larger than a football field, with no windows, just high ceilings and bright fluorescent lights. There was no sense of time in the Casino, and it was rumored that executives pumped in extra oxygen to keep everyone alert.

I'd like to say that I chose this group because I was passionate about their business, but that's not how Goldman worked. They were the first group I interviewed with, they had an opening for an analyst, they offered me a job, and that was that. I was just excited that I nabbed the elusive role of Goldman Sachs analyst and had the opportunity to make my family proud. I would've worked anywhere at the firm as an analyst, the role too prestigious and lucrative to pass up.

Sprinkled throughout the building were the "Chosen Ones," the must-hires, because of their connections or pedigree. From the gal who left early every Friday to catch her private jet to Nantucket, to the guy who came in late every morning hungover, this crew lived by different rules while the rest of us worked our tails off. Michelle and Sofia fell into this Chosen Ones group. When I mentioned that I'd had thirty-five interviews before I got an offer letter, I thought they might pass out. Turns out they each had only a few interviews. But Michelle's dad was a Goldman client; Sofia's played golf with a Goldman partner. They thought getting a job at Goldman was no big deal.

For better or for worse, this was now my world. And stocks were now my language.

When people asked, "So, what do you do at Goldman?" at first I'd tell them I was a sales trader in Global Securities Services, a group of 200 professionals. If they asked for more information, my answer would produce yawns and glassed over eyes. Terms like "short selling," "term funding," and "rehypothecation" were laced with a sedative. To keep it simple, most people know that in the stock market you want to "buy low and sell high." Well, in my business it was a flip of that order—it's "sell high and buy low." People, or more specifically hedge funds and crazy rich people, would sell a stock that they felt was overpriced, expecting it to drop. Once the price fell, they would buy it back. But here's the thing: They didn't actually *own* the stock to begin with. That's where I'd come in. I'd lend them these stocks, and they'd pay me a fee, like a rental charge, which was sometimes large, so they could sell them in the market. I borrowed these stocks from my institutional clients, large pension funds and mutual funds, endowments, and insurance companies, who owned the stocks in their portfolios. I stood in the middle of these trades, with hedge funds on one side and institutions on the other, and I—or, rather, Goldman—would take a cut.

When I explained all of this to my liberal arts friends from Bryn Mawr, they'd look at me like I was playing a pointless video game and ask what the point was—why would anyone *want* to short a stock? Some of my clients just felt the stock was overpriced and that there was money to be made in that assessment. Say, for example, XYZ stock is trading at $100 a share. Some hedge funds would research the company and think, based on their earnings and balance sheet, that the stock should be worth only $60. So they sell short at $100 and wait for the price to come down to $60. This wasn't a given—it's like when you buy a stock in the hopes it increases in value, you can't guarantee it actually will. So, if the stock drops to $60, they would buy it back and make the $40/share difference, minus my fee, and I'd return the stock to its original owner. Short selling is a well-established strategy, and although these speculators don't get it right every time, most get it right enough of the time to post amazing returns to their investors.

For others, shorting stock is part of a larger trade. This happens in arbitrage, when funds buy and sell securities simultaneously in order to take advantage of differing prices for the same asset. For example, in a merger, when one company (the acquirer) announces they are taking over another company (the target), many days or months pass between the announcement of a merger and its completion. When the deal is official, the two companies become one, with the same stock. By buying or selling both the original companies' two stocks at the same time, funds try to profit from the difference between the price of the acquirer's stock and the price of the target's stock—they buy the target and sell the acquirer, during the window between the deal's announcement and the deal's closing and at the end it becomes the same stock.

But you don't have to be a Fortune 500 insider to be privy to the practice. I spot arbitrages all the time, even at Dunkin' Donuts. For a time, there was a great arbitrage on their donut holes. The box of fifty was priced at $9.99, but the ten-pack went on sale for $1.50. So, you could buy fifty donut holes for $7.50 if you just bought five of their ten-packs. You'd end up with the same product but $2.49 cheaper. This is what arbitrageurs do—they're essentially just buying ten-packs of donut holes.

When I first started at Goldman, though, I didn't directly handle these trades so much as log them for my colleagues. I arrived by 6 a.m. and didn't leave until at least 8 p.m. The days were long with lots of button pushing, a simple job that I mastered within the first week. It didn't require a lot of thinking, so I listened to Brian, a senior guy who sat next to me, talk to his clients. I'd ask questions here and there to pick up some knowledge about what stocks the hedge funds wanted to short, and who had them to lend.

I picked up on other things, too. A few weeks after I started, the firm gave everyone a "Facebook" of sorts, a small booklet with every new analyst's ID picture. The traders I worked with read it more closely than *The Wall Street Journal*. Whistles, hoots, and hollers filled my ears every time someone brought out the booklet.

One memorable day, Jerry, a trader at least ten years older than me, waved it at his friend Vito. "Hey, Vito, do me a favor, would'ya?" he said. "Let's throw some quantitative analysis on this. Build me a macro in Excel to graph this stuff. Research needs to be done on these ladies. I want tit size, ass shape, and leg length. We can't rank on fuckability by just a black and white picture." Vito smiled wide, like a dog that had seen a bone. I gritted my teeth and pretended I hadn't heard, staring at my screen keying in trades.

I hadn't been completely clueless about Wall Street's reputation, but I expected something different from Goldman. They seemed the gold standard of Wall Street, when I was first introduced to them on campus, so I was surprised by how brazen these guys were. At the training program, even Tom had made a huge to-do about the fact that the standards were higher at this firm and at our jobs. Was that all just bullshit?

I thought back to the Goldman partner, Genevieve, who had come to Bryn Mawr's campus my senior year to recruit applicants, after I decided to focus on a good paying job instead of social work. "Our mission statement is just three words," she'd said. "Minds. Wide. Open. We're tired of hiring male economics majors from Wharton down the street. We want liberal arts majors, varied backgrounds, different experiences. Come as you are. All are welcome."

I remembered everything about that night at the career center. When Genevieve had taken the stage, I'd been mesmerized. She was older, at least my mom's age, and she looked experienced, almost regal. Her white-blonde hair was in a tight bun on the top of her head. She wore bold red shiny glasses that matched her lipstick. Her neck was wrapped with a string of large diamonds and smaller strings dropped from her ears. When the spotlight hit them, they turned them into white fire. It was like watching magic.

Genevieve started to rattle off Goldman's various rankings. It was hard to follow, as I had no idea what it was being ranked on, but I did understand that Goldman was number one in everything. "Join me, join us," she said in a hushed tone, like she was letting me in on a secret. "We want sharp, smart women from Bryn Mawr. We want women with grit and a never-give-up attitude. We want to bring in a new crop of hardworking and powerful women. We want to blast through the glass ceiling! We want you."

Afterward, I couldn't get Genevieve out of my mind. Yes, she was dazzling, but there was something more. She held court in that room, a tough and strong leader. When I spoke to her one-on-one afterward, I saw she was also friendly and welcoming. I didn't think there was a world where a woman could be all those things. At that moment, I realized I wanted to be like her and work at Goldman Sachs.

There were several partners across Global Securities Services, and I worked for Mike, the one who had tested me on the probability proof during interviews. He seemed nothing like Genevieve. Brian, Vito, and Jerry weren't like her, either. I couldn't imagine Michelle or Sofia ever being as poised and self-confident as she was. I looked around me at the boys congratulating themselves on their "fuckability" jokes and wondered, did Genevieve even really exist? I never saw her after that night at Bryn Mawr and sometimes I wondered if she was an actress hired by the PR department, paid as a spokesperson, like the kind I'd see on infomercials.

My sinking feeling only grew worse the next week, when I noticed Melissa, an analyst on the team who was a year ahead of me, was away from her desk a lot. We shared the same phone line, and I took loads of messages for her. I knew she had lunch meetings with clients sometimes, but it seemed like every day she was gone for at least an hour.

"I hope Melissa's okay," I said to Jake, a trader who sat near me, as I put another "while you were out" note on her desk. "She's been off the desk a while, and I just took the tenth message for her."

"She's fine," Jake shrugged. "She's out fucking George from Lenders Trust at the Marriott. How else do you think she wins the business?"

I'd noticed Melissa wore low-cut lace tops, but showing off cleavage was one thing, sleeping with someone was another. Plus, wasn't George married? My face reddened, much to the amusement of my colleagues.

"I think I'm gonna call you Sister Jamie," Jerry teased. "Our prude little nun." More traders on the desk got in on the fun, laughing at my embarrassment.

"Don't you know how Wall Street rolls, Sister?" Vito said into my ear. "At Goldman, sex will propel you further than an

Ivy League diploma." They laughed and high-fived each other. Sure enough, I soon discovered that Melissa not only slept with clients, but also with one of our department's partners, Mike.

The latter was something I picked up on over time. Those first few months I was always the first to arrive and the last to leave. Brian even dubbed me "FILO," the accounting term for "first in, last out." I was such a constant fixture on the desk that oftentimes my coworkers didn't even notice me. But I started noticing them and picked up on their schedules and idiosyncrasies. How Jerry would argue with his wife every morning on the phone. The way the office assistant reapplied her lipstick several times an hour. How Brian ordered a bacon, egg, and cheese sandwich every day for breakfast. I also noticed Melissa and Mike. How often she was in his office, how they walked out together every night, and how she bragged that Mike's driver would give her a lift home.

As I started to try to live with my "Sister Jamie" identity, I realized that Melissa's "slut" label might make her uncomfortable too. I wondered why we had to have labels at all. I began to notice this was a mostly homogenous group, almost all white, who pressured one another to conform, if they weren't already acting the part. But the guys didn't seem to be put into buckets, instead just living their lives, where the women were treated differently. Like I was "Nun Barbie" and Melissa was "Slut Barbie" and we were poseable dolls the men played with in their world. Although Melissa and I weren't best buddies, I knew there was more to her than her "slut" label, just like there was more to me than a "nun."

❦

My schedule left little time for life outside of work. Most of my fellow analysts lived in the city and had time to go out and meet people. After market close on some days, it would get quiet and I'd hope that maybe I could get home at a decent hour. Then, as Brian packed up to leave, he'd place a thick stack of papers on my desk. "After-hours trades to input." I'd smile and nod while I cringed inside. All I did was work, commute home, sleep, and do it again. My dad reminded me to "keep an eye on the prize": Get in good with a company and have a job for life. In the meantime, I had no life, no friends, and was too tired to do anything on the weekends.

But there was one silver lining. My salary. In just a few months I'd amassed a small fortune—much more money than I'd ever made in my side jobs in college; as a waitress, a math tutor, and piano teacher to the affluent children who lived along the Main Line. And I had few expenses. I paid some rent to my parents but saved the rest of what I brought home. Grandma had taught me well. Like she said, I'd never know when I'd need it. I felt giddy whenever I checked my bank account balance. At least I had something to show for all the hours. This was no social worker salary, and it helped cement my decision to work at Goldman.

Soon the holidays rolled around and the trading desk buzzed with excitement. It was bonus time. I knew what my bonus would be, so I wasn't too worked up. As a new hire it was in my contract that I'd get $40,000. I planned to use some of it to replace the 1987 Honda Civic that I'd bought myself junior year in high school.

On Bonus Day, all of the partners called everyone one by one into the conference room to tell them their bonus amount. I watched from the corner of my eye as each person walked in and out. I was like an undercover detective as I tried to read their expressions, but their faces were blank and stoic. I'd heard it was taboo to show any emotion on bonus day.

As I wrapped up the day, Mike stood at the door of the conference room and called me in.

"Jamie," he said and squinted at the paper in his hand. "Your contract says you'll get a $40,000 bonus your first year." The wind whistled through the large floor to ceiling window behind him. The towers of the World Trade Center in the distance framed the sides of his body. It had just started to snow, and wild flurries blew in swirls in the dark gray sky. "But your contract states that bonuses are discretionary," he said, "and I'm not obligated to give you one." My breath caught in my throat. I felt like I'd been slapped across the face. I didn't remember the word "discretionary" in the contract, but I didn't look it over with a fine-tooth comb either. I couldn't believe that I'd missed such an important detail. What a fool I was to count on something that might not even exist.

"Okay, I understand," I said. I wanted my words to sound sincere. I didn't want to seem ungrateful. My salary alone was a lot of money, even without a bonus. I pasted a firm smile on my face and clenched my teeth, hoping it masked the disappointment churning in my gut.

"But Brian says your work has been outstanding," he continued, "so your bonus this year is $80,000."

I leaned in toward him and then froze. This must be a mistake. The contract said $40,000 and this was double that. Was this a joke? Mike had a large smile on his face, and I could see the pink gums around his teeth. "Earth to Jamie," he said. "Are you with me?"

The phones rang from the trading desk outside the door, the

sound reverberating in my head and echoing in my ears. "Yes," I said. "I just don't get it."

Mike shook his head and laughed. "There's nothing to get," he said. "I doubled your bonus because you're the best analyst we have. Welcome to Wall Street."

My eyes opened wide as I heard it a second time. This wasn't a joke. It felt like the Monopoly game I played with my family and I just collected the huge stack of pink funny money as a rental fee for Park Place.

"I don't know what to say," I said hoarsely. I sounded like an idiot. A thick frog sat in the back of my throat.

"A thank you would be sufficient," Mike chuckled.

"Of course, of course," I said. "Thank you so much." He stood up to shake my hand. I realized how cold my hand was as I felt his.

I headed to the bathroom, knowing I couldn't go back to the desk like this. My pulse rushed in my temples and my face burned hot, but my fingers and toes were numb. I stood in front of the sinks, splashed cold water on my face, and looked in the mirror. Maybe I could compete with these people after all. It made me believe, if only for a brief moment, in the meritocracy that Goldman proclaimed to be.

I grabbed a paper towel and wiped the drops of water off my face, wiping away some of the frustration from the past year with them. Now that I had something to show for all the sacrifice, I could see maybe it wasn't a sacrifice after all. My mom once said that she forgot the pain of childbirth when she held us for the first time. It was like I'd given birth to this bonus, and all the pain I went through to get there dissipated like smoke. I wasn't sure if that was a good or bad thing.

I couldn't wait to get home from work that night to tell my parents and Grandma about my bonus. When I raced through the front door two hours later, I found them watching TV in the family room, with my grandma crocheting as usual in her rocking chair and my parents on the couch. I stood in front of the TV and smiled at them.

"I have some news," I announced. My fast heartbeat echoed in my chest. "It was bonus day today, and I was supposed to get $40,000."

"l still can't get over it," my dad said. He was leaned back on the sofa, in jeans and a T-shirt, his arms crossed in front of him, lit cigarette hanging out of the corner of his mouth.

"Well," I said. "Mike said I was doing such a great job my bonus is $80,000. My total pay this year will be $135,000."

Their jaws dropped in unison. My grandma's metal crochet needle hit the wooden floor and rolled across the room. Loud laughter roared from the TV behind me.

"You're kidding," my mom said. She covered her mouth with her hands.

"I can't believe it," my dad said. "It's like you hit the lottery." My mom jumped off the couch and hugged me and then my dad and Grandma joined.

"We're so proud of you," my mom said. "Our girl, conquering Wall Street." She grabbed my hand and squeezed.

I felt like the football quarterback who just threw the final touchdown to win the game and got swarmed by proud team-mates. After our celebration hugs, we all sat back down. My dad shut off the TV and put out his cigarette.

"You know," he said, "our whole lives, your mom and I never made that much money in one year." My dad stared out the window behind me, and I saw dark shadows under his tired eyes. Smoke from the extinguished cigarette rose in front of his face. My parents were almost sixty and had worked for close to forty years. Dad's mouth was turned up in the tiniest smile, but I wondered if it was a smile at all.

A strange sense of reality set in. My parents had careers that they built over decades, while they raised a family, including taking care of me with all my health issues. They started from nothing and built a great life through hard work. And in one fell swoop, I passed them. I knew we were a family and a team, and that I'd made them proud. Their investment in me had just paid a huge dividend. But I also felt like the new quarterback who had just caused the beloved veteran, who'd led the team for years, to retire.

CHAPTER THREE

The night after Bonus Day, the firm had its annual holiday party at Windows on the World, the restaurant overlooking the entire city from the 107th floor of World Trade Center's Tower One. As a kid from Jersey, the towers were a familiar sight. I'd seen that pair of buildings all my life from afar, but I'd never been inside.

We boarded the elevators and shot up so fast that my ears clogged from the pressure of the thousand-foot climb. I touched my ears as if I could rub away the discomfort with my fingers. The elevator attendant, a thin man in a black suit and tie who sat on a stool next to the elevator's controls, locked eyes with me. "Swallow hard," he smiled. I smiled thanks at the man as I felt a pop and the pressure release, and noticed dark circles under his eyes, the skin hanging from his jowls as if exhaustion pulled them down.

The elevator dinged and the doors opened. "Welcome to Windows on the World," the elevator attendant said as he gestured his arm toward a large reception area. He winked at me as I nodded with a smile. The room was circular and a chandelier hung above a tuxedo-clad pianist playing a baby grand in the center. A high-pitched soprano vocalist in a long red ball gown stood at his side singing Christmas carols.

I'd only walked a few steps from the elevator when a man in a tuxedo and white gloves came up to me, took my bag, and helped me out of my coat. I flushed from embarrassment. I felt like I'd walked onto a movie set as an extra.

I looked for the colleagues I'd walked over with, but they'd vanished in the crowd. I was alone, unable to hide behind the piles of work on my desk. Groups of people mingled and chatted around me in little pods of friendship. Suddenly, I was back in sixth grade standing alone in my middle school's parking lot while a group of popular girls stared at me. They all had smooth straight hair, clothes from the Gap, and clear skin. I knew they were looking at my back brace, which was hard to miss since it covered me from my armpits down to my butt. Rebecca, the group's leader, waved at me. I waved back, trying to tone down the smile growing on my face. "You're a disgusting freak," she said. The girls' laughter filled my ears and I wished I could melt into a puddle and drip into the nearby sewer grate.

"Miss?" said a tall man with a deep voice, waking me from my trance. He carried a silver tray filled with champagne flutes, handed me one, and then walked away. The flute, rimmed in gold and etched with a diamond design, felt heavy as a rock, so much thicker than the ones my mom used for Christmas dinner. The cool condensation of the glass dampened my fingers.

I turned around and almost bumped into another waiter, this one carrying a silver-beaded tray of scallops wrapped in bacon. They looked too pretty to eat, but once I took a bite, I got over it—I'd never tasted something so delicious. My eyes scanned the room. The eager waitstaff with their shiny white smiles moved with such perfect synchronicity as they took coats and offered food and drinks that it looked like the scene in the movie *Annie*, where the servants danced around her when she first entered Daddy Warbucks' estate, attending to her every need as she sang "I think I'm gonna like it here."

When the lights flickered on and off, we were shepherded into the Grand Ballroom where the largest chandelier I'd ever seen sparkled and reflected small beams of white light throughout the dim room. Seats for hundreds surrounded round tables covered with crisp white linens, napkins folded into origami fans, and chairs with covers that were tied with royal blue bows, the color of Goldman's logo. The centerpieces were works of art, roses and lilies piled high. Across the room a ten-piece band and a few singers performed mellow background music at the side of a dance floor. Was I at someone's wedding or a company holiday party?

Entering the ballroom felt like a threshold to another world, and I wasn't sure I was ready to cross over. I knew I couldn't have been the only person at the company who hadn't experienced wealth, but I hadn't met them yet. Instead the people I knew had an ease about them that came with knowing wealth, they knew the customs, dress, and actions, coming across as comfortable in their own skin, while I second guessed every word and gesture, like I was in a foreign land and not a native speaker, just one word away from getting it wrong.

But I felt pulled inside. Maybe it would be as amazing as those scallops. This was my chance to get a taste of the country club lifestyle that I'd been hearing about all these months. I wanted to trade my Payless shoes for glass slippers, play Cinderella, and see what I'd been missing.

I took the last empty seat at my table with my department, as assigned. A menu on thick cream paper in ornate calligraphy sat atop my plate. It was written in English, but I only recognized half the words. When the waiter asked me, "Chicken, fish, or beef," I was so relieved I wanted to kiss him. We had langostinos, which, when I saw them on my plate, I realized were just a type of lobster, and the beef I had requested was called chateaubriand. Regardless of their names, they were delicious.

Liquor was abundant, and I nursed my champagne while the guys from my desk pounded glass after glass of Macallan 25 scotch. They said each one cost more than $100.

Much of the dinner conversation centered around bonuses. Not the amount, which was taboo to disclose, but how people planned to spend their newfound windfall. For Brian, it was a Rolex watch for himself and diamond jewelry for his wife. For Vito, it was a new Porsche to race on weekends. Jerry held up his glass of scotch in a toast. "I'm still working on my Fuck You Money status," he said, "but for my next vacation I'm chartering a private plane. No more sitting with the regular fat ugly Joes in commercial." Everyone at the table had a huge grin on their face. Part of me was disgusted by Jerry's condescension, but I had to admit I was also excited about my own bonus.

Other than a newer used car for myself, I planned to give my family some money and get them nice Christmas presents. I'd get my parents tickets to an opera in the city. They'd love it! If it weren't for them and everything they'd done for me, I wouldn't be here. Then I'd save the rest to make Grandma proud. If asked, I decided I'd say, "Oh, I'm still considering my options." I wasn't, to my relief.

The party continued and I soon discovered that the regular

Goldman employees went as hard as the trainees had during boot camp. The drugs in the bathroom and drinks at the bar stripped away more judgment with each hour. In the lobby one of the newly minted partners of the division was on the couch being straddled by his secretary. In the ballroom, the dance floor was packed with people and looked more like a frat party than an upscale corporate event.

"Loosen up, Sister Jamie," Jerry smirked. He was on the dance floor next to our table, bumping and grinding with one of the assistants. She smiled in delight as he studied her cleavage. His hands cupped her ass and I could see his wedding ring shine off the band's strobe lights as he squeezed. I thought about his wife, who was probably putting their four kids to bed at that moment. I nodded, raised my glass to him, and gave him a feeble smile. No wonder spouses and dates weren't invited. What was this world?

I may have been discomfited, but I have to admit I was also fascinated. I watched the goings on around me like I was in the audience of a Broadway performance, taking it all in. The over-the-top jewelry and fur coats, the drinking games along the bar, the boisterous alcohol-induced laughter. What would happen next? I moved around the room constantly, looking for different angles, different dramas unfolding around me.

Toward the end of the night, I wandered toward the far edges of the ballroom and looked down into the city. I'd never been so high up in a building before. I took a sharp breath in. It was like I was on an airplane as it made its final descent. The teeny tiny taxicabs and people that milled on the city streets below reminded me of the little miniature toys from my childhood dollhouse.

Here were the Gods of Goldman, looking down from their

perch on top of the world at all the little people below. Did the fact I was standing here mean I was one of them now?

⸻✴⸻

"Come on Jamie, you promised me you'd come," my sister, Janine, pleaded. I was at my desk the morning after the Goldman holiday party and it was 6 a.m. I looked across the trading floor out the window, the sky still pitch black. Not the only early bird in the family, my sister had called to remind me of our plans for that evening—going to her company's holiday party.

"I know," I said, "but I'm so tired." It had seemed like a good idea when she asked me a few weeks ago, but I was exhausted from the party the night before.

"Pleeeeaaase," she whined. "I want to introduce you to everyone." Janine was a senior member of a small business and this was their first holiday party. Employees were encouraged to bring friends and family. I couldn't remember the last time I heard her so excited.

"Fine," I agreed. "I'll come."

The party that night was held in the basement of the Methodist Church in Clark, New Jersey. I fought off exhaustion as we entered through the heavy steel gray service door in the back and walked down a metal staircase, alongside cream painted walls with moldy dried water stains. Curled, frayed flyers plastered the walls, advertising Sunday school, prayer groups, and bake sales. Portable rusted metal coat racks lined the hallway, which guests had started to use for shedding their outdoor layers. I went from the top of the tallest building in New York the night before to a basement in New Jersey, but at least I could hang up my own coat.

The party was in a large multipurpose room, which sported round tables covered with red and green plastic tablecloths, and metal folding chairs. A self-serve buffet offered sausage and peppers, baked ziti, and a tossed salad. Everything was served on red plastic plates with green plastic utensils. On the other side of the room, a DJ played in front of a makeshift dance floor. Cans of beer, soda, and opened bottles of wine filled plastic tubs around the room.

My shoulders relaxed as I walked in. Even though the only person I knew at this party was my sister, I still felt at ease and reminded of the large family reunions we had each year. I slipped into the familiar simplicity of it all like a pair of old comfortable shoes.

At the start of the night the company president addressed the crowd and thanked the employees. He announced that everyone would receive a holiday bonus gift, a $100 Visa gift card. The room lit up with laughter and cheers. As the applause drowned out, I felt sad for them, wondering what $100 could possibly buy.

Jamie! I sounded like Jerry from work and that scared the crap out of me. A $100 bonus versus $80,000. The disparity of it blanketed me in shame. But I discovered that underneath that blanket, I was warm and cozy with my bonus money. How could I be ashamed, yet proud of myself at the same time?

Janine was in a happy mood, introducing me to all her colleagues. Everyone I met was down-to-earth and our conversations were easy, mostly about the stresses of last-minute holiday shopping. Instead of Rolex watches and Porsches, they'd bought sweaters and picture frames.

Midway through the night, my sister grabbed my hand and pulled me aside. She teetered on her red high heels, tipsy giggles escaping her lips as some of her drink sloshed onto the floor. She leaned into my ear, half-whispering, "I have someone I'd like you to meet." She walked me through a throng of people and that's when I saw him. My stomach dropped past my knees. My black tank dress felt tight, the pearl choker around my neck cut off my breath. He was tall, more than six feet, and handsome. More than handsome, he was beautiful, and that wasn't a word I'd ever used to describe a guy. With light blond hair and large blue eyes, he had a smile that made his eyes crinkle and revealed dimples on both cheeks. He held out his hand to shake mine and I prayed he wouldn't notice that it trembled.

"Jamie, meet Dan," Janine said.

A large proud smile sat on my sister's face and I realized she planned this all along. I searched Dan's face for disappointment as he looked at me. Part of me would forever be the dork in the back brace.

My sister lingered and watched us until Dan gave her a wide-eyed stare and waved his hand goodbye. Janine walked away from us, and I knew she was beaming.

"Janine said she might bring her sister," Dan said. "I'm happy to meet you." He smiled again. Ugh, those damn dimples. Then his face flushed. Was he nervous too? The tightness in my chest released and a smile blossomed on my face.

"Nice to meet you too," I said.

We started to talk about where we grew up, went to school, and our families. He had an easy way about him, bright eyes with soft edges and a face that seemed to accept whatever came his way. His eyes locked on mine and didn't waver for a minute. He nodded and smiled at all the right times. He pulled the words out of my mouth one by one with his interest. I was surprised at my lack of reticence and fear. This wasn't like conversations with the analysts at work; I didn't feel embarrassed or ashamed to talk about myself. I hadn't felt this way around someone my age since college. The rope of nerves that wrapped around me loosened and words gushed out. After we'd exhausted our personal histories, we turned to our jobs.

"So, what do you do for work?" Dan asked. We were in the middle of the party room at the edge of the dance floor. My joyful mood was extinguished like a bucket of water on a fire. I didn't want to admit what I did. I didn't want to seem like a cocky Wall Streeter like the people I worked with. I didn't want that to cloud his opinion of me. I could feel the floor vibrate through my black heels and up my ankles from the loud music. "I work at Goldman Sachs," I said.

I took a long draw of my white wine while I watched him. He cocked his head to the side, and his eyes brightened with curiosity. I clenched my teeth and braced myself for the wave of judgment about to crash down. "Sorry, I've never heard of it," he said. "What do they do?"

The wine burned my throat as it went down, feeling both relief and embarrassment. How cocky was I to assume everyone knew Goldman? But also, how refreshing was it that this guy had no clue?

"They're an investment bank," I said.

"Cool," he said. "Do you like it?" Such a simple, benign question, yet after all the months I'd worked there, nobody had ever asked me that. I considered the question for a moment, but I didn't have an easy answer. I decided to go with noncommittal, shrugging, "It's okay, I guess."

After talking for more than an hour, I felt like it could go on forever, when one of Janine's colleagues came to my side. She whispered in my ear that my sister needed help. Just like at Goldman's party, alcohol was abundant, and much of it flowed into my sister. She was always on a diet and drank all night on an empty stomach.

I walked away from Dan into the bathroom where Janine was on her knees, her red heels discarded next to her. Her hands gripped the sides of the toilet bowl as she threw up. Vomit was splattered everywhere. I pulled Janine's hair back off her sweat-covered face as alcohol and bile poured out of her. I fought back the urge to gag. When she finished, she started to cry, the sobs echoing off the tile.

"Get me out of here," she said into the toilet, her voice hoarse and raspy. "I'm so embarrassed." Janine had driven us to the party and I wasn't familiar with the area. This was years before GPS and I had no idea how to get home. "Okay, be right back," I said.

I ran back into the party room to find Dan right where I'd left him. "Hey, my sister is sick, and we have to go," I said. "Would you tell me how to get to the highway so I can get her home?"

Dan looked at me, both his eyes and his mouth turned down. "Sorry you have to leave," he said. "Meet me in the parking lot. I'll get in my car and you can follow me out."

I went back to Janine, cleaned her up, and walked her to her car. She crawled into the backseat, curled up into a ball, and was asleep within seconds. I got into the driver's seat and Dan walked up to the car as I rolled down the window.

"The highway is just down the road," he said as he peered in the backseat and saw Janine. "But follow me, it's kind of tricky."

"Thanks," I said. "As you can see, Janine is out for the night."

We laughed and I began to roll up my window, when Dan placed both his hands on it, and I stopped.

"I really liked meeting you," he said. "Could I call you some-time?"

This adorable guy, who seemed nice, too, liked me and wanted to call me. His blue eyes were expectant, his cheeks flushed pink.

"Sure," I smiled. "I'd like that."

He smiled back and got into his car. He led me to the highway as wispy snow swirled and danced in the sky. My body felt alive all over, like someone went into the cold dark basement of my body and turned on a circuit breaker. I couldn't remember the last time I'd felt so excited. My body warmed and a large smile glowed on my face as I traveled through the wintry night.

CHAPTER FOUR

In the New Year I was assigned a mentor named Molly Provenzano—a vice president in another division—through the Goldman Sachs' Women's Network. She invited me for coffee in the lobby one afternoon, and I let Brian know I'd be off the desk.

"Here we go again," Jerry said as he eavesdropped. "Mentoring! Another thing they do for the women and not the men."

"Jerry," Vito chimed in, "would you be my mentor?" His hands were pressed in prayer. He batted his eyes like a middle school Romeo overacting his part.

"Yes, young one," Jerry said. "I'll show you the way to success." They laughed and high fived while I clenched my hands into fists.

As I waited in the lobby for Molly, I hoped that we'd hit it off. I needed a trusted advisor at Goldman. Although I was doing well and felt more confident each day when it came to the nuts and bolts of my work, the personalities and politics were beyond me.

"You must be Jamie," Molly said as she walked through the

lobby toward me. She had a large smile that revealed bright white teeth framed with rich plum–painted lips. Her short brown wavy hair was styled into a bob. She wore a tailored black suit with a plain white blouse, but her jewelry stood out: large rubies and diamonds sparkled from her wrist, neck, and ears.

Despite the bling, Molly and I had a lot in common. She was new to Goldman too, having joined from a competitor a year before I did. We were also neighbors in New Jersey, as she lived just a few miles from my parents' house. She told me about a better way to commute to work, by ferry instead of train, which would save me a half hour each way. She was so down to earth, also an Italian American, and we talked about all the seafood dishes and pastries we'd made with our families over the holidays. Our conversation was so easy, and our time together flew by. After we finished our coffees, we headed back to the elevators.

"Wall Street can be tough," she said, "especially at the beginning of your career. Let's keep in touch, I want to help you succeed."

"I'd love that," I said.

We parted ways and my body felt lighter. Maybe I had just found a friend, a confidante who'd help me navigate this crazy world of Wall Street.

My day to day was improving too, because a new analyst joined the team and I was able to pass my data entry responsibilities onto him, enabling me to have clients of my own for the first time, instead of just supporting my colleagues and their clients. Finally, I had the opportunity to use my brain rather than simply perform rote administrative tasks.

"Here's your client list," Brian said as he placed a sheet of paper on my desk. "See what you can do with them." I was so excited, like it was the first day of school, a blank slate with nothing but opportunity ahead. I skimmed the list of client names and their current balances, the market value of what we had borrowed from them. I'd never heard of most of them and, looking at the sheet, we hardly did any business with them. This was my opportunity to build relationships and borrow securities from them that the hedge funds desperately wanted. I was no longer the best supporting actor in this world, I was front and center. I had a new role, I was the face of Goldman Sachs to clients. I started calling them to introduce myself and adopted my new persona: I was now "Jamie from Goldman."

I knew I wasn't going to be handed large accounts at first, and that was fine with me. I wanted to be long-term greedy—a phrase I'd heard back at training along with some advice to think of my career as a marathon and not a sprint. I focused on making the most of the clients I had with the hopes that I'd be recognized and get more opportunities with bigger clients in the future.

My new accounts were mostly small regional retail banks, scattered across the country, from Oregon to Minnesota and Ohio. The people who worked there were not the big obnoxious heavy hitters from New York, Chicago, and San Francisco that Jerry and Vito covered. They were my speed, and I developed a great rapport with them. We were on the phone so much that we talked more than just business, we talked about our lives, hobbies, and families. I felt I knew some of my accounts better than I knew my colleagues since I spent all day talking to them, borrowing the stocks we needed and negotiating the fees.

Many of them weren't even familiar with lending stocks before I came along, but they were already clients of Goldman's in different businesses. Maybe Goldman did all their trading, but they weren't involved in lending. So I created a simple presentation and spent time educating them on how the process worked: they already owned the stocks, so our work together would be a low-risk transaction. I would just borrow the stocks, to lend out to our hedge fund clients, and then pay them back a fee. This would be on top of the earnings they would get from any price appreciation or dividends of the underlying stocks. It was a win-win; they didn't have to do anything, just allow me to borrow their shares and they'd enjoy a bump in revenue. I ended up signing many of them to lend to us.

For a newbie like me, they were great starter accounts, and since nobody had touched them before, there was only upside potential. Each morning I got to the office early and pored over their holdings—the stocks they had to lend. It was like mining for diamonds among loads of dirt and rocks.

One morning, Vito stood over my shoulder. "Why do you even bother with these accounts?" he asked. "They're nobodies from nowhere. They don't have enough stock to make a dent in what we need, they won't make us enough money to spend your time on them." I looked at him with a small smile and shrugged my shoulders. I knew better than to engage Vito; nothing I could say would change his attitude.

Guys like Jerry and Vito dealt with large mutual and pension funds that were dubbed the "big whales." They had "size" positions, or huge quantities of stock. And he was right, my small fry clients never had many shares of any stock, but each share of a hard-to-find stock added up. It reminded me of my grandma's advice about saving spare change from when I was a kid. "Every penny has value," she'd said, "don't think they are worthless. If you pick up enough of them, you'll have a dollar."

In our business, we differentiated ourselves in two ways: getting hedge funds short by finding the stock they wanted, and keeping them short. They wanted to short these stocks because they felt they were overpriced, or they wanted to short them as part of an arbitrage trade, but they were impossible to find. Many of the trades were "crowded" at the time, like Enron and Overstock.com, meaning every fund wanted to short them, and every broker wanted to borrow them, but there weren't many shares available. Each share mattered, and even though the hedge funds were trading in big blocks of shares, I would find them one share at a time. I picked up pennies, just like my grandma had said, and hoped that over time it would make a difference.

One morning, as I'd sifted through my account's holdings, I got a call from Jackie, a woman around my age who worked for a small bank in Iowa. Over the past months of talking, we realized we shared a love of reading and had started our own little book club from afar. "I think I have something you want," she said in a sing-song voice. "We just took receipt of the stock, so you won't see it on our holdings. I wanted to make sure that my girl Jamie from Goldman got every share." I was so excited I thought I'd explode. Borrowing this stock was like hitting the jackpot, getting something for Goldman that so many of our hedge funds wanted. The fact that Jackie kept it just for me, and didn't lend it to anyone else at Goldman or to another broker on the Street, that was the icing on the cake.

"Who just picked up that Lernout and Hauspie stock?" Mike yelled a few hours later. He stood at his office door and looked over the trading floor, his eyes narrowed, like a detective wanting to solve a mystery. The phones kept ringing, but the desk chatter silenced, and everyone scanned the floor to see who'd been able to find the most elusive stock of the month, the shares of a Dutch telecom company whose stock was tanking because the market felt their earnings were overstated. Hedge funds were dying to short it, and since nobody had borrowed shares in days, nobody could. But I just got some, which meant hedge funds could short again. I could feel the heat creep up my neck into my face as I raised my hand. "It was me," I said.

Everyone's eyes turned to me, and I felt like a beacon as my cheeks flushed. Mike's face lit up with a smile and he walked over and slapped me on the back. Hard. "Well done," he said. "Where the hell did you find them?"

"I pieced them together from those smaller accounts I just signed on," I said.

"The team can learn from you," Mike said, as his eyes scanned the floor, loud enough for everyone to hear. "You're hungry and scrappy. I like that." I saw Jerry and Vito roll their eyes, and a small part of me loved getting a rise out of them.

I worked hard to make the most of my small clients, and I had fun doing it. It was exciting to build something out of nothing, to bring in revenue to the firm that hadn't existed before, that everyone had previously overlooked. And I loved working with my clients and being the face of Goldman Sachs to them, that they looked to me for guidance and information. Jamie from Goldman was wise and experienced even though I was only twenty-three. I fell in love with being her.

After a few months, I wrote up a report that summarized the revenue from these clients, and Mike pulled me into his office to review it. "You know, I'd never thought these accounts could be so profitable," he observed. I couldn't help but smile. "It must be because you are working with them," he added.

"I don't know," I said. "I just think that somebody finally had the time to work with them." I wished I could suck the words back into my mouth. Why couldn't I own my accomplishments? Sometimes I wished I were one of the cocky guys on the desk, who was their own biggest fan, who could accept a compliment, who could advertise their own success. But that wasn't how I was taught. In my home, humility was valued more than pride, but that's not how it worked in Goldman's house. Mike smiled and shook his head.

"No, Jamie," he said, "it's because of you. You're a chameleon, you can talk to anyone, blend in anywhere. With those little Podunk banks in the middle of nowhere and the big institutions in New York. Many of the guys wouldn't have given these accounts the time of day, but you saw potential in them, created great relationships with them, and it made a difference." My face flushed and I felt so light, I thought I'd float out the door. To me, there was nothing better than being good at something, and impressing someone, especially a partner at Goldman Sachs.

❯✳❮

I'd kept in touch with Michelle during the past year, but not with Sofia because she had been transferred overseas. Michelle and I grabbed dinner one night at a local tapas bar to chat about our experiences at the firm so far.

"Well, working here is not what I thought it would be," she sighed. "I don't think I belong here." We were sitting at a table in a dark corner. A single candle between us lit up Michelle's blue eyes and long blonde hair.

"What do you mean?" I asked, surprised that someone from Goldman's country club world felt this way.

"I feel like I've been boxed into a role. The guys on the desk see me as a party girl, a blonde bimbo with connections. Like I have nothing else to offer. They don't take me seriously and don't challenge me. I've hardly learned anything."

Seeing her sad eyes, I frowned. Once again, I thought about labels. Here was "Sister Jamie" meeting "Bimbo Michelle"—such rigid definitions, so few roles offered, based on so little. My mind went back to Melissa, too. I'd bet that most of us Goldman women didn't feel comfortable in any of these assigned roles.

"I'm going back to grad school," Michelle admitted, "to redefine myself."

But Michelle hadn't defined herself—Goldman had defined her.

I ended up having a lot of these "closing dinners" over the years, where I'd dine with Goldman women before they'd leave the firm. One woman saw no opportunity for her, since all the meaningful work that would propel her career was given to the men. Another woman asserted that her values didn't align with the firm, and that when she looked at senior management, it concerned her that she didn't want to aspire to be any of them. Then there was another woman who was told she wasn't polished enough to cover large lucrative clients, when she was surrounded by rough men who told crude jokes. It was as if Goldman women had a limited shelf life, unable to succeed long-term like the men could.

As for me at that moment, I had pushed aside my discomfort with the rigid roles that women were put into—the lack of diversity, the macho culture, and how foreign this whole life felt—and instead focused on how much I'd accomplished my first year at

Goldman. I'd also grown up and toughened up, being initiated into this frat-like culture, shedding some of my initial naivete. The banter on the desk and crude jokes shocked me less and less. I found that I was good at my job, and my success filled me with some satisfaction. The days were fast-paced and challenging and seemed to end before they began. I thought, *I can do this. The girl who didn't know a stock from a rock is making it at the most competitive shop on Wall Street.*

But the hours were grueling, and I was tired and stressed all the time. On the weekends, the thoughts that I pushed down during the busy workdays would seep into my brain. As much as I enjoyed being a good trader, I didn't enjoy trading. I felt like a flower child, wanting to make the world a better place, not make rich people richer. Again, I thought about being a social worker and wondered what would have happened if I'd had the guts to stand up to my parents. I wondered if I would have been happier and if having passion for my job would have made up for the lack of money. Then I'd judge myself for not being more grateful for the job I did have. I always ended up feeling confused and exhausted.

So, I thought, *Yes, I can do this.* The question was, did I want to?

CHAPTER FIVE

Everyone I knew had an opinion about my life and career—my parents, siblings, friends, even the woman who lived across the street. Everyone, that is, except for Dan. We had started seeing each other right after my sister's Christmas party, and he'd quickly become my best friend. His advice was never direct—he wasn't a fixer, he was a listener. He'd nod and wince at all the right places as I'd vomit my work frustration all over him. But he always encouraged me to trust my gut, which put him distinctly in the minority.

One night I met up with my friends from high school, Maddie and Lily, and their verdict about Goldman was clear.

"You need to just leave," Maddie said as she handed me a glass of chardonnay. Her wrist, lined with bangle bracelets, jingled. "Life's too short to not be happy. Think about the quality of your life. Do what you want to do, follow your dreams."

Maddie had just left her job because she couldn't stand her hour-long commute. She took a pay cut to get just thirty minutes of her life back. I couldn't get over her decision. It seemed so indulgent to me to sacrifice money for an inconvenience of time. Maddie wasn't a trust fund kid, either; she came from humble beginnings like me, and I knew she didn't make a ton of money. I wondered what her parents had thought. I didn't think phrases like "quality of life" and "follow your dreams" were in my family's vocabulary.

"Jamie," Maddie went on, "there are other companies that would hire you. I just left my job and got another one. Goldman isn't the only game in town."

"With such little experience, I'm hardly marketable," I said. "Where am I going to go? I feel like any appeal I have comes from the Goldman name."

Lily stared at me through her black framed glasses. "No offense, Jamie," she said, "but they are Jedi mind–fucking you. Making you think you're nothing without them. It's so unhealthy, you've got to get out of there."

She had such clarity. But I quickly dismissed her advice, rationalizing that she came from family money, and with her parents still supporting her, she wouldn't feel the same way if she were in my shoes.

And then there was my family.

"Tell everyone what you brought in, Jamie," my dad said at a Sunday family dinner not long after bonuses were given out. My grandma, parents, brother, sister, and I sat around the dining table. I hated sharing what I made with my family—the money was too excessive, like chocolate so sweet it stings your teeth.

"Come on," my brother Tony urged. "Spill it."

I swallowed the lump in my throat. "I made $175,000 this year," I gulped. I hated hearing the words come out of my mouth. They made me feel dirty. I was too small of a person to be the big earner of this family. Tony looked at me wide-eyed as his fork dangled over his mashed potatoes. He was my big brother; he taught me how to ride a bike and how to live life, he always gave me advice, sharing the wisdom he had from being on this planet ten years longer than me. I'd never seen him look at me like that. It made me happy, scared, and sad at the same time. Who was there to look up to when your idol starts idolizing you?

"If it makes you feel any better," I stammered, "I don't really like what I'm doing."

Tony scoffed at me and rolled his eyes. "Jamie," he said, "it's called work, not fun. Nobody loves their job. But you do it for the money, and then with that money you enjoy your life."

"I guess," I said. *So that's life?* I wondered. We do what makes us the most money, and then we use that money to "enjoy life." But what happens when we work so hard and long that there's no time for enjoyment? That sounded like a bad trade to me and hell, I was a trader, I should know.

"You listen to me, kid sister," he said with his fork pointing at me. "Don't be a fool and leave. People would line up to make the money they're throwing at you. Hell, I'd take your place in a heartbeat."

"Listen, Jamie," my dad said in his soft voice, his attempt to diffuse the situation. "I know you don't love what you're doing, but this money is really setting you up."

He wasn't wrong. I thought of my daily drive past the Jordache clothing factory. Dozens of people walked toward the building—a two story cement block. Their heads hung down from slumped shoulders as they carried their paper lunch sacks in hand, ready to start their shift. These were hardworking people who probably made minimum wage. They would slap me upside the head if they knew I doubted my path. I was making money that would change my future, and the life of my family. I could provide for my parents as they got older, which was the least I could do after all they'd done for me. All the trips to the hospital, the expensive spinal surgery, the treatments and therapies. I owed them so much. Also, I hoped I'd have a family of my own someday, and I wanted to be able to take care of the needs of my future children without struggling like my parents had. And if life indeed was a marathon and not a sprint, why not just suck it up these early miles, and then be able to coast the second half of the race?

Though my mom had grown up in poverty, and she valued the security that money could provide, for my dad, money meant something more. His father, my grandfather, as a new immigrant from Italy, had achieved success as a tailor and was able to move his family of six out of a small apartment in Newark, New Jersey, to a single-family home in the suburbs, complete with a fenced-in yard. He left the poverty of his past behind and made it in the Land of Opportunity. Unfortunately, it didn't last long, as his business dried up, while his needs multiplied. He overextended himself, counting on income that never came. The financial demands for the mortgage, utilities, food, and clothes never ended, so he did the only thing he felt he could to make the responsibilities go away—he ended his life. After, my widowed grandmother and her children, including my then–ten-year-old dad, went right back to a small apartment in Newark, as if their windfall, and my grandfather, had never existed. My dad's mom, who died when I was five, lived the opposite story of Cinderella, going from living a more affluent life to spending the rest of her days working as a maid. For my dad, having money wasn't just a matter of stability. It was a matter of life and death.

My dad looked at me like a judge about to give a disappointing verdict. "I'm sorry," he said, "but you've got to suck it up, toughen up, and be grateful."

Suck it up, toughen up, and be grateful, push through the pain. It was a familiar sentiment in my family. It was an oft-repeated mantra after my spinal surgery, when I know they said it as much for themselves as for me. There's nothing quite so hard as seeing someone you love in pain. It was their way of coping, their way of trying to help me be strong.

My whole life, I'd felt like my family was the wind at my back, supporting me and pushing me forward. But forward toward what? I'd followed their advice, I'd been grateful, I'd pushed through and sucked it up, but now I'd landed somewhere I didn't want to be. I was their baby, I was their last chance, I was their communal masterpiece. A canvas where everyone had a right to make their mark, even if they painted right over me.

And then there was my grandma, who stayed silent at dinner but who'd had Goldman's number since day one. I will never forget her reaction when I told her I'd gotten a job there, the day after the math problem fiasco. I'd rushed into the family room to tell her while she crocheted her latest blanket.

"Why would you want to work there?" she asked. "The people you met seem so unkind and rude."

"But Grandma," I said, "everyone wants a job there and they chose me. I'll make a lot of money there."

She stopped crocheting and looked at me. "I know it's a lot of money, Jamie," she said, "but what's it going to cost you?"

⟶✳⟵

A few months after the family dinner, Grandma's health started to deteriorate. She was well into her nineties and couldn't climb the stairs to her room without gasping for air. My parents got a hospital bed and she started to sleep in the family room. Grandma and I were close; she was a constant in my life. She'd moved in with my parents when my mom was pregnant with me and had helped take care of me since. Throughout my childhood and even into college, when I had bad dreams, I got into bed with my grandma. Yes, a healthy, grown woman who would crawl into bed with a tiny old lady for protection! But it wasn't her size that extinguished my fears; it was her strength. Her knowledge, confidence, and wisdom were the threads that weaved the safety blanket that she was for me.

Now I slept on the couch next to her, wrapped in one of her crocheted blankets. It smelled like her perfumed powder. "Night, Grandma," I said. I watched her chest rise and fall as the soft yarn touched my face. My chest tightened as I pictured the room with the bed gone, with her gone. "Goodnight, baby," she said.

A few weeks later, her breathing got so bad that my parents said she had to go to the hospital. I helped her pack some things. "No matter what happens," she said, "remember how much I love you." We sat on her bed in the family room, her St. Jude candle burning next to us. I held her hands, which were covered with age spots, swollen knuckles, and bulged blue veins. I focused on the warmth of her touch and wanted it burned into my brain. A tear fell down her wrinkled cheek. I kissed her hands and put my head in her lap. She combed my hair with her fingers and sang me an Italian lullaby, just as she'd done for decades. "Always choose happiness for yourself," she said. "Above all else."

I couldn't sleep that first night she was in the hospital and when the sun rose, I panicked. I didn't want to go to work, I wanted to be with her. But Goldman was clear about time off—and I thought it was decidedly *not* okay to take a day off to be with a dying grandparent. I called Molly, who'd become more than a mentor over those months; she'd become a friend.

"Don't think twice about it," she said. "Go to the hospital." It was the best advice I'd ever get in my career.

When I arrived, I discovered that Grandma's condition had worsened and she'd lost consciousness. I sat vigil at her bedside and held her hand all day as she faded away. Her breaths slowed with each hour and her skin grew paler, her lips drier. I wished she wouldn't die, I wished she could be with me for my whole life, I wished my heart was strong enough to beat for the both of us. My eyes were glued to her heart rate monitor as I felt her hand grow colder and colder. Finally, at 9 p.m. that night, a nonstop high-pitched beep filled the room.

As I headed toward the hospital lobby to leave, my body trembled as I fought back sobs, tears pouring down my face. I heard someone call my name and found Dan standing at the hospital's entrance. He wore a hooded gray sweatshirt and jeans, his hands pushed into his pockets.

"I needed to see you," he said. "I'm so sorry." His face was pale, and tears lined his cheeks. I had called him right after she'd passed, and he must have headed to the hospital immediately after. I ran into his arms and cried into his chest. We hadn't said it, but I knew I loved him, and he loved me. I wondered if my grandma brought him to me so he could take her place.

The next morning I got ready for work, heavy with sadness, my eyes swollen from all my crying. As I walked out to my car in the driveway, I heard the hum of an engine. It was so early, the sky so dark that it looked like the middle of the night. I never saw another soul up in my neighborhood at that hour. I walked with hesitant steps toward my car, then I saw Dan standing in front of his, wearing a chauffeur cap and holding up a sign marked "Fiore," just like the Goldman drivers did.

"What are you doing here?" The headlights from the car lit up his face. He was bright-eyed like it was the middle of the day, which I couldn't believe since I'd kept him up the previous night, talking for hours.

"Today of all days, I wanted to do something nice for you. Hop in. I'll drive you to the ferry today." He smiled at me in that sweet way of his, with a small arch of his full lips and his dimpled cheeks. I got into the car and kissed him.

"But wait," I said as he pulled away and I noticed the back of my car. "How am I going to get home?"

"It's a round-trip service," Dan said. "You must be exhausted. Close your eyes and try to sleep."

I looked at his profile as he focused on the road, my chest so filled with gratitude I thought I'd explode. The truth was I couldn't imagine how I was going to get through the day. I had to be "on" all the time. I was alert on the drive to work, alert with my client trades, alert with the office politics. There was no room for error, and no time for rest. But I felt safe to be off around Dan.

Grandma knew the deal with Dan the night she met him. My

parents had invited him for dinner and my mom and grandma stood at my side as I answered the door. Dan stood there with three bouquets of flowers, one for each of us. I blushed as my mom sighed, and my grandma smiled wide, her dentures bright and shiny. As my mom pulled Dan into the living room, my grandma took my hand and held me back. "I like him, Jamie," she said. "He's got a soft kind face, and a nice smile."

Grandma had said to choose happiness, and with Dan, I knew I was doing just that.

CHAPTER SIX

"What the hell was that?" I said. I heard an explosion, and the whole trading floor seemed to vibrate, the lights flickered, and the client call I'd been on was disconnected. I looked up from my desk into the glass walled conference room. The floor-to-ceiling windows faced north and our location on the forty-eighth floor gave us an unobstructed view of the World Trade Center. One of the towers was on fire. The bright blue cloudless September sky from earlier was now gray, tinged by smoke.

The whole desk rushed into the conference room and pushed up against the windows to gape at the fire. The windows were like a movie screen; it just didn't seem real. The conference room TV blared, and Tom Brokaw announced that a commercial airliner struck the tower. Over my shoulder, I heard whimpers and I turned around.

Leah, our new trading assistant, sat on the ground outside the conference room and sobbed. She hugged her knees to her chest, her red ringlets cascading over her purple blouse. I got on the floor and put my arm on her shoulder.

"Leah," I said. "Are you okay?" I could smell her vanilla perfume.

"My dad works in the North Tower," she said. "On the ninety-fifth floor." Her words knocked the wind out of me.

"Oh Leah," I exclaimed. "I'm so sorry." When I put my arms around her and squeezed, her trembles vibrated against me. "Have you called anyone in your family yet?"

Her mouth turned down and I could see her full lips quiver. "I'm too afraid to," she said.

I got up and held out my arm. "Come on, let's go and try to call your mom."

She followed me and we got to her seat, the last one on the trading row. I sat next to her as she put on her headset. Her view faced west, and I could see the sun illuminate the Statue of Liberty. It was so surreal; from this perspective you wouldn't have thought anything bad had happened.

Then I saw it. I shook my head and hoped that it was a figment of my imagination, hoped it was a bad dream, hoped it would disappear. But there it was, right out the window, an airplane. To see it fly so low didn't make sense. I saw the United Airlines emblem as it passed me. The image defied all logic and order in my mind. The plane traveled north toward the World Trade Center. I ran into the conference room and heard screams as the plane approached and then sliced through the South Tower.

I was stunned into silence, thick with shock. I couldn't make a sound. I was no longer grounded in reality; I was a feather that could float away on the breeze. This was no accident, this was no mistake, this was planned.

I scanned the room for Leah, and I saw her run off the floor.

It was like a bomb had gone off in the office, full of chaos and fear. My colleagues, usually put together, were wild animals, screaming and crying as they ran around the floor. I got in my seat and called my mom and then Dan. They both begged me to come home.

The emergency speakers dotted along the walls crackled to life: "This is the security department. Our building is secure, and you are advised to stay where you are." The trading desk was in disarray. Few people were at their seats, their chairs empty and pushed toward the middle of the room. Some had left, others huddled in small groups around the floor. Garbage cans lay on their sides, discarded breakfasts spilled out on the office carpet. Cell phones buzzed and rang. My boss, Mike, called out from his office door. His voice was calm and measured, like it was any other Tuesday morning. He wasn't wearing shoes, just bright red socks as the shoeshine guy next to him polished his wing tips. "Everyone hang tight," he said. "We'll have a team meeting in a few minutes."

I sat at my desk, took a deep breath, and bit my lower lip. I didn't want to stay, but I felt like I needed permission to leave. I was too much of a chicken to take a stand for myself. I feared for my life, yet shockingly the fear of punishment at Goldman held the same weight.

Just then Molly called. "Listen to me," she advised. "You grab your stuff and leave. Don't wait to talk to Mike, just go." She told me what I wanted to hear, but I wasn't convinced.

"But I don't want to get in trouble," I admitted as I felt tears starting to push through. I was desperate to leave, but also terrified of what I'd face outside. I just wanted to wake up from this nightmare.

"Jamie, you need to trust me," she said. "If there are any issues from you leaving, I'll take the blame."

I hung up the phone. With all the uncertainty around me, I felt some relief that I had a plan. I grabbed my stuff and headed to the elevators, hoping nobody noticed. I considered taking the stairs, but walking down fifty flights versus a short elevator ride made my decision. If the elevators were running, I was getting on one. I needed to get off the high floor, get out of the building, and get my feet planted on the ground. My heart pounded so hard in my chest I could hear it as I walked into the elevator. There was only one person in there with me, the woman from the reception desk; at least I thought it was her, since she sobbed the whole ride holding her head in her hands.

Outside was like another world. The once clear sky was now gray and smoky, and a fine mist of ash floated in the air. Papers rained down, some intact, and others singed and shredded, like a ticker tape parade gone wrong. It smelled like a chemical fire, burning rubber and metal. I tried to call Dan and my mom, but my cell phone had no service, and the pay phone at the corner had a line down the whole block. People yelled and moaned as they ran through the streets. They looked like extras in a horror movie, chased by a serial killer or a wild beast.

The tall skyscrapers of downtown that once made me feel powerful and protected, now penned me in like a zoo animal. Thick with claustrophobia, I headed down the street toward the river. I needed to see as much sky as possible so I could keep my eye out for more planes.

I ran along the path toward the ferry terminal. Drops of sweat fell down my face. As I neared the ferry, the pathway became congested with people, so I slowed to a walk and looked at my watch; a ferry to New Jersey would arrive soon and I hoped I could catch it. When I got to the pier I stopped; I'd never seen it so crowded. It looked like everyone in Manhattan wanted to get on a boat.

My mind raced with alternatives, how to get home if I couldn't catch the ferry. I wondered if I could swim to New Jersey. Instead I got in the long line for my ferry to Jersey City, so crowded that people were practically standing on top of each other. Next to my slip a boat to Hoboken started to board, and a man in line argued with the deckhand who had told him the boat was full. I watched as the man pushed him, and the deckhand fell onto the metal ramp. The man stepped over him like he was a discarded ferry ticket and boarded.

My breath came in fast and shallow. I grabbed my phone and tried to call Dan, but I couldn't get through. I counted the people in the line in front of me, as I guessed what the capacity of the incoming boat was, praying that there would be room for me on it.

People started to board and the deckhand at the boat's entrance had a clicker that counted passengers. I went forward and with each step my body relaxed knowing that in a few minutes I'd be in New Jersey. Right as my leg reached the boat, the deckhand put his hand out. "Sorry, we're at capacity," he said. My shoulders slumped, and I could feel the last of my energy fizzle out of me. I wanted out of New York, I wanted safety, I wanted to be home.

"This is bullshit," the man behind me said. I could feel his hot breath on my ear. "There's plenty of room. Let more people on." I cringed, not wanting to be in the middle of a fight. When I turned toward him, my eyes widened. He looked like he'd been dragged through a pile of gray ash—the only bright part of him was his glassy blue eyes. He reminded me of Bert the chimney sweep from *Mary Poppins* and I wondered what he'd been through to get here.

"Come with me," he said as he grabbed my hand. He pulled me past the deckhand and onto the boat, just before the captain backed away from the dock. The deckhand glared at us and groaned as he threw his hands up in surrender.

The man pulled me up the stairs to the boat's open top deck. I just held his hand, this stranger covered in soot. I didn't want to let go.

We stood in silence, shoulder to shoulder, against the deck railings as we made our way to New Jersey. I couldn't take my eyes off the buildings and as we went around the tip of Manhattan we were right in front of the Towers. Things fell from the top of them, and I wasn't sure what they were at first. Then the realization came over me like a rogue wave: it was people. How scary it had to be in that building, surrounded by fire and smoke, unable to breathe, unable to see, unable to think. How desperate the situation that that was the choice they made. If I'd had a work breakfast at Windows on the World, if I worked at another broker whose office was in those towers, that would have been me. I covered my mouth as my stomach stretched and shrank and then I hunched over and threw up. My vomit covered everything, my sneakers, the man's loafers, and the white boat deck floor. The man's hand rubbed my back as I continued to retch the contents of my breakfast. The air smelled of spoiled milk and smoke.

I got off the boat in New Jersey and watched it pull away. I looked around the dock for the man but he and the rest of the passengers were gone. I sat on the bulkhead as my feet dangled over the river. I was full of relief, full of fear, full of sadness. Then I heard loud and desperate screams, like the cries of a wounded animal fighting to survive. The sound filled my ears, rattled my brain, and only seconds later did I realize the sounds came from me.

I ran toward my car like something chased me. I don't remember the drive, or arriving home. I just remember sitting on the family room couch, curled into a ball as I stared at the cream wall. I heard the news from the TV, decrying "the events of September 11," I heard the telephone ring, I heard my mother's pleas for me to eat. But I just stared at the wall, at the crack that ran from the windowsill up to the ceiling. I'd never noticed it before, but I stared at it all day and all night. I'd become an expert on that crack, knowing where it widened and thinned, where it took out chunks of sheetrock and where it faded into the ceiling into nothing. Over the next days I studied that crack backward and forward until I felt I knew that crack better than I knew myself.

The stock market closed for the rest of the week, the first time in history that trading halted for so long. I didn't have to go to work so instead I found refuge on the family room couch. Day after day I stared at the wall and rocked myself.

My mom hovered over me offering food, drinks, and conversation. I didn't want to eat, I didn't want to talk, I didn't want to do anything. Dan came after work and sat on the couch and held me, like he was a human vest thrown out to rescue me.

"Talk to me," he said. I stiffened. My silence was the piece of gum that covered the hole on the bottom of my boat. If I removed it, I'd sink and die for sure. "I can't," I said. "Not yet."

Sleep became my enemy. Terrors filled my nights: I'd burst out of my office window with shards of glass stuck to me and then my bloodied body would drop to its death. Or I'd choke on rancid gas, my hands clasped around my neck. Or I'd catch on fire and flames would wrap around me and I'd throw myself into the harbor to douse them. I'd wake up in the middle of the night so soaked with sweat that I thought I'd wet the bed.

One morning my mom came into my room. I was still in bed and couldn't get out. "You need to talk to someone," she said. Her hands were on her hips as she looked down at me. I smelled onions and I realized it was my body odor. "I made you an appointment with Dr. Taft today."

Dr. Taft was my internist and I'd known her since I was a kid. I went to her when I had a cold or needed a physical, not for something like this. Dark circles lay under my mother's eyes and her face was white. I realized I wasn't the only one who felt like hell. "Okay," I agreed.

When I arrived at the appointment, I went to the doctor's office and sat across from her. Busy floral wallpaper covered the walls and the room smelled of spiced potpourri, which gave me an instant headache.

"How are you feeling?" Dr. Taft asked. Her eyes were wide open, like she'd seen a ghost.

My face was slack, and I didn't have the energy to smile. "Not good," I said.

She bit her lower lip, like I had a disease she wasn't familiar with. "Tell me what happened," she encouraged.

I told her what I'd seen, a graphic play-by-play. Despite my protests to keep them in, the words flowed out. Dr. Taft handed me a box of tissues and leaned in and watched me like I was an interviewee on *60 Minutes*. When I finished, her eyes dropped down and her lips were thin. Then she gave me a hug, which is something that in all my years of knowing her, she'd never done.

"I'm going to write you a prescription," she said. "It will help. Especially the first days back." I heard the scribbling of her pen as she wrote on the thick prescription pad. I wondered what she could possibly give me. Did a pill exist that erased memory?

"You need to take it step-by-step," she said. "Focus on what you can do to feel comfortable going back."

I looked at her, puzzled. There wasn't anything that could make me feel comfortable going back to work. "Okay," I said.

I brought the prescription home and ripped open the bag, desperate to feel better. The bottle contained Xanax, which I'd never heard of. I popped a pill in my mouth, swallowed it dry, and waited as the bitter taste hung on my tongue.

Half an hour later the magic happened, where everything about my body and my mind slowed down and softened, like sandpaper had rubbed over me and smoothed my sharp corners and took away my splinters.

I thought about Dr. Taft's advice, and what I could do to make me feel comfortable. The only answer, I decided, was to prepare for my worst nightmares.

Dan and I looked for gas masks and traveled two hours to get one in upstate New York, since all the local Army Navy stores were sold out. While there, I picked up a set of emergency fire blankets. I also searched for personal parachutes in case I needed to jump out of the building, but I couldn't find one. I wondered if they even existed. If not, I figured someone would invent one soon.

The night before I was due back at work, I called Molly. She knew I'd gotten home on September 11, but we hadn't talked since.

"I'm not sure I can do it," I said. Thanks to the Xanax, my heart no longer raced, and my words came out calm and smooth. But just the sound of her voice brought me back to New York and the office. Even with the medicine and the emergency supplies, I wasn't sure if I could pull it off.

"Respond, don't react," she said. "Reaction is a knee-jerk thing like fight-or-flight. Responding is thoughtful, where you base your decisions on the long term." I just wanted her to tell me to quit because I didn't want to return.

"I'm not saying you should or shouldn't go back for good," she continued. "I'm saying that you should try, because once you leave, it's over. You can only leave Goldman once."

I sat on my bed after the call and her words echoed like a bell in my brain. *You can only leave Goldman once*. This would be the refrain I'd hear through my entire career.

I couldn't imagine looking back at my life and knowing I left a job because of fear. That wasn't my family's way. I'd always been taught to push through fear and anxiety, not to be pushed around by them. Whether it was my childhood medical challenges, anxiety over college exams, or my fear of flying, I was always told to dig in and face difficulties head on. I wasn't going to answer fear with retreat, I was going to be brave and strong, and pray like a fiend. I didn't want this event to derail my life. I didn't want to just rashly walk away.

The next morning, I got dressed for work and looked at myself in the bedroom mirror. My reflection was the same, but I was different, like a reused piece of tin foil, no longer shiny, but riddled with cracks and folds. I jammed my gas mask and fire blankets into my workbag, pinching the sides together to zip it up. I washed down a Xanax with my coffee and headed to lower Manhattan, with my rosary beads clutched in my fist. *I can only leave Goldman once*, I told myself, *and it won't be today*.

As I waited at the dock in Jersey for the ferry, I saw the big smoking hole where the Towers used to be, transforming the entire skyline, making it look like a kid who lost their front teeth. When I got into New York, the air was so thick it felt like I was breathing in ashes. It smelled rancid and I reached for my army grade mask, but then thought that was foolish since no one else wore a face cover. The mask was for chemical warfare anyway, and I didn't want to waste the filter. Instead, I took out the surgical mask I'd also purchased, the kind doctors wear in hospitals. It didn't help, and within a few minutes my head started to throb.

At every street corner there were large armored vehicles flanked with armed soldiers. It reminded me of the videos on the news of the war-torn Middle East. The soldiers stood like the guards at Buckingham Palace, frozen in place and looking past me like I wasn't there. They each carried a machine gun with a string of bullets that hung across their bodies.

I'd hoped getting back to work would be a return to normalcy. That the anticipation of it would be worse than the reality. But the whole downtown scene made all my nightmares seem logical and plausible, and none of my preparations seemed to help.

Everyone at the office was the same but different. There was little banter, little laughter, little life. They did their work as fast as they could and then high-tailed it out of there, as if being in lower Manhattan was a bad omen. Close to 3,000 people died on September 11, but there were some miracles amidst the devastation. I found out that Leah's mom had asked her dad to pick up a prescription at the pharmacy that morning. That errand delayed his arrival to the Towers and saved his life. Despite that, Leah never returned to work after that day. In fact, many never came back.

I was a nervous wreck as I went through those first days back. The benign sound of moving furniture on the floor above me was a bomb detonating. The unknown smell of someone's hot lunch was air warfare. Exhaust smoke that rose from the rooftops of buildings was a weapon of mass destruction. Every oversize bag that someone carried on the ferry was a bomb, ready to blow me to shreds. I felt like I had two full-time jobs; my regular one and worrying about being a victim of a terrorist attack.

I trudged through the next months with Xanax in my bloodstream and darkness on my back. Dan was the one light I had, and I looked forward to Friday nights with him where I'd show up at his door exhausted and he'd recharge me with Chinese take-out and funny movies.

One night I stood at Dan's kitchen sink looking out the window as I washed the dinner dishes. The wintry night was heavy with snow flurries in the black sky. I rinsed the last dish, and as I turned to put the towel away, I saw Dan in front of me on one knee.

"I almost lost you that day," he said. "It made me realize I can't be without you." His blue eyes were shiny, and I hadn't appreciated how much 9/11 affected him until that moment. He held an opened black velvet box with a solitaire diamond ring. "Will you marry me?" he said.

I'd thought about this moment a million times before 9/11 but I hadn't since. It was hard to imagine anything joyful after that day. The sight of Dan, though, with his sweet dimples and his raised brows, changed all that. "Yes," I exclaimed. "Yes!"

CHAPTER SEVEN
Four years later (2006)

"We're supposed to wait three minutes," Dan said. He held the directions and looked down at me as I hovered over the test stick. "Start a timer," I instructed. We stood in the bathroom and faced the counter hand in hand. My bare feet felt cold against the cream tile floor. That white stick, a worthless piece of plastic, held a priceless answer. Dan's watch timer rang. "You look," I said. "I can't do it." Dan reached over and grabbed the stick, turned it in his palm, and then looked at me. I held my breath and tried to read his blue eyes, and then a large smile crossed his face.

The thought of having our own family was an everlasting Gobstopper, layers of excitement wrapped in layers of fear. The idea of having a child with Dan filled me with sunshine, but I was afraid of my body. I wondered if all the spinal X-rays I'd had as a child ruined my eggs and if the rods in my back could stand up to a growing baby inside me. I wondered if my busted-up body was a safe and strong enough vessel for another human. I was scared about work, too, since my career gave me little free time. I wasn't sure if being a Goldman working mother was possible, since few senior women in my department had kids. I wondered if there was a reason why.

A few weeks later, we went for an ultrasound. I couldn't wait to see our baby on the screen and get a little picture to keep for the pregnancy journal I'd bought. We were sent to a patient room where I put on a gown and jumped on the paper-covered exam table.

"This is it," I said as goosebumps covered my arms. The room was cold and smelled like rubbing alcohol.

"I can't believe this is happening," Dan said and smiled. Soon a sonographer named Gabby came in. She had a large smile with dimples so deep you could stick your finger in them.

"Let's take a look at your baby," she said. I giggled as I shifted down on the table and put my legs on the stirrups.

"You'll feel some pressure first," she said as she held up the vaginal wand. I nodded and grabbed Dan's hand. The sensation of the wand made my teeth clench, but I stared wide-eyed at the screen. The picture was fuzzy, like a TV in the middle of the night before the advent of cable, but the sound was music. The *tap tap tap* filled my eyes with tears. "That's your baby's heartbeat," Gabby said. Dan squeezed my hand as I felt a rush of relief that my body had pulled it off.

As we were walking out, Gabby stopped us and said, "Dr. Cohen would like to meet you before you go." Dr. Cohen was the head radiologist, and I hadn't expected to meet him. His office was musty and damp, with outdated wood panels and little light. It was like walking into 1975. Dr. Cohen sat at his desk, and we took seats across from him, the sonogram picture held tightly in my hand.

"So, about your scan," he said. He gestured to a screen on the wall where I saw the image of our little baby. "From what I see," Dr. Cohen said, "I wouldn't bet the ranch on this pregnancy." My eyes remained on the screen because I couldn't face him.

Suddenly, I was twelve years old again, looking at a spinal X-ray, not an ultrasound, at the children's hospital in Delaware. "There's nothing more we can do," my orthopedist Dr. Schaefer had said. "If we don't operate soon, Jamie's spine will crush her heart and she'll die." I could hear my mom's cries as I sucked my lips into my mouth so deep that my braces dug into my flesh. Despite the years since that surgery and the successes I'd had, I'd never be able to shake my shadow of defectiveness.

"I don't understand," Dan said, bringing me back into the room. "We heard a heartbeat." His voice cracked.

"Yes, there's a heartbeat, but the embryo is hardly growing," Dr. Cohen said. "It'll take a miracle for this pregnancy to stick."

We got in the car and Dan held me as I cried. It was like Dr. Cohen had detonated a bomb inside of me, the countdown to the death of our baby. I lived in fear that every twinge and discomfort was the beginning of the end. I prayed for it to survive, even as Dr. Cohen's negative words played in a loop in my mind.

A few weeks later, when I woke up to use the bathroom, I saw blood in my underwear. My doctor sent me for another ultrasound and Dan and I were ushered straight to an exam room.

The room smelled of Lysol and anticipation as the overhead speakers pumped in sounds of trickling water. The sonographer came in and conducted the ultrasound, focusing on the screen, which she turned away from us. Dan and I sat in silence as she withdrew the wand from inside me.

"Is the baby okay?" I asked as Dan squeezed my hand. His jaw was so clenched that I could see the tendons that ran across his neck. The sonographer stood at the foot of the table, and blood covered the wand in her hand. "I'm sorry," she said. "There's no heartbeat."

I don't remember much after that. They ushered me out via the service elevator, my cries were so loud that they didn't want me to upset the perfect pregnant ladies in the waiting room.

It was a Thursday and the doctor scheduled a D&C, an outpatient procedure to remove the rest of the pregnancy from my uterus, for the next day. I was grateful I'd have the weekend to recover, and I emailed Brian and asked that he tell Mike that I'd be out a few days for medical reasons. I didn't go into details, but I knew rumors would spread since a young female newlywed out sick had "reproductive issues" stamped all over her.

When I got home, I crawled on the couch to watch TV even though I couldn't concentrate. Maybe this was a message that I wasn't mother material, or it was a sign to focus on my career, something that I was good at. I searched the house for my bottle of Xanax and found it at the bottom of my dresser drawer. I couldn't remember the last time I'd taken one, and it was like seeing an old friend. I popped one in my mouth and fell asleep.

When I returned to work the following Monday, I got an email from Mike asking me to meet him. I prayed it had nothing to do with my sick days. Mike sat at his conference table, and I joined him with my pen and notebook in hand.

"I've got good news." He smiled wide, like it was my birthday and he'd just handed me the biggest present. "I'm promoting you to manager of the Institutional desk." My mouth gaped open, and my eyes widened, so shocked that words wouldn't come out.

"Higs, your star is rising," Mike said, using the nickname he'd coined since I'd gotten married. "This is going to be the first of many promotions." Mike was known as a hard ass and very stingy with compliments, so as I smiled, bubbles of excitement burst in my belly. I wished it had been my baby instead, but at least this was something.

"Eric will be working for you, but he doesn't know that yet," he said. I squinted in confusion since Eric had managed the group for years and was a fixture in that business. I'd assumed he'd gotten promoted to a bigger job.

"If you're wondering what happened to Eric," Mike said, "let's just say he isn't serious about his career." Mike's lips had a slight curve to them, too small to be a smile, like the wicked grin of the Grinch. "Once he started to leave early to coach his kid's T-ball team," he said, "I knew he wasn't manager material."

I nodded, now knowing why so few working mothers existed in this place. For a flash I was relieved I wasn't pregnant, then my eyes burned at the twisted thought, and I wanted to throw up.

"I could never get rid of him though," Mike explained. "I can't afford to lose his golf connections." He leaned back in his chair and wrapped his hands around the back of his head, threading his fingers through his thick brown hair. A framed photo of a golf green was over his shoulder. Eric had something better than a 4.0 from Harvard; he was a scratch golfer and the Connecticut State amateur champion. His connections with golf pros around the world got Mike tee times anywhere. Mike laughed, and his large midsection jiggled.

"You can handle Eric, right?" Mike said. "He might not be cooperative." It made Eric sound like a wild horse that had to be broken in.

"Yes, I got it," I said.

"And I need total devotion from you," he said. "No personal distractions, understand?" His large brown eyes were on my waist, like they were trying to send my womb a message. I wanted to wrap my arms around my stomach, to pretend it wasn't there, to protect it from Mike's glare, and to comfort it from its loss. "Yes," I said. "I understand."

"Tonight, I want you to come out to a client event, just so you can meet some folks. Eric's going to be there obviously, but he doesn't know about his demotion yet, so just play it cool."

That night I went to the industry-wide event at a big hotel, attended by hundreds of our clients. I was with my soon-to-be team from Goldman, but nobody knew that yet. When the bartender announced last call, Eric bought dozens of beers for everyone. I'd been nursing a few glasses of wine all evening so I could stay out and be social, but not get drunk. Most people had left, including Mike, and it was mainly Goldman people left at a cluster of tables in the dining room.

Eric, who sat next to me, started shot-gunning cans of beer, a sight I'd last seen at a college frat party. Again and again he'd pierce a hole in the bottom of the can and drain it into his mouth with such efficiency, his Adam's apple didn't even move.

The lights were turned up, a signal that the staff wanted us to leave, and Muzak played from the speakers that dotted the room. Eric finished the last of his beers and looked at me with bloodshot eyes as he licked his lips. Then I felt his hand rubbing my knee as he leaned in for a kiss.

"Come on now, Eric," I said in an awkward sing-songy voice as I gently pushed him away. I scanned the table, grateful that everyone was too drunk to notice.

"You come on, Jamie," Eric slurred. "I've had a thing for you for months. Let's grab a room tonight." He smiled, showing off his crooked yellowed teeth, and I had to keep myself from wincing.

"Sorry, Eric, not going to happen," I said. "I think it's time I headed out." Eric placed his hand on my knee again and squeezed so hard that I felt his nails digging into my flesh. I took in a sharp breath.

"You should really think about reconsidering," he said.

I stood up so fast, his hand released from my leg and I walked away. I wanted to smack him in the face, but I didn't want to make a scene, not with my promotion on the horizon. I didn't bother saying goodbye to anyone, hoping nobody noticed our exchange. I hightailed it into one of the town cars waiting outside. As I replayed the events of the night on the way home, I couldn't believe it, and I realized it would make Eric working for me even more awkward. I prayed he was so drunk he'd forget about it, and I wouldn't dare say anything to anyone. I'd told Mike I'd handle Eric, and I would. I chalked it up to a stupid mistake on his part and was hopeful that he'd get in line once he knew I was his boss.

The next morning Mike met with Eric in his office. I could see Eric's face through the glass walls and knew the exact moment he found out about his demotion, because his pale face flushed to a deep shade of crimson.

After that meeting, news of my promotion spread like wildfire. I didn't receive congratulations or handshakes, just glowering stares. I saw my reflection in all their eyes, like I was somebody different. No longer Sister Jamie who plugged away in the background. Now I was front and center, now I was a manager, now I was a threat.

Later in the day, I went into the kitchenette to grab a coffee. Vito and Jerry stood in the corner, huddled over their paper cups, covered in whispers. They looked up when I entered.

"Congratulations," Jerry mumbled. He stared at my feet and sounded like a boy whose mother made him apologize for something.

"Thanks," I said. He walked out of the room so fast that I wasn't sure he heard me.

Vito stayed, and I felt the pressure of his glare as I poured my coffee. "Jerry should be a manager, not you," he said. My fingers warmed from the hot cup of coffee in my hand, and I wanted to throw it in his smirking face. "The only reason you got it," he said, "is because of your vagina."

He walked out before I could react, but I didn't know what I would've said. I took a sip of my coffee and it burned as it went down. I wondered if Vito was right and if I got the manager spot to fill some quota, but I refused to let doubt disorient me. Men, including Vito and Jerry, had tried to bring me down for years. They were just jealous that as a manager I was now more senior than they were. Regardless of why I got the promotion, I'd show that I deserved it.

The next day I scheduled one-on-one meetings with my new team members. I started off with Eric because I wanted to get it over with. I could only imagine how pissed off he was; going from managing a team to working for a woman half his age, that he'd just unsuccessfully hit on. We met in a conference room and sat at the round wooden table across from each other.

"Thanks for meeting with me, Eric," I said. I smiled wide while my stomach churned, praying he wouldn't mention our encounter at the bar.

"I'll make this easy on you," he said. "I can't afford to leave. So, I'll do a good job and play by the rules." I nodded and relaxed a bit; maybe he wouldn't give me a hard time after all. Eric's face was pale, and the skin sunk under his eyes. Mike said my star was rising, and it was clear his was falling. I felt a pang of sympathy. "But to be clear," he added, "everyone's on my side, and we won't help you."

Eric walked out of the room, slamming the door so hard that the office wall vibrated from its force. I looked through the glass wall and, relieved nobody was around, put my head on the conference room table, grateful for the cool wood against my hot face. Everyone was on his side, and the good old boys made up most of the team. Even though Eric wasn't their boss anymore, they'd be loyal to him. How could I run a business where everyone was against me? How could I manage people who didn't want to work for me? How could I succeed in this situation? It was like I was the quarterback, and Eric was my receiver. He'd suited up, he was on the field, but that was it. I couldn't expect him to catch the ball, I couldn't expect him to run a play, I couldn't expect him to score a touchdown.

Mike would judge me on my team's performance and profitability. This was my first time managing, and if I didn't deliver and if Mike thought I couldn't hack it, I could kiss any future opportunities and promotions goodbye.

I tried to relax while I waited for my next meeting. Maybe Eric's comments were idle threats, and I could win the others over with time. Then Chris, another member of the team, entered the room and took a seat at the table. He had thinning brown hair and deep wrinkles around his eyes, and I realized I wasn't just younger than Eric, I was one of the youngest people on the team.

"Chris," I said, "I'm excited to work with you." I gave him my winning smile, as if the smile alone would ensure the meeting would go better than the last. Chris looked at me, his brown eyes squinted, his lips pursed. "You spoke with Eric," he said, "so you know where I stand."

I bit my lip hard, and my toes became roots that burrowed into the office carpet. I refused to let his harsh words flatten me. "Well, I did hear from Eric," I said sitting up straighter, "but I want to hear from you. Ideas you may have about how we can make our business better." Chris's face was blank; the only life was the freckles along his nose that flushed red.

"They can call you my manager," Chris said, "but I'll always work for Eric." His words were monotone, like he was a robot that Eric had programmed. The tick of the office clock filled the room, and I hoped the quiet would break his façade and soften his resolve. "So, am I free to go?" He shrugged.

"Sure," I relented.

After he left, I felt tears burn the corner of my eyes. I had told Mike that I could handle this, but I was doomed if everyone was against me. A knock on the conference room door shook me from my overwhelming stupor. It was Pete, a junior member on my team, who came in and started to talk before his butt hit the chair.

"So, I've got to say how psyched I am to work for you," he said. His bright smile matched his words and I stopped myself from looking around the room for a candid camera, because I was sure I was being pranked. "Someone who'll judge me on my work," he said, "and not my ability to shot-gun beers."

I must have looked confused, because Pete continued, "That's what it feels like to work for Eric. It seems all that matters is my knowledge of football and my alcohol tolerance."

I laughed and eased back into my chair. "You won't have to worry about that from me," I said.

"And something else," he said as he leaned into the table, like he wanted to share a secret. "I know this team looks like a locker room filled with Eric sympathizers. Some of us, though, are happy to work for a professional for a change." I took a deep breath, relieved. Maybe there was some hope in this new team after all.

"That's nice to hear," I said. "Tell me about yourself."

"Well, I started working here three years ago," he said, "right after I graduated from Notre Dame." Pete had a baby face, but his head of thick silver hair made me think he was older. "I have a toddler son at home with another baby boy on the way." My eyebrows raised. He seemed too young to have kids. Pete held his hand up and gestured toward his ring finger. "I married my college sweetheart," he explained, "and we got pregnant right away."

"Wow, that's wonderful," I said, though I felt a pang of jealousy.

"I want you to know," he said, "that I'm good at my job. I'll work my butt off, but a career at Goldman isn't in my long-term plans."

Here we go, I thought. I waited to hear about his dream to start a hedge fund with his dad's money.

"I've always wanted to be a guidance counselor," he explained, "but I couldn't walk away from the money here. I hope someday to leave, move back home to Indiana, and pursue my dream." I didn't know what shocked me more, the fact that there was someone here, like me, without a passion for finance, or that he had the guts to admit it to his new boss.

"That's amazing," I said.

"I've got many more years here before I'll have saved up to do it," he said. "Kids aren't cheap, so I'm not going anywhere anytime soon."

We chatted for a bit more, then Pete went back to his desk, and I waited for the next meeting. Pete's words ignited a fire in my gut that had been extinguished for so long I'd forgotten it was there. Maybe it wasn't too late to do something meaningful with my life. I thought back to my dinner with my family— viewing my life as a marathon and not a sprint. I was only thirty after all; maybe I could be like Pete, put in my time at Goldman in these early miles and have a meaningful second act toward the end of the race.

My mentor Molly, who'd just retired and moved to Florida, had shown me the Goldman way, and I was grateful to her. But meeting someone like Pete was even better—he was a kindred spirit, someone who dreamed about doing something more meaningful someday.

My new role as a manager was a challenge those first few months, but with Pete's help, especially, it went well. Eric, Chris, and much of the rest of the crew did the bare minimum to keep things afloat, but Pete and I worked overtime to push the business forward. Here I was the quarterback, with a team of players on the field, but just Pete and I were playing. I'd throw the pass and he'd run all over the field, doing everything he could to score the touchdown, while the other players stood, arms folded, staring at the sky. Pete and I created new technology, improved workflow, and developed stronger client relationships. Pete became more than just an employee; he became my right hand and a close friend.

One night, we were working late on our business proposal. "So

I've got to share something with you," I uttered. We sat shoulder to shoulder as we looked over a spreadsheet on my computer. I'd wanted to tell him since the day I met him, but I'd been afraid to share my secret within Goldman's walls. I'd needed to know that Pete was a decent and loyal guy and in those past months, as he put in the long hours by my side, he'd proven that. I trusted him, and it was the first time I felt safe sharing my values and dreams at work because they were similar to Pete's. Before this moment, I hadn't spoken them for fear of penalty, because the only values that mattered at work were Mike's values. Empty bags of chips and soda cans littered my desk. "I have a dream to leave Goldman, too," I disclosed. "I've always wanted to be a social worker."

He turned to me and a big smile crossed his face. "That's awesome!" he declared. "And it doesn't surprise me at all. Let's face it, we're not Wall Street people."

"Definitely not," I agreed. At that moment I felt bonded to Pete with an invisible adhesive, the glue of our aspirations.

"Let's make a pact," he suggested. "Let's work our asses off here, save as much money as we can, and then leave so we can do what we want." He held out his hand and I smiled as I shook it. Then he picked up his can of Diet Coke and I grabbed mine.

"Let's toast to freedom from Goldman someday," he said as we clinked cans.

"Yes," I said. "To freedom."

That pact wasn't some throwaway comment—we took it seriously. In the coming weeks we each created a "Spreadsheet of Freedom," an Excel document that tracked financial goals we wanted to accomplish, like saving for mortgages and retirement. We wanted something serious backing up our dreams, and our spreadsheet showcased our efforts and highlighted our progress. It became the fuel that kept us going day after day. I was excited to have a goal to work toward and a partner to reach it with.

A few months later, my phone started ringing off the hook, but it wasn't clients trying to reach me—it was Eric's wife, Dana. I'd only met her once before, when she stopped in the office before going out to dinner with Eric, and we'd had a nice conversation.

"Jamie, it's Dana. I need your help," she said the first time she called, her voice cracking into sobs. I looked across the desk at Eric, who was laughing with Chris. "What's going on?" I asked. I made sure my call was on private since we shared a phone bank on the desk, where the lines were open and anybody could jump on anyone's call at any time.

Dana told me that Eric was having an affair with one of his clients, a recent college graduate who worked at Patriot Bank, based in Chicago. I wasn't surprised, since I'd heard rumors from people on the desk about it. Their relationship was the worst kept secret. Even Pete reported seeing them go into the same hotel room during a work trip to Chicago. Although romantic relationships with clients were against firm policy, I didn't feel it would be appropriate to tell Mike unless I was sure.

"You have to help me," she said, "and you're the only one I can go to. He keeps denying it and I need proof. I feel like I'm going crazy." I heard the cry of a baby in the background. Dana and Eric had two young kids and I heard she'd just suffered a miscarriage, which pulled on my heart strings. But what could I do, spy on her husband, my employee? I didn't want any part of it, but I couldn't hang up on a crying woman, so instead I just listened and told her I was sorry.

Then she started calling more, several times a day, which started to impact my job. She sounded more hysterical with each call and then her speech started to slur. I was sure she was drunk, and I worried for her and her kids.

After a week, I couldn't deal with the disruptions anymore, so I met with Mike and told him everything. As I recounted the story, my face flushed, like I was guilty by association. I'd told Mike I could handle Eric, but I didn't think mediating his infidelity was part of that. I felt sad for Dana, but I didn't want this drama, especially as I embarked on my new management role. Mike looked at me, his arms crossed and his eyes narrowed. "I can't get rid of him," he said, "but I can tell him to control his wife. You just pull him off the account so there won't be a conflict of interest, but don't mention the affair."

Eric should have been told to stop the relationship or be terminated, but it didn't seem he was. The situation should have been reported to our division's human resources department, but I didn't think Mike would. Instead, Mike spoke to Eric—or I assume he did, because Dana never called me again. I was relieved but still worried about her and her kids. That afternoon, after market close, I pulled Eric into an office to talk about account coverage and to move him off Patriot Bank. I had learned at Goldman to relay difficult messages at the end of the day because if the person is pissed and makes a scene, no one will be around to see it.

"Since I'm still new to the team," I explained, "I've decided to reshuffle account coverage." I didn't want to make it obvious that I was just singling out Eric and Patriot Bank so I'd mixed up all the accounts. We sat next to each other at a conference table, and I went over the new account list, which had him covering our largest institutions. Yes, he was losing Patriot, but he was getting another comparably sized client to replace them.

Eric looked down at the account list, and I saw the tightness in his jaw as he crumpled it up and threw it at me. Fight or flight kicked in, as I stood up and headed toward the door, but he grabbed me and pinned me against the wall, his hand wrapped under my jaw. "Who the fuck do you think you are?" he screamed into my face, his spit showering my nose and cheeks. "If I could, I'd rip your fucking face off." His lips were wet and drool rolled down his chin. His face was bright red. My heart pounded so hard I was sure he could hear it. He kept me suspended against the wall, my toes brushing the floor. I held my breath as the blood rushed out of my face; I thought I'd pass out. His eyes were wild, like he'd kill me right there on the spot.

Remain calm and just tell him what he wants to hear so he'll let you go, I thought. I looked at him and spoke in a hushed whisper, my lips quivering.

"Okay, Eric, I didn't realize this would make you so upset," I said calmly. "I can definitely think about this and come up with another solution."

He looked at me wide-eyed and then a wave of calm came over his face, like he'd been shot with a tranquilizer gun. He morphed into a totally different person, like I was on a movie set and the director had just yelled "Cut!" He placed me on the ground then turned around, opened the door, and headed toward the elevators.

I went back to my desk to grab my stuff, grateful that nobody was around. My body trembled as I headed home, and when I made it to my car in Jersey City, I called Dan and burst into tears as I recounted the story.

Dan and I spoke at length about it, but I didn't know what my next move should be. Goldman didn't like "troublemakers," people who made waves and were involved in drama. They wanted people who put their heads down and made money for the firm. Plus, Eric was friends with all of senior management due to his golf connections, so if it were a "he said/she said" battle, I didn't think I'd win. And I'd told Mike I could handle Eric, though I wasn't sure navigating assault applied. I just felt dirty, like Eric's disgusting behavior rubbed all over me. But despite all of this, by the end of the day, I decided that I needed to say something.

The next day I watched Eric as he walked onto the trading floor. He was all smiles, high-fiving the guys as he walked down the row, as if nothing had happened. Meanwhile, my fingers trembled as I emailed Mike to ask for a meeting.

"I'm sorry, Jamie," he said after I'd told him what happened, "and there are channels at the firm to report this conduct. But remember, I'm not getting rid of Eric, so imagine what managing him will be like after you report him to human resources." His nostrils flared and he looked at me through his silver-wired glasses. Then he leaned forward, resting his arms on the table. "I'll tell you what. I'll make sure he stays off Patriot Bank and you don't report him, agreed?" My stomach tightened as his words sank in and the smallest smile crossed Mike's lips. He was bargaining with me on something that shouldn't be negotiated. I was shocked, but part of me was not surprised one bit. Mike was making it seem like I had a choice, but he and I both knew I didn't.

I wanted to call human resources right away, but I knew I wouldn't. That would end my career and bringing Eric's and

Mike's behavior to light wasn't worth the risk. I just got this promotion and I remembered, *You can only leave Goldman once.* I'd pushed through the aftermath of the 9/11 terrorist attack, I could push through the terror of Eric. I swallowed the lump of disgust in my throat.

"Agreed," I said.

Drama with Eric calmed down in the ensuing weeks, and he seemed to make peace with losing Patriot Bank. We never addressed the incident, and our conversations were brief and professional. Like great actors, we pretended it never happened.

A few months later it was bonus day, and, since I was now a manager, I was excited to hear my number. I met Mike in his office. "Jamie," he said, "your total comp is going up 100 percent this year, from $500,000 to $1,000,000."

A wave of cold washed over me. My comp was *doubling*? He was paying me a million dollars? A million goddamn dollars? I was speechless, like I just won the Powerball. I knew people on Wall Street made a lot of money, but seven figures? I froze in place and my mouth hung open with shock. Mike gave out a big belly laugh, enjoying my deer-in-the-headlights reaction. "Congratulations, Jamie."

I didn't have much time to compose myself because as a manager, I now had to present my team's bonuses to them. Since I was new to the role, I wasn't part of the compensation discussions that led up to this point, so this was the first time I saw what they made. Mike handed me a stack of papers, one for each person on my team, with their compensation totals that I'd share with each of them.

What I noticed right away was the pay disparity between the men on my team and me. I was a manager now, and I knew I was viewed as a high performer, since I'd gotten promoted. But before I was a manager, guys like Chris were considered my peers. Yet, he'd pulled in $700,000 last year. Of course, I'd heard rumors that men made more than women at Goldman, but now I saw proof in writing. And even though all the salaries, even the smallest ones, were huge by the world's standards, the disparity still pissed me off.

The last person to enter was Eric, and I picked up his sheet. My eyes widened as I saw his numbers and I almost choked on my words as I read them.

"Eric, your compensation is going up 11 percent this year," I said, "from $900,000 to $999,999." Eric gave a small smile, nodded, said a quick thank you, and walked out, like he was just handed a latte from Starbucks and not a check for a buck short of a million fucking dollars. Mike then left and as I sat alone in the quiet office, everything became clear.

I'd like to say I got that big pay day because I did a great job managing a new team, signing up new lenders, increasing the spread on our book by more than 20 percent, developing new workflow that saved time and increased the teams' productivity, and navigating all the Eric drama with grace, but that wasn't why. It was because they wanted to pay Eric, the guy who had affairs with his clients and assaulted his boss, a million-dollar salary. They simply bumped up my comp to match his, plus a dollar more because an employee can't make more than their boss.

I was psyched about the money, but also outraged. I felt that my bonus was just a big pile of hush money to keep the scratch golfer's career intact despite his egregious actions. I couldn't believe that someone's weekend hobby had such an impact on their livelihood.

CHAPTER EIGHT

We weren't splitting atoms on the trading floor each day, but skill was involved in what I did as I advanced at Goldman. I arrived by 6 a.m. every morning and scoured the news to anticipate the next stock a hedge fund would target. Then my team and I would search through the holdings of our lenders, which showed the stocks they had available to lend, to make sure we borrowed what we needed. Then we'd marry the two, lending our borrowed shares to the hedge funds, making a cut (called a "spread") on each trade. The fees we charged on each individual loan didn't make a ton of money, but our total of borrow and loans were valued in billions, and it added up. I did this all day, just getting up to grab food and water and use the bathroom. Unless we were out with clients, we ate breakfast and lunch at our desks. After the market closed, I'd call my operations group to confirm all the trades settled, meaning that we'd actually received the stocks that our clients agreed to lend us. After all that, I'd do a little prep work for the next day.

Most evenings we went out to dinner and drinks with clients, since good relationships with these institutions were crucial to our business. Sometimes, these institutions gave stock to the brokers that they liked the best, but more often to the ones who treated them with steak dinners and expensive wine. We often called our client dinners "steaks for stocks" because the morning after we wined and dined them, we'd get even more shares of the stocks we wanted to borrow. I'd get home at midnight or later, and then get up at 4:30 a.m. to do it over again. I originally thought I was compensated on the spreads I made off my book of securities, and the great relationships I developed with clients, but instead I started to feel like I was mostly paid for dealing with the grueling lifestyle and the bullshit at the office. I called it my "hazard pay."

One morning, right after our yearly bonuses were announced, Mike walked up to our group holding a basket filled with bananas. He handed them out, one by one, with a saccharine smirk. Everyone gave Mike an awkward smile as we took our banana from his hand, and then we all exchanged confused looks. Nobody would dare ask why we were getting this gift, but we knew it wasn't an act of kindness.

Mike handed me the last banana but held on to it as he looked at me. "Just a reminder," he said, loud enough for the team to hear, "that you're all monkeys in my book. You're overpaid and I could replace you at any second. Your asses are taking up prime real estate in my world, so make sure you're earning your spot. Remember, each day my expectations are higher than the day before. Goldman isn't lucky to have you, you are lucky to have Goldman, without us, you're nothing."

Then his eyes scanned the team, and everyone stood at attention around him, like he was the general and we were foot soldiers, holding our bananas instead of our rifles, ready to go to battle.

We had just been paid bonuses for our efforts from the year before, based on our contributions of earnings for the firm. Mike was the one who had decided our pay, and now, just a week later, like a bad case of buyer's remorse, he deemed us overpaid. He *wanted* us all to have imposter's syndrome. After pumping us up and acknowledging our efforts through our bonus, now he needed to minimize us and push us down, making us feel that our bonus was just dumb luck, having nothing to do with our abilities or accomplishments. Our personal value at Goldman Sachs was reset to zero, as it was at the beginning of every fiscal year, and we started from scratch again. We had millions just wired into our personal bank accounts, but Mike saw us as worthless and he wanted us to know it. It didn't matter how hard we worked, how many shares of stock we lent, how much money we made for the firm. Goldman wasn't lucky to have us, we were lucky to be at Goldman.

At Goldman there was always talk about "culture carriers," employees who lived by the well-crafted business principles penned by the executive office decades earlier. The fourteen principles contained wonderful sentiments, focusing on honesty, integrity, and teamwork. These culture characters stood for the meritocracy that Goldman was supposed to be. But in Mike's world, we first had to be recognized by him. And in order to do that, we had to carry not the *firm*'s culture but *Mike*'s culture, two vastly different things. We had to act and think and be like him. We had to follow his sports teams, like to drink bourbon, and enjoy sailing. We had to be the first in and the last out each day. We had to make it look like we were busy well into the evenings when we could've been home enjoying our families instead. Whole sections of the employee population who didn't try to look or sound or think or behave like Mike were sidelined. Their achievements weren't noticed because they weren't noticed.

I lived in fear that I wasn't worthy of the real estate I was taking up on the trading desk; I walked in every day trying to earn my spot. Even as a manager with all my experience, I felt each day was an interview to keep my place at Goldman Sachs. Like the children who followed the Pied Piper in a trance, I followed Mike; instead of playing a melodic tune, he guaranteed money, status, and success. I began to adopt some of Mike's values and dipped my toe into his culture pool when I felt I had to. I didn't go to crazy extremes—like a woman in another division that I knew, who bought the same type of Porsche as her partner (not Mike—but close enough) so she could race him on the weekend. But I did follow the Packers during the playoffs and learned how rare and expensive Pappy Van Winkle bourbon was. And I was grateful that Dan sailed a lot as a kid, because he gave me terms and trivia to pepper into conversations with Mike. I became the queen of "face time," a constant fixture on the desk so Mike could see me, even though I could have been home hours earlier.

Mike monitored everyone's comings and goings. Like a sentinel, he'd walk around the desk in the early morning and in the late afternoon, keeping track of everyone. On days where there was inclement weather, especially snowstorms, Mike had a field day. He'd stand guard by the door so that if someone came in late, due to train delays or bad traffic, he'd be the first face they'd see. "Good morning, snowflake," he'd shout, and start a round of applause, a standing ovation that the rest of the desk joined in on. As I stood up and clapped my hands, I felt terrible for the poor schmuck who'd just walked in, but I was just as grateful that it wasn't me.

But what I became most of all was Mike's culture enforcer. I made sure his rules, as silly as they seemed to me, were known.

Nick, a guy who worked for me, started to leave at 4 p.m. on the dot, right when market closed, to see his kids. He'd just been through a divorce and didn't have primary custody, so he wanted to see them as much as he could. It was during review season, which was our yearly professional assessment and those results impacted bonus numbers. I worried for Nick and didn't want his review, and ultimately his pay, to be affected by his departure time.

"Mike's noticing that you're leaving early," I said as I stood over his desk. The closing bell had just rung, and he was powering down his computer. "You need to put in more face time. It's going to affect your bonus."

He looked at me, his lips pursed, his nostrils flared. I hated being Mike's messenger. Nick was one of the most productive people on my team. The hedge funds and institutions loved him. I never had an issue with any of his trades, and his spreads were huge. I didn't care when he left, but that didn't matter because Mike cared.

"When it comes to my kids," he said, "I don't give a shit about my bonus." He got up, pushing his chair back with such force that it hit the desk behind him, and walked out. I felt sick for him, like I just allowed a drunk person to get into a car to drive himself home. He was going to get into a huge accident and I couldn't stop it.

Weeks later, Mike called me into his office to review bonus numbers together. He handed me a spreadsheet with everyone's compensation totals.

"I don't agree with Nick's number," I said. "It's a total outlier.

He should be up like the rest of the group." Nick was being paid down 20 percent when everyone else on my team was up 10 percent. Our business had a great year and each of my traders had a profitability metric tied to their name, which was the average spread they made between the fee we paid on the securities they borrowed and the fee we charged our hedge funds when we lent them. Nick had the highest spread on the desk, and therefore was the largest contributor of our profits.

"He's a part-time worker," Mike retorted. "When he starts working a full day, I'll give him full pay. And he's overpaid as it is, where's he going to go?" He looked at me, waiting for my answer, but I just stared at him. "Nowhere, he's going nowhere," he answered. "He's nothing without Goldman Sachs."

I looked down at Nick's line on the sheet, considering. As a manager I was supposed to advocate for my people, to fight for them. The silence took up space between us.

"So, do you want to fight me on this?" Mike asked point blank. He looked at me over his silver wire glasses, his eyes angry slits, daring me. I wasn't in the business of fighting battles I couldn't win. After all, he was calculating my bonus too. My stomach felt queasy.

"No," I admitted. "I don't."

The day Nick found out about his comp, it didn't go over well. After I told him his numbers, he walked out and slammed the door so hard that everyone on the desk heard. Even though Mike made the decision, and had all the power, Nick only blamed me. I was just the messenger, but it didn't matter. Weeks later, Mike called me into his office and wanted to hear how Nick was doing.

"He's fine," I said, "but he's still bitter about comp."

"But don't you see, Jamie," he said. "Nick didn't leave. Even though he thought he was underpaid, he's still here, which means we were overpaying him. It's just like I told you. We own him. And we saved some money on his comp, which is money that could go to someone else, someone like Pete, someone like you."

I felt disgusting. Yes, I enjoyed the financial rewards of the job, but not what it was doing to my character. And if Nick was owned by Mike, then I was too, because I didn't feel I could leave. So of course I wanted success for Pete and me, but I wanted it because we earned it. I didn't want it to be a zero-sum game, for us to win because Nick lost. But to Mike, this was all one big game, where we were all pieces on his chess board, and he loved to pit us against one another, and play with our lives and livelihood.

※

The following spring, Mike called me into his office. "Human resources needs me to nominate an up-and-coming vice president to run the summer intern program," he said. "I'm selecting you. Don't make me regret it, got it? You are representing me. Make me look good."

I smiled widely. Though I was a vice president, that wasn't really a big deal; if you worked at Goldman six years or more, you got that title. For most that's where you'd stay, a vice president lifer—thousands and thousands of VPs were at Goldman. Only a select few, about 8 percent, were on track to become a managing director, or MD. This nomination was a signal that I was being considered for that title someday, and this was my shot to prove myself.

"I won't let you down," I said.

The day the program started, I gave opening remarks to the 200 hopeful college students in the same large meeting room where I reported on my first day. I scanned the crowd: they looked so eager, in their new suits, shiny shoes, wide eyes, and large smiles. They hung on every word I said, like I had the secret code needed to unlock a successful Wall Street career. I couldn't help but be proud of myself. I felt competent, I felt like a role model.

I thought back to Tom White, the tall man with the booming voice who scared the crap out of me when I was a trainee back in the day. Somewhat to my surprise, I used some of his old tricks on the interns. I told myself I was doing it for their own good, that it was my responsibility to indoctrinate them into Goldman's cutthroat culture. How else were they going to survive? I found that I even enjoyed it. I got a bit of a kick seeing the fear in their eyes as I walked in the door, locking it behind me. I collected apology notes from them signed by the partners who ran their departments, without a bit of sympathy. I didn't even feel bad when I kicked crying interns out of Open Meetings for not knowing the exchange rate between the pound and the dollar.

Every evening, before we went out to networking events, I met with a bunch of interns one-on-one to give them feedback on their performance and advice so they could find a permanent job at the firm.

"The convertibles desk has great things to say about you," I heard myself saying to Patty, an intern from Stanford. "But your nail polish has got to go. This is Goldman Sachs, not a night club." As my words reached her ears, a blush traveled down her face and she moved her hands from the table to her lap. Even though my stomach was in knots, my body pulled up straighter as I saw hers crumple.

I still had a brain, so I realized that the color of her nail polish had nothing to do with her intellect or ability to be successful at Goldman Sachs. Why did I feel like I had to mimic Tom White's shenanigans when they were not useful or productive? Throughout the whole program, I felt disgust by my actions, but also vindication. As much as I hated myself for acting this way, I thought I was doing it for the interns' own good—they'd never make it at Goldman without this tough love. Like the long-bullied kid on the playground who becomes the bully, I had become a part of the cycle of abuse at Goldman Sachs. And, the truth is, it felt good to be on the other side of the Open Meeting for a change: the powerful side.

Mike wanted daily briefings on the intern class from me, specifically, who the sharpest and smartest kids were so we could hire them for our own department. I was like a breeder, and he wanted the pick of the litter.

"I really like Tammy from Middlebury," I said. "She doesn't know a ton about the business, but she's super bright and has great potential. I've been working with her a lot." We sat at his meeting table, my ranking of the interns printed out before us. Mike tossed his copy toward me. "Cut the Mother Teresa shit," he said. "It's a shark tank here. It's eat or be eaten. Don't do too much to help her survive. Then she'll always be needy. We need to weed out the weakest ones before we hire them."

I chuckled that I was Mother Teresa now, which at least was a promotion from Sister Jamie. Tammy was a great candidate—

she reminded me so much of myself. She knew nothing about Wall Street when she arrived but had read every book I'd recommended and had gotten up to speed fast. I wanted to hire her and have her join my team, but I wasn't sure if I had her best interests in mind. Sure, I thought she'd succeed at Goldman, but I wondered if I just wanted someone else like me there, like my misery wanted a little of her company.

I thought Tammy was as naive as I had once been, and that she'd follow me right in the door, but she was more sophisticated than I gave her credit for. The last day of the program, she stopped by my desk to say goodbye. "I learned so much from you this summer," she said. "I can't thank you enough for all of your support."

I couldn't tone down my huge smile because she was getting an offer from us the next week. I was dying to tell her, but I couldn't, as it was against protocol.

"But the biggest lesson I learned," she continued, "is that Wall Street isn't for me. I'm going to apply to law school instead."

My shock showed, and she explained. "It's just that I've realized that finance isn't my passion, and during my time here I kind of feel like I'm a round peg in a place with only square holes." Phones rang all around us, and I could hear Jerry, Vito, and Eric's cackling laughter as they tossed a foam football to one another. All I did was nod and give her a tight hug. I was happy for Tammy, but my stomach panged with jealousy, that she was wise enough to figure out that lesson before it was too late.

CHAPTER NINE

D an and I still wanted to have children, but with the pressures of being a manager now, I was terrified of having another miscarriage. I also knew that promotion season was coming, and there was a chance I'd be considered for the managing director title. I thought back to Mike staring at my stomach and warning me of "distractions," so I couldn't afford to have any complications that would make me miss work. I just wanted to get pregnant and have a healthy baby; there wasn't time for anything else. Dan and I made an appointment with my OB to discuss options.

"What can we do to prevent another miscarriage?" I asked Dr. Drake, an OB/GYN I'd recently started seeing. We sat in her office as she held our chart and looked at me, her brown eyes framed by thick black glasses.

"Healthy eggs and healthy sperm make healthy pregnancies," she said. "There are no guarantees, but if you do IVF, we'd be able to make sure the eggs fertilize properly."

I'd heard all about IVF, the shots, procedures, blood tests, and costs. Making a baby in a lab and not in a bed seemed cold and unnatural to me, but if I could avoid a miscarriage, that's what my career and my sanity needed. It turned out that Goldman wanted that for me as well. My Cadillac insurance plan covered eight rounds of IVF free and clear. The finance person at the doctor's office said she'd never seen coverage so good. It was like Goldman's way of fast-tracking motherhood, which it approached the way it did business—with extreme efficiency.

So IVF seemed like a no-brainer for us: we could plan our family by timing it around my career, reduce the chances of miscarriage, and it wouldn't cost us a penny. The clinic even opened at 5 a.m. so I was able to get all my scans and procedures done and not be a minute late to work.

We got pregnant the first cycle, with twins.

I loved being pregnant, and I couldn't believe it when I got great reports from my doctor, appointment after appointment. My body, with all its struggles when I was younger, was able to keep up with two growing humans, and I was relieved and grateful.

Unfortunately, while my pregnancy was smooth, the markets weren't.

The year 2008 started off tough, as the unemployment rate rose. Then in March, the Fed intervened to save Bear Stearns, one of our competitors. Bear was overexposed to mortgage-backed securities and other toxic assets, which were tanking. To make matters worse, they purchased them with leverage, which is fancy talk for borrowed money. But the markets rebounded by May, and we all breathed a sigh of relief.

Then over the summer, Fannie Mae and Freddie Mac stocks started dropping. As their main line of business was residential mortgages, there was no other source of income when home prices began to plummet. They lost close to $50 billion in their mortgage business, and they had to use their capital reserves, and the well began to dry up. Fearing the disintegration of the housing market, the U.S. government took control of Fannie and Freddie and supervised them under the newly created Federal Housing Finance Agency. The Dow continued to fall, and all eyes were on the market.

I was at my desk one morning when I heard, "Higs, my office now!" Mike was at his door, his face beet red, his large frame filling the whole opening. I looked over at Pete, wide-eyed. I was five months pregnant, but because I was carrying twins I looked and felt like I was full term. Between the higher risk twin pregnancy and the markets, I felt like I was about to snap.

"Relax," Pete mouthed. I grabbed my notebook and pen and waddled into Mike's office.

Mike was turned away from me, staring at the CNBC broadcast and his Bloomberg terminal. He rubbed his temples again and again.

"I'm getting calls about liquidity," he said. "We need to round up some terms and round them up fast." Just like Fannie and Freddie, the entire global financial system experienced urgent demands for liquidity, or good old-fashioned cash. All the investment banks worried about their internal funding since their mortgage portfolios were dropping. Though the bread and butter of our business was borrowing securities that the hedge funds wanted to short, we also lent securities we had on our books, long positions that our various clients owned. When we lent securities out, we received in cash as collateral. The firm needed to secure cash, and it would be up to my team to lend large quantities of securities out to brokers to bring some in.

"Okay, Mike, we'll get on it," I said. I walked out of the room, my shoulders heavy. Mike was counting on my team, and it felt like the whole firm was. My team watched me with wide eyes as I returned to the desk, waiting for information and instructions. This was a big moment, the challenge was huge, and I found that part of me reveled in it. Like an army sergeant, about to lead her troops into battle, I revealed our strategy and assigned everyone a different role. Then we went to work, made calls to all our institutions, and in the next few days we packaged large quantities of securities to lend and we received the cash we needed as collateral.

The work didn't end after we got the loans on the books, though. Now we had to maintain the contracts through marking them to market. Marking to market is a process that maintains a loan's value and the collateral we received. When the original loan was established, we received money as collateral based on the price of the stock that day, so if we lent a stock worth $20 we'd get around $20 cash. But stock prices fluctuate, and as the price of each security goes up and down, we needed to receive more money on the loan or return some. And with the crazy market fluctuations that summer, with stocks trading wildly up and down, we were constantly maintaining the loans to make sure we had the cash we needed each day. I started leaving for work at 4:15 a.m. and drove straight into the city, getting to my desk by 5 a.m. I often didn't leave until well past dinnertime.

"Jamie, this can't be good for the babies," Dan said when the alarm went off one morning. I was lying in bed, trying to fight the forces of gravity and exhaustion to get up. I knew he was right, but I didn't have a choice. I had to perform. This was my chance to differentiate myself, in a time of crisis, the likes of which Wall Street hadn't seen in decades. Mike was counting on me. Failing might cost me my career, though I was also afraid that my efforts to succeed might cost me the pregnancy. I pushed myself out of bed.

"I know, Dan," I sighed heavily. "I know."

In mid-September, Lehman declared bankruptcy. Then the next day the Fed bailed out insurance giant American International Group (AIG). In the weeks that followed, money market funds, where most businesses parked their overnight cash, lost close to $200 billion.

We all lived in fear that Goldman was the next to go. My team did their part but that's all I had control over. My eyes were pinned to the partners in the glass offices those weeks as I tried to read their body language. I would say a silent prayer of thanks when they'd smile or laugh.

In the end, Goldman Sachs did survive that horrible year, but unfortunately many colleagues didn't. All through the fall, Mike pulled me and the other managers into his office. We all sat around the oval walnut table, our collective breaths held as we watched him.

"The firm needs to cut costs," he said, "so welcome to our first round of layoffs."

He gave a report to each of us, a list of twenty people from our group of 200, their corresponding salary, and their latest review score. "These are the lowest performers of our department," he said, "we need to choose our first four."

Like the brackets in March Madness, they were put head-to-head and analyzed; except the final four weren't going to the national championship, they were getting fired. The first person discussed was Kyle, who also happened to be one of the few Black people on our floor.

"Well, we can't touch him," Mike shrugged, "given his *status*," which he punctuated with air quotes.

"And the funny thing is," Jack, a manager from the hedge fund team said, "the dude's an Oreo." Laughter filled the room.

I cringed inside. As an employee active in recruiting, I knew the firm recruited from historically Black colleges and universities (HBCUs) to find new hires. Hiring Black, Indigenous, and people of color (BIPOC) candidates, especially at the entry level, was a priority from the executive office. In fact, in 2019, after I'd left, Goldman set a goal that 25 percent of their new hires should be Black and Hispanic/Latino. Looking back, I could count on one hand the number of BIPOC people I'd closely worked with at Goldman in two decades. So even though the company hired diverse candidates, they couldn't retain them; but with this environment, that didn't surprise me.

The same went for the LGBTQ+ community, although as of 2019 the firm didn't have a quantifiable goal. Rather, they were "exploring new ways to increase representation." As a manager, I signed up to be an "ally" of the firm, and I received a table tent for my desk to indicate my support. From the first day I had it, though, someone started messing with it. It was knocked over on its side, hidden behind my computer terminal, stashed in my desk drawer . . . anything to make it disappear without stealing it. I never proved it, but I figured it was Jerry and Vito. A few days after I got the tent, the firm made all employees attend a mandatory LGBTQ+ sensitivity training. As I headed to the meeting, the duo walked in front of me, telling each other gay joke after gay joke, with gay slurs sprinkled throughout. I never had one LGBTQ+ person approach me in all those years. Nobody was officially out on the desk, but chances are someone or many were. These close-minded, outdated colleagues silenced them.

Debate on the names continued. We whittled down the list and were between the last two people, Ben and Jocelyn. Ben was in his mid-thirties, a vice president lifer with two kids who worked for Brian, and Jocelyn was a junior associate, single, in her mid-twenties who worked for me. From a numbers perspective, not only did Ben score worse in his review than Jocelyn, but Jocelyn made way less money than Ben. For me it was a clear call. The babies pushed on my bladder so hard I thought I'd wet myself.

"I assume Ben is the one who has to go," I said.

James shook his head. "It's gotta be Jocelyn," he scoffed. "Ben's got a stay-at-home wife and two kids. Jocelyn's single with nobody to support."

My eyes widened and my mouth fell open. Goldman always touted that it was a meritocracy, where people succeeded or failed based solely on their abilities, not anything else like their marital or parental status. My eyes swept around the table, all men except for me, their faces without expression, looking at Mike.

"You're right, James." Mike nodded in agreement. "We can't fire a guy who has a family to feed. Jocelyn's the one. Thanks, everyone." Then just like that, he got up from the table and left the room, and everyone scurried behind him back to their seats. As much as I needed to pee, I couldn't get up, unable to process what had just happened. I was angry at myself for not putting up more of a fight, but it was clear that Mike was going to do what he wanted. I thought back to Nick's compensation, and how even though I tried to stand up to Mike about it, it didn't matter. When Mike made up his mind, there was no changing it. Although I could voice my concerns, he wouldn't have changed his mind. If anything, challenging him might piss him off and make me an additional target. I wanted to remain in good standing with him and keep my job, so I kept my mouth shut, even if I hated myself for it.

I wondered how Jocelyn would have fared if she had kids to support, but I knew the answer. Although around 50 percent of the firm's new hires were women, and the firm was focused on promoting them, by the year 2020, only 25 percent of MDs were women and 18 percent were partners. No wonder so few women lasted at Goldman long-term, since it seemed to me that they always protected the men. When I walked into the bathroom, I saw Jocelyn standing at a sink, and we exchanged smiles and small talk. My pregnancy heartburn flared as another reality set in—I had to be the one to fire her.

A week later, we had layoffs. The meetings were in a confer-ence room tucked in the back of the floor, away from the trading desks, right next to the elevators. It was the perfect spot with total privacy in case the meetings ended in hysterics, and its close proximately to the elevators allowed security to quickly get the victims out of the building.

My phone rang at my desk. "It's your turn," Mike said. He was in the conference room and wanted me to bring Jocelyn there. Layoffs were the worst kept secret, and everyone was on edge that morning. I hung up the phone and glanced at Jocelyn, who stared at her computer screen, reading the news. Everyone's eyes were on me, a walking hurricane as I approached her desk and double tapped her shoulder. Her head dropped toward her chest. It was the wordless signal that on this day only meant one thing. She looked up at me, tears already forming in her eyes.

"I'm sorry, Jocelyn," I said, "but we have to go for a walk."

The long walk from the trading floor down that hallway to the meeting room was dubbed the Green Mile, from the 1990s movie about death row at a penitentiary. Jocelyn and I walked as she choked back sobs, "I just don't understand this place," she said. I remained silent, understanding everything, but unable to share my knowledge.

During the next few months, more rounds of layoffs happened. One minute the employee would be at their desk, the next Mike's assistant would be packing up their belongings in a banker box.

Those months I thought of one of my grandma's lines of wisdom: "There are two ways to have money," she'd say, "you either save it or make it." During these tough times at Goldman, the company saved money by reducing headcount. Now it was time to make more of it.

Part of my job, once we got our hedge funds short, was to *keep* them short. That meant we always had to borrow the stocks that the hedge funds wanted to short. In return, the hedge funds would pay us a fee, a percentage rate applied to the market value of the trade. The harder the stock was to find, the more expensive the fee. Clients would pay high fees (upwards of 100 percent). Since there wasn't a published market for short fees, you couldn't just look it up on an exchange like a stock price. The broker quoted the fee at the time of the initial trade, but they could change day to day.

I had to look over the fees we charged our hedge funds and

adjust when necessary. Mike got involved in the stocks that had the largest market value of shorts, because a change in fees would have a significant effect on our profits.

"Jack these up another 200 basis points," he instructed one afternoon as he looked over the short report, a list of stocks with the largest hedge fund short positions. With a red marker he circled several securities and tossed the report back to me. For many of these stocks we were already charging double digit percentage rates—20 percent, 30 percent—and he wanted to increase fees another 2 percent.

"But we just raised their fees," I said. I knew what he wanted was legal, but I thought it was excessive. We were already making a huge spread on these stocks, and I'd just moved the fees the day before. We weren't the only broker to charge high fees, the whole Street did. It was the cost of doing business, but it felt wrong. The funds were stuck. Their only option was to get out of the position, to not be short; but for many of them, they hadn't made that much money on the trade and they wanted to stay short. I felt we were taking advantage of that because we were under pressure, after the market's tough year, to post decent earnings, and there was nothing the funds could do about it.

"Yeah, I know we did," Mike said. "But where are they going to go?" He smiled wide, and his flushed full cheeks looked like two ripe apples. Our hedge funds always complained about short fees, but Mike knew they couldn't find the shares anywhere else.

"They won't go anywhere," I acknowledged. "They can't leave." They wouldn't be able to find the shares to short anywhere else, so they had no choice but to stay and pay the fees. My stomach sank as I stared down at the report. I thought back to Nick when Mike slashed his pay and he didn't leave. Nick was stuck here, and I was too. Even though part of me knew how toxic this place was for me, I truly felt I couldn't leave. I was so enmeshed in Goldman's world, even my identity was tied to it. I answered the phone "Goldman—Jamie" and my clients knew me as "Jamie from Goldman" as if Goldman was my surname, Mike my dad, and I worked for the family business, unable to quit. Although it was for different reasons, I realized then that I had a lot in common with these hedge funds.

On the flip side, many of the institutions I borrowed shares from weren't that market savvy. Oftentimes they didn't know how special the stocks they had were, how desperate people were to borrow them. Many didn't realize that they could raise the fees on our borrows, like we jacked up the loans to the hedge funds. I'd developed great relationships with some of the smaller lenders, and they'd look to me to let them know if they were charging us the right fees for their stocks. After all, those stocks belonged to pension funds and mutual funds, and with the chaos in the market, they would have appreciated any additional opportunities to make money for their clients.

"Don't even think about telling them how valuable that stock is," Mike said to me one day. I'd just told him I'd seen a block of a stock that was hard to find on a small lender's inventory that morning. "If they are too stupid to know how much to charge us for their stock, then that's their problem." I ended up borrowing the stock, paying way less than I felt I should have. These tactics, which I thought were underhanded, made my pregnancy heartburn even worse.

The industry's reputation hit new lows after the Emergency Economic Stabilization Act of 2008—often just referred to as the "Bank Bailout of 2008"—was passed in Congress. Then 2008 closed with the Bernie Madoff scandal and the opinion of Wall Street was worse than ever. Protests popped up around the country and some of them made it to Goldman's front door. These protests morphed over the years into the "Occupy Wall Street" movement.

Pete and I went outside after market close for a coffee one day and faced the protestors for the first time. They chanted "Goldman Sucks" while they pushed handmade signs that said, *YOU GOT BAILED OUT, WE GOT SOLD OUT!* and *SATAN CONTROLS WALL STREET* in our faces. We didn't acknowledge them until we'd made it across the street.

"I hate how my identity is wrapped up in Goldman," he said as we waited for our coffee. "People now view me differently. They see that I work at Goldman and make awful assumptions, when I'm nothing like these people. I'm a member of a club whose values I don't believe in. But the money's too good, and with the world falling apart and people losing their homes and going bankrupt, there's no way in hell I can walk away."

But many of our colleagues celebrated their affiliation with Wall Street, like the one guy who dressed up as a 1% milk carton on Halloween, strutting by the "99%" protestors, shoulders back, chin up. I wished someone had beat the crap out of him on the way in, but he entered the trading desk unscathed. Thank goodness someone in human resources had the sense to send him home to change, but not before he got a standing ovation on the trading floor.

I was confused, feeling more kinship with the protestors than with my colleagues. I couldn't defend the industry—I looked at our business with great skepticism and oftentimes with revulsion—

but yet, I was part of it. And worried, as the financial world was collapsing, unemployment skyrocketing, homes foreclosing all around me. With the money they shoved in my pockets and the babies in my belly counting on me, I was just too scared to walk away.

CHAPTER TEN

O ur twins, Abby and Beth, arrived at full term and were completely healthy. After months of reading about twin pregnancies and all the risks, I couldn't believe there weren't any complications, and I was grateful they didn't have to spend a moment in the NICU.

Those first weeks I was in awe of what Dan and I had created. They were so tiny and looked like the baby dolls I'd had when I was a kid, with their delicate fingers and toes. I'd find myself spending hours just holding them and staring at them, but worried that there was something wrong I wasn't aware of. I'd read that oftentimes twins had issues and developmental delays, sometimes so slight they aren't initially picked up. I watched them like a hawk, charting their sleeping patterns, their poops and pees, and the ounces of breastmilk they drank.

"Jamie," Dan said, "they are fine, honey, perfectly normal. You've got to relax." He'd caught me red-handed, as I was feeling up and down Abby's spine for crookedness, though I wasn't even sure if scoliosis could be detected this early. I just wanted to be prepared, and not overwhelmed like my parents had been.

I was twelve years old the day we were told that I needed spinal surgery to save my life. When we headed back to New Jersey from the hospital in Delaware, Dad drove while my mom looked through the medical forms she'd just received.

"Put on your Walkman, honey," my mom said. "It'll take your mind off things." I sat in the back seat, which smelled like my dad's Salem cigarettes and wintergreen air freshener. I put on my headphones but didn't press play. Instead I leaned forward, trying to hear my parents' conversation.

"It'll be okay, Tony," my mom said. "We have some insurance."

I looked at the back of my dad's head; his tanned neck had flushed bright red. "I know, Angie," he said, "but this is only the beginning. The deductible alone is several thousand dollars. Then we'll need time off work for her surgery and recovery. We won't have any income coming in and we'll also have to get meals out and pay for hotel rooms. Then she'll need physical therapy after her surgery. The expenses won't stop. All on top of Tony and Janine's college tuition."

I curled up into a ball and smelled the smoke that was absorbed into the plush tan cushion. "This is spinal surgery, remember," my dad added. "It's not like she's getting her tonsils out."

My parents didn't just have an American dream, they *were* the American dream. They'd put themselves through college, worked hard at their jobs, and moved their family out of the poverty they were born into. And then through the randomness of bad DNA, my crooked spine risked costing them everything.

As I looked down at Abby and Beth, I understood what my parents sacrificed—and why—more than ever. These babies were so fragile, so dependent, and so trusting. I'd do anything to protect and provide and care for them, including sucking it up and staying at Goldman Sachs.

Dan and I reviewed our "Spreadsheet of Freedom" and, although we'd saved well, I still feared it wasn't enough. I found myself creating more items on the spreadsheet to save for, making the end goal number larger, moving the finish line further away because I was afraid to finish this Goldman race. For years I'd been told this was a once-in-a-lifetime opportunity, that I'd never make this kind of money again, that *I could only leave Goldman once*, that I was nothing without their name. I'd come to believe all these things and was petrified to leave, afraid that I'd regret it once I walked away. I also had a new family obligation spurring me on—the responsibility of providing for the girls—and my interests and dreams took a back seat to theirs.

While I had four months of family leave, I was on the phone with Mike most days. The firm policy that parents should be "unplugged" from work during leave was bogus. The birth of my kids didn't end the financial crisis, so I logged in to work, dialed in to conference calls, and talked to Pete daily about the business. I felt like I had to do it, if I wanted to protect my job and my standing. Other women had done it too. I thought back to the woman who was called from the office while she was in labor, and the other one who felt pressure to return after a few weeks, her Caesarean scar barely healed. They didn't want to do it, but they felt they had to, so they told their managers it was okay. And then there's Mike, who had considered Nick a part-time employee because he left an hour early each day and paid him down accordingly. What would he think of me, after being out of the office one-third of the year?

As I prepared for my return to work, my biggest focus was finding childcare for the girls. Dan, who had just started his own IT business, couldn't care for them, but my mom had just retired and offered to watch them for us. I paid her of course—I was making the money to afford a nanny and as a retiree she needed the extra money. Plus, my grandma had meant everything to me, and she'd watched me while my mom worked. It felt so natural and fitting that my mom would do the same for my kids. Although I didn't want to leave them, I was happy they'd be in her safe hands.

Breastfeeding was my next focus. I knew from day one that I wanted to do it. Goldman had a lactation center, an entire floor with hospital-grade pumps, private lockers, a full-size kitchen, and lactation consultants available 24/7. I'd miss the girls, but if I pumped, I knew I'd feel connected to them.

A few days before my return, Mike called. "HR informed me that you signed up for the lactation rooms. That's going to be a problem," he said. "Don't you want to make managing director? You need to be at your desk working, not pumping." I sat on my family room couch, as the girls slept in the double pack n' play next to me. My limbs were so heavy I wanted to climb in with them. *People would die for your job, Jamie,* I told myself as I bit my lip. "Yes, of course," I said. "That's what I want."

"You'll want to get home as soon as you can," he said. "If you're pumping half the day, you'll have to make up the time. You won't see the girls at all." He was right. On a good day, I didn't get home until 7 p.m. If I had to make up the pump time, I wouldn't get home until after 8 p.m., which meant I'd never see the girls awake during the week. I looked out my sliding glass door and said nothing.

The irony is that HR most likely told Mike about my breast-feeding plans so he could support me, but it had the opposite effect. The most frustrating part of Mike's call was that I knew I could've been productive while I pumped, since I'd have access to a phone and my email. These decisions weren't based on reason and common sense, but on Goldman's value system. If your values aligned with the men in the glass offices, you were fine. But if you had different interests, look out. Leaving your desk to get your wing tips shoe-shined was a worthwhile endeavor. Providing breastmilk for your infant at home? Not so much. Those men in the offices clutched on to their old boys' club values with white-knuckled fists. As long as they were in power, there wasn't a chance that someone who looked like me, with interests like me, could be successful there.

"So we agree?" Mike said. "No breastfeeding."

Tears blurred my vision. "Yes, Mike," I said. "No breast-feeding."

I shoved all my pump stuff in a plastic box and stuck it in my basement. I bought powdered formula and cried while I mixed it. Without stepping one foot in the office, I'd failed my girls already. I reminded myself that the purpose of my working was to provide for them financially. Bonuses, not breast milk, did that.

There'd been changes at work during my leave. The executive office recognized Mike for his performance during the crisis and promoted him to a larger role, overseeing more businesses. Mike then hired a few MDs to work under him, including a guy named Rich from Chicago, so now I had two bosses. Rich reorganized the department, and Jerry and Vito, after years of trying, were now managers.

My first day back, I felt like a new employee. I'd become the unofficial poster child for "The Goldman Working Mother." Like a magnet, junior women were drawn to me, seeking me to mentor them. I thought back to my first meeting with Molly and marveled that I'd become her. Now I had the opportunity to pay it forward.

Their questions were endless. "How do I get promoted?" "How do I handle a difficult boss?" "How do I outperform my peers?" "How do I manage career and family?" As time passed, I grew close to these women, like they were my younger sisters in a Goldman sorority. I loved leading them, showing them how to navigate the environment, sharing mistakes and observations I'd made along the way. Helping them became the best part of my day, and it was no wonder why: It was the only part of my job that resembled social work.

A few months after my return, *mentoring* became the new buzzword at Goldman. It seemed like everyone was being assigned mentors, and Mike set up an official mentoring program in our department. It seemed unlike him to care about mentoring—he was a "kill or be killed" kind of guy—but rumor had it that department heads received financial incentives for setting them up. The program paired each manager with an analyst.

I ran into Jerry in the pantry one morning. "So, I'm mentoring one of *your girls*," he said, "Lizzie Dobson. Our first meeting is today." The way he said "your girls" made it sound like a disease. Lizzie was energetic and hardworking, and Jerry was right that we'd become close. I worried he'd hold that against her since he still held a grudge that I'd become a manager before him.

"Great," I said. "She's an awesome analyst."

He nodded, and a small smile crossed his lips. "You think so, huh?" he said. "We'll see about that." I watched him walk away, and my gut twinged. I wished I'd kept my mouth shut; now I worried the fire of hatred he burned for me would spread to her.

Sure enough, a day after they started working together, Jerry came by my desk. "That awesome analyst Lizzie?" he said. "She's an entitled bitch." He walked away before I could respond.

Lizzie asked me for coffee soon after. "I have a problem," she said. "Jerry's telling my clients to give business to other brokers outside of Goldman and not me. Vito's in on it, too." Her large brown eyes sagged, and her lips were thin. I wasn't surprised Jerry wanted to mess with Lizzie, but I couldn't believe he'd cost Goldman business to do it. Lizzie's clients were "good old boys" who'd been in the business for years. They liked Lizzie, but they loved Jerry and would likely do whatever he told them. Nothing cemented client relationships like visits to strip bars; Jerry provided that, while Lizzie couldn't.

"Let's not jump to conclusions," I cautioned. "We'll keep an eye on it and follow up in a few weeks."

I felt like a used car salesperson who sold an old lady a lemon with bad brakes. I was supposed to be the poster child, married with kids and on track to be a managing director. I was proof that someone like Lizzie could succeed here, but I knew that wouldn't matter if Jerry had it in for her.

Two weeks later, Lizzie left a graph of her trade volumes on my desk. Since Jerry started as her mentor, they had dropped off a cliff. Soon after, at the managers' meeting that afternoon, we discussed layoffs. Every spring the firm fired the lowest performers and the process had begun.

"I'm not a fan of Lizzie," Jerry offered. "Her trading volumes are down. I've tried to mentor her, but it's no use." We sat in

Mike's office, ten managers around his conference table, all men except for me. Vito sat next to Jerry and, like an old married couple, they'd begun to look alike with their pudgy faces, stocky arms, and balding heads.

"I'm not a fan either," Vito said. "We should can her."

I wanted to scream and flip the table over, *Real Housewives of New Jersey*–style, but I needed to be strategic, so I said nothing at the moment. Instead, I decided to talk to Rich, the new managing director in our department. He wasn't a "bro" like the other guys. He was more intellectual, the type to engage you in a conversation about politics or philosophy rather than football.

"I need to talk about Lizzie," I said when I caught him alone in his office. "Her trading volumes are down, but I think Jerry is funneling business away from her and Goldman."

"Are you sure, Jamie?" he inquired. "Maybe she's just a poor performer and making excuses for herself."

"You're kidding me, right?" I said, my voice growing louder with each word. Hope dissolved before my eyes. "It's so obvious what's going on. We need to help her. This kind of crap has to stop."

"Listen, I know you care a lot about these analysts," he said, "but you can't save everyone. You need to spend more time thinking about yourself and your career."

Rich turned back toward his computer, and I stared at the stubble on his neck. I didn't want to walk out a failure, but I felt defeated, like there was nothing I could do. This Poster Child act was a lie, and I was a sham.

The next day, Lizzie told me she'd started to look for a new job. I should've discouraged her because we needed good women at Goldman. Wasn't that just what Genevieve, the woman who had given the talk at my college, had promised all those years ago? I still thought it was possible, that we could somehow build teams of Genevieves. But in this environment, good women didn't seem to succeed unless they were like me, someone who felt like they accepted, tolerated, and perpetuated the harassment and abuse. If she didn't leave, I knew Lizzie would get fired, and I couldn't stomach that.

A few weeks later, Lizzie resigned. Mike called me into his office.

"Lizzie said in her exit interview that this department is bad for women," Mike told me, "and that Jerry and Vito made her life miserable. Is this true?" We sat at the oval table in his office.

"Yes, she was miserable," I acknowledged. "And yes, it was because of Jerry and Vito." He nodded, as if deep in thought, and I suspected that Lizzie had filed a lawsuit.

Soon after, Mike asked to talk to me again. "Our legal team is going to call and ask how you're treated here as a woman," he said. "I trust you won't say anything negative. You're my star, Higs, and soon I'll make you a managing director. What's negative about that?"

I heard the phones ringing on the trading floor behind me as I took in what he'd said. Managing director level was rarified air, and those promotions were given only every other year. While there was a separate hierarchy among MDs, with some managing others, the only role higher was partner. My competitive side reared its head—I wanted that promotion. After all this time, I wanted to get to that elusive level, especially as a working mother. It would be a way of sticking it to the Aarons from my boot camp days, and all the naysayers since, who didn't think someone like me could cut it. It was my answer to all the people in my life who'd said, "You'll never." And I also wanted to make the money that went with the title so I could save it and get the hell out.

"Of course, Mike," I said. "I'd never say anything negative."

Mike nodded and smiled. I walked out of his office straight to the ladies' room. I was so tired of lying, I just wanted to believe the stuff I'd told those junior women. I locked myself inside the handicap stall and turned the faucet on. This place was killing me, and my morals were dying first. As the water rushed out white noise, I started to cry.

Later that year, managing director promotion season began, which was a cryptic process, like a secret society. Rich told me I was up for it and that was that. If I was cut during the three-month selection process, I'd be told. If not, on the second morning in November, I'd get a call from the head of the division welcoming me into the MD club.

I worked long and hard during those months. Pete helped where he could, and Rich spent countless hours providing feedback and encouragement. I wrote business plans, forecasts, and budgets, and Rich was always there, reviewing my work, listening to my presentations, and introducing me to senior people in the division. Most nights I had client dinners and for a month I only saw the girls on the weekends.

One night I was finally able to get home early. Dan held Abby in the kitchen while Beth sat in her highchair. I grabbed Abby and smothered her with kisses, my nose buried into her pink sweatshirt as I took a deep sniff of her baby lotion. "Want Dada," she said. "Not Mama." Her face scrunched and she reached for Dan, and he pulled her into his arms.

Then I leaned over Beth and kissed her cheek as her large blue eyes stared at me. Then her mouth pouted as she wiped her cheek with her hand, my kiss right off her face. My heart was shredded. I'd counted down the hours to kiss them, to snuggle them, to see them. I felt so beat down I didn't know if I was standing anymore.

"Don't take it personally," Dan said. "They're just used to me now." In just weeks, while I put in those long hours, they'd gotten used to life without me. I know Dan meant well but even he seemed like a stranger. By the time I got home the kids were long asleep and I was so tired Dan and I hardly talked, let alone hugged or kissed. We'd discussed having more children at one point, but that seemed impossible now.

In mid-October I went to a conference in Florida with Rich and Pete. It was my final shot to impress the Goldman gods, so I packed my schedule with meetings and meals with my clients to show how strong my relationships were.

The last night ended at the hotel bar. It was past 2 a.m. when I decided to turn in. Pete had left hours before. My fitted black cocktail dress and high black patent leather heels were uncomfortable after the hours of wear. The dark bar was still crowded, people letting off steam after the long week. Even I'd had more than my usual two drinks and felt dizzy from all the white wine. Hearty laughter and slurred speech rang through the room as cigarette smoke wafted in from the patio next door.

I did a farewell tour of the bar, the alcohol that pumped through me and everyone else making us warmer and friendlier with one another. As I neared the bar's exit, I saw Rich, alone, in his blue suit and white shirt, still crisp despite the late hour. He peered into his glass of scotch, served neat, as he swirled it.

"Rich, I'm turning in," I said. "Thanks for your help this week." He looked up and smiled.

"Night, Jamie," he said. I went in for a quick hug when his arms wrapped around the small of my back and pulled me in. My eyes widened as my chin cupped his shoulder. His stubble rubbed against my check, and I smelled his musky cologne. My heart knocked into the sides of my chest, my breath stripped from my mouth. I wondered if people saw us and if it looked as intimate as it felt. I wanted to pull away, but I was shocked that I also wanted to see what would happen.

I'd always felt a pull toward Rich—his confidence, his dry, witty humor, and his intellectualism. He was different from the other guys at work, the kind of person who others stopped what they were doing to listen to. Rich wore an easy sense of power that drew others to him, and now, my arms encircled his neck.

Rich turned his head toward mine, and his skin brushed against my cheek until his mouth was over my ear. The sensation of his breath sent electric pulses down my neck. The worries about what others thought evaporated as he tightened his arms around me.

"You're so beautiful," he said in a deep whisper. "I'd give anything to be with you."

I closed my eyes and exhaled; my breath fell on his neck. I felt each connection between our bodies—his arms on my lower back, the texture of his suit against my cheek, the heat from his body on mine—like they were live wires.

Then, as if awoken from a trance, I separated from him. Rich's hazel eyes were pinned on me, a light brown tinged with golden flecks, such a unique and gorgeous color that I'd never noticed before. His gaze held a charge that made my stomach drop to my toes. I turned around and walked out of the bar. Once in the lobby, I ran to the elevators.

My mind felt severed in half, as if my good side split from the evil side. Good was relieved that I ran away, putting images of Dan, at home with the kids, in my head. Evil felt angry and cheated, wanting to stay and be held by Rich and hear his whispers.

Just three hours later, I stood in the lobby with Pete, hungover and exhausted. While we waited for a taxi to the airport, I told him what had happened.

"What a pig," he said, rolling his eyes. "He should be ashamed! You're both married. Just another creep who wants to screw anything he sees."

I warmed with shame. What kind of wife was I? What kind of mother? I couldn't tell Pete that, just for the moment, I had felt so desired. Not that Dan didn't make me feel that way, but with Rich, it was just different. I was no longer the girl in the back brace or the worker who led with her smarts and not her looks. A smart, confident, powerful man like Rich found me attractive, which ignited a flame in me that had been dormant.

I was such a cliché—a working stiff burned-out mother of two. I was thirty-three, with a body covered with cellulite, stretch lines, and wrinkles. I loved my husband, but we hadn't been intimate in months. With twin toddlers at home and the pressure on at work, romance was on the backburner. It seemed like the best days of my life were behind me. I regretted not having a more exciting life in my twenties. I'd graduated from college, lived at home, met Dan, went to work, got married, and had babies. I skipped the chapters that some of my friends had lived, the ones club hopping with friends and flirting in dark bars.

When I went to work Monday, my stomach rumbled with nerves, anticipating seeing Rich after what happened. When I got to my desk, my phone rang. "Come to my office," Rich said.

I couldn't believe we'd deal with this first thing. I leaned in toward Pete. "Rich wants to see me," I said.

He rolled his eyes. "I hope the pig apologizes."

When Rich saw me at his door, he waved me in. "Have a seat," he said. "I have to tell you something." I went to his meeting table and braced myself.

"Listen," he said as he got up from his chair and closed the door. "It's just not your year for MD. It was Mike's call and I'm sorry."

My eyes opened wide, and confusion shook my head, like I was an actor who lost her place in the script.

"Don't overreact," he said. "You'll get it next time."

After all that work, after a twelve-year career, after the ways I'd supported and protected the department instead of people like Lizzie, after the bargains I'd made with the dark side, it appeared there was more bargaining to be done. I'd have to wait another two years. What a fool I was to think he wanted to talk about our meaningless bar embrace. I wanted to run to the bathroom and have a good cry, but instead I took a deep breath.

"I understand," I said. "Thank you for letting me know." I was pissed, but I knew that Rich's rejected pass had nothing to do with Mike's decision. Rich was supportive when it came to my promotion, even though it made his own position more precarious. I'd heard rumors of Goldman's unspoken "one in, one out" rule. In order to manage the number of MDs tightly, to keep the role exclusive, when a new managing director was promoted, an existing one was asked to leave. Only Mike knew the real story of why I didn't make MD, and I wasn't about to ask him.

Rich followed me as I walked toward the door.

"Keep in mind, people will watch your reaction," he said. "You need to be professional."

I turned around and our faces were inches from each other. I smelled his cologne, and it made my stomach turn.

"Professional, huh?" I said. "That's your advice?"

"Yes," he said. "Compose yourself, no tears, no reaction."

I couldn't believe the irony. He was my boss and had hit on me just days before, yet he was advising *me* to be professional.

I forced a smile. "Naturally," I said, and walked out the door.

CHAPTER ELEVEN

"Sister Jamie." I had almost started to believe in my moniker—the innocent woman who was scandalized by all the crazy behavior around her at the office.

They often say catastrophes aren't caused by one singular action, but rather through the sum of many smaller missteps. And the affair that threatened my marriage didn't begin with some juicy scene, but rather with toys on the living room floor.

The year after I'd gotten passed over for the MD promotion, Dan and I had another child—our son, Luke, who was a breath of fresh air in our lives. We all fell in love with his sweet disposition and his head full of brown ringlets. The girls loved being big sisters and our family felt complete. But having three kids aged three and under was harder than we'd expected. It was more than my mom expected, too, and she told us it was too much for her to handle. Dan and I interviewed prospective nannies in our area, but after having my mother watch my kids, none of the candidates seemed competent enough. They either had too little experience, or couldn't work the hours we needed, or seemed overwhelmed by how many little ones we had. Eventually, Dan and I decided that until we could find someone we liked he would step back from his work as an IT consultant in order to split the time with my mom and give her a break. Plus, it was soon MD promotion season again, and I had to make sure I got it this time around. It would justify all the sacrifices Dan and I had made, which seemed like even more now as we both felt like we were working nonstop.

One late night, I got home and found Dan on the couch, in front of the TV, with a beer in hand, and empties covering the coffee table. Toys were all over the family room floor, my big pet peeve, so I got on my hands and knees to clean them up. I picked up dress-up shoes, oversize Legos, and stuffed animals as I searched under the couch and table. Anger rose up inside me as I tossed them into the toy box. "Could you pick up your legs?" I said as I knelt in front of Dan, reaching for the baby doll under his feet.

"Would it kill you to clean up before you got on the couch?" I said as I stood up. I was tired to the bone. Managing director promotion season had kicked off again—between work and client dinners, I hadn't been getting home until 10 p.m. or later for weeks.

"You're kidding, right?" Dan said. "I got home at 1 p.m. to relieve your mom. I only worked four hours. I dealt with the kids all day. Fed them, dressed them, played with them. Changed diaper after diaper. Then it was bedtime, which is almost impossible for one person. It's not like I enjoyed a steak dinner, like you."

I squeezed the baby doll so tight I thought I'd pop her head off. "I don't see the kids all week!" I said. "I'd do anything to change places. I can't believe that you can't clean up toys, while I've busted my ass all day."

Dan's eyes were bloodshot, and a flush of red spread over his face. "You want me to clean up the toys?" he said. "No problem!" He grabbed the ride-on car in front of me, opened the sliding glass door, and hurled it into the night. It crashed onto the deck and the neighbor's dog barked. "There you go. All cleaned up now!"

"You asshole!" I said. The TV blared and my fingernails dug into the plastic doll skin. "I work all day and I come home to more work at home. I'm killing myself to get promoted so I can make more money for us, and this is the thanks I get?" Dan sat back on the couch and stared at the TV. We were mere feet apart, but I felt alone. I tossed the baby doll in the toy box and went to bed.

The next day was Friday and the weekend couldn't come fast enough. As I left my desk at the end of the day, Rich asked for a lift. It wasn't an unusual request, because his place in New Jersey was on the way to mine, and I often gave him a ride. And it was the least I could do, we were in the middle of promotion season, and once again he was by my side, helping me with special projects, introducing me to senior people across the firm, and giving me opportunities to work with new clients. When we got to his house, he asked me in for a drink, which again, wasn't unusual. Rich, his wife, Lara, and I would sometimes catch up over a glass of wine before the weekend. This time was different, though, because they'd split up a few months before and she'd left. The house was on the market and for the time being, Rich lived there alone.

"To you," Rich said as he poured us wine. "This is your year. We're going to make MD happen." I smiled and we clinked glasses.

"I hope so," I said. The wine felt warm in my throat and chest.

"You know, I don't say it enough," he said, "but I admire you so much. The way you perform at work, while being a great mom to your kids. You manage so much and do it so well." He winked as I melted inside, and then he leaned toward me. "I really hope you are taken care of," he said, "because you deserve that." His tie was off, and the top buttons of his white dress shirt were undone, his salt and pepper chest hair peeking out.

I wanted someone to take care of me, I wanted someone to lift the burden, I wanted someone to say *thank you*, because I couldn't hang on much longer. My cell phone sat face down on his kitchen table, and I'd shut the ringer off. "I should go," I said.

On the drive home, my mind felt muddled with what had happened and how I felt. I saw the scene from the hotel bar two years before in my head. I thought Rich was drunk then and didn't remember. But whether he did or didn't hardly mattered, because I'd never forgotten.

The next morning, Abby and Beth had a soccer tots game. I stood next to my camping chair on the sidelines and held Luke as he slept, his head nestled into my neck, the bright morning sun warming my face. My phone buzzed and once I saw the caller ID, I looked over at Dan as he coached on the field.

"Hi there," I said. My singsong voice didn't sound like me.

"Hey, I was just thinking of you," Rich said. "What are you up to?"

"Boring stuff," I said. "What about you?"

"I'm in the city at my new place," he said. He'd told me the night before about his new rental in the Meatpacking district.

"An artist friend has an opening tonight in the Village. Come with me."

"Are you nuts?" I said and laughed. "It's the weekend and I'm with my family. You know, my husband and three kids?"

"Don't remind me," he said as my pulse raced. "Tell Dan you're going out with friends. You deserve a night out. My driver can pick you up. A sushi restaurant just opened near the gallery. They have miso cod, your favorite."

I closed my eyes and envisioned a different life as I overheard parents on either side of me chatting about baseball tryouts. "I can't," I said. "I'm sorry. I gotta go." I dropped the phone like it had a disease.

The kids were tired by the afternoon, so we fed them dinner early and put them to bed. Dan watched a baseball game and drank beer on the couch and I went to my room to watch a movie with a bowl of Cheerios. I put on my pajamas and *Moonstruck* and as I took a spoonful, received a text: a picture of miso cod next to a glass of wine. "Eating here. Alone. Wish you were here."

I closed my eyes, and I was there, in my black cocktail dress, eating cod, drinking wine, and talking with Rich. I opened my eyes, and I was alone, in my fleece Mickey Mouse pajamas, with my bowl of Cheerios. The movie's opening scene began, and images of New York City flashed on the TV. I wasn't sure what kind of life I wanted, but I knew this one wasn't it.

❦

Two months later, in November 2012, managing director announcement day arrived. I hadn't received any bad news so, with cautious optimism, I got to my desk to wait for the call from Liam, the head of our division. I knew the drill: at 7:30 a.m., all the current partners and MDs reviewed the list of the new MDs, and afterward, Liam made the congratulatory calls.

I waited—headphones on—and stared at my phone turret, willing it to ring. At 8:07 it did and Liam, in his Dutch accent, said, "Congratulations on making managing director. You'll be getting an email about training." Then he hung up, and that was that.

I turned toward Pete, who sat next to me. He smiled like a kid on Christmas morning.

"You did it!" he said.

"It wouldn't have happened without you."

After fourteen years at the firm, I felt like I just completed the Iron Man as Pete and I hugged tightly. Soon after, people crowded my desk. Junior kids whom I'd mentored greeted me with squeals and hugs. Other vice presidents, who were now my former peers, offered me limp handshakes and mumbled congratulations. Jerry and Vito never came by, even though they sat in the next row; instead they each sent me a blank email that said "Congratulations" in the subject line. They were still managers, of course, but only vice presidents. Between visits, calls, and emails, I was bombarded all day and didn't have a moment to myself, so I texted Dan the news. I waited for Rich to come by, but I never saw him. Late in the day, though, he texted: "Sorry I missed your big day. I was out with divorce stuff. Dinner tomorrow with me and some others to celebrate."

At the end of the day, Mike called me into his office. It was time to kiss the ring and say thank you. He greeted me at the door with a handshake.

"So tell me," he said, "how does it feel to be my worst performing MD?"

I sat across from him, the room feeling warm and smelling of burned coffee. I thought I'd misheard him because I'd expected we'd be high-fiving and celebrating. This was supposed to be the biggest day of my career, the reward for the past fourteen years of hard work and loyalty.

"You were my top vice president," he went on to explain. "But since you're my newest MD with zero experience, you're in the fourth quartile."

The dreaded fourth quartile. During review season, each person is ranked among their peers and put into one of four performance buckets called quartiles. The fourth was the lowest and most of them were fired. Mike coughed back a laugh. "How are you going to climb out of this hole?" he said.

My business plan was burned into my brain from the past months of meetings, so I replayed it like a broken record.

"Sounds great," he said when I finished. "Let's hope you can pull it off. Remember, the bar just got way higher."

"I got it," I said and went to leave.

As I was midway through the door, Mike said, "And about your bonus this year. Ask your friends about the MD tax."

I was still confused by that parting statement when I made it to the ferry. So I approached fellow ferry commuter Matt, an MD in another department. "So, Mike mentioned something about a tax today," I said. "Do you know what he's talking about?"

"Ah yes, the MD tax, another lore of Goldman and a typical power play," he said. "The first bonus after your promotion you might take a hit. It's Goldman's way of saying *making MD is enough, don't expect to get more money*. Plus, they gotta pay the VPs who didn't get it."

"Are you serious?" It didn't make sense to get a promotion and a pay cut at the same time.

"Afraid so," he said. "They paid me down 20 percent the year I made it, but don't worry. It evens out after a few years." The boat rocked as it made its way across the river and I felt nauseous, even though I never got seasick. This promotion was supposed to mean more money, not less; it should've brought me to the finish line of the "Spreadsheet of Freedom." Then I could leave, then I could pursue a fulfilling career, then I could spend more time with my family, then I could be happy . . . but instead I was playing an epic game of Sorry and I'd just been moved halfway back across the board.

The house was quiet when I got home, but then I heard the commotion of bath time upstairs. All three kids were in the tub, covered in bubbly suds as Dan poured water from a green plastic pitcher over their heads.

He looked up at me and said, "Hey, I thought we'd get Chinese to celebrate." Tub water dripped onto the cream tiled floor and pooled under my heels. "Would you mind ordering and picking up? I don't care what you get."

I changed into yoga pants and a T-shirt and, as I drove to get dinner, my body slumped from disappointment. I knew Dan's days were full and I appreciated he was home with the kids, but I'd hoped for something more festive, maybe a balloon or two, or a homemade card. Everything I did at work was for this family, and I didn't even get a proper congratulations. I knew I sounded like a big baby. I was a grown woman and didn't need a party, but at the same time, I couldn't help it. Maybe my mood was because of my conversation with Mike. I felt like I just scored the winning touchdown, but nobody was in the stands cheering for me.

I returned home with the food and set the table as the kids barreled down the stairs. I cut up Beth's wontons, gave Abby some fried rice, and placed a forkful of lo mein on Luke's highchair tray. Dan opened a beer and served himself some wonton soup. I watched as everyone took their first bite without complaint and then I poured myself wine and made a plate for myself. Then Beth toppled her wonton soup onto Abby's lap, who shrieked.

"Congratulations to me," I mumbled as I removed Abby's soaked pants, cleaned up the table, and returned her back to her seat. Dan smiled and took another swig of beer.

"Welcome to my world," he said. "Cleaning up while you make the big bucks." He leaned back in his chair as I chugged the rest of the wine.

"About big bucks," I said. "My bonus will be cut this year. That's the price for making MD."

The skin between his eyes wrinkled. "What?"

"That's what I heard today. It's called the MD tax," I said. "Since they promote you, they feel they don't have to pay you."

"Are you kidding me? After all the work and sacrifice, they're paying you *less*?" His volume raised with each word. "How much of a cut will it be?"

"One guy said he was down 20 percent," I said.

Dan stared at me wide-eyed as the kids chattered with one another, and his reaction made real for me how much the situation sucked. Here I was, a big MD now, and when it came down to it, I couldn't bring home the bacon.

"What a waste," he said as he shook his head.

A waste, the whole thing was a waste; the projects, presentations, and client dinners, the lack of sleep, and never seeing the kids. It was like Dan put a mirror to my face and showed me who I was. I brimmed with self-hatred, and anger seeped out of me.

"This was supposed to be the biggest day of my career," I said. "You don't care about me. You only care about money."

"That's BS!" Dan said. "It's about more than money. I gave up my career for you. You finally got to the big leagues and we're getting less. Preschool tuition isn't going down 20 percent, mortgage payments aren't going down 20 percent. I took a step back so you could move forward and now we're all falling behind."

"Mama, help," Abby said, her words cutting through the room like a razor. Lo mein covered her hair and face, fresh out of Luke's fist.

"Could you clean Abby up while I do the dishes?" I said.

"Sure," Dan said. "It's just another day in paradise."

Later, I lay in bed and replayed the day, which should've been amazing. At work, I was behind, and at home, I was a failure, missing out on so much with nothing to show for it—no memories made with the kids, no mortgage paid off, no 529s funded. This promotion was supposed to get me closer to freedom, but instead it pulled me down like quicksand. It felt like a no-win situation. I wanted to be with my kids and to make them happy, but I also wanted my career to provide for them. I wanted to be a leader and a go-getter, but I also wanted to be appreciated and adored. I wanted the same deal that had been offered to men a generation earlier, the one where I'd be celebrated for my professional achievements, rewarded with a paycheck, and coddled by a spouse. I drifted off to sleep full of resentment that that deal wasn't offered to me.

⤙✳⤚

The next night Rich and I headed out for dinner. I knew it seemed silly, but after my dinner with Dan and the kids the night before, I wanted a do-over celebration, and I was happy people wanted to join me.

"Where are we meeting everyone?" I said as we exited the building.

"Oh, it'll just be us," he said. "Lines were crossed and tonight didn't work for the others." He winked and my stomach did somersaults and then felt punched with guilt. I knew it was wrong, but the thought of being alone with him warmed my body.

We got into his driver's Cadillac Escalade. "Louie, Nobu tonight," Rich said. It was my favorite sushi restaurant in the city.

When we arrived, the hostess, without asking our name, seated us at a table for two in the back corner of the room. The overhead lights were dimmed, and small votive candles burned around a vase of white roses. The sommelier arrived with a bottle of Cristal and we raised our glasses. "For all you've done," Rich toasted, "and for all we'll do together." His hazel eyes locked on me like lasers.

The server came with menus, and Rich brushed them away. "We don't need those," he said, smiling at me. "Your job is to enjoy yourself. I'll take care of everything."

I sat back, drank champagne, and watched Rich order. He

didn't have to ask me what I wanted; after all the years of client dinners, he knew.

Within moments our first course arrived—tuna and salmon served in chilled silver dishes, garnished with white orchids. The server left and the plate sat waiting. Nobody's little hands grabbed for it, I didn't have to cut anything for anyone. It was just mine.

I placed a piece of tuna in my mouth, the sauce so flavorful that my taste buds ached. I started to reach for my second piece while I chewed the first, and then I put my chopsticks down, not wanting to rush a single moment. After all, I didn't have to.

"Is everything all right?" Rich said.

"Yes, it's amazing." We talked about the day and laughed about something that had happened in a meeting. We shared so many inside jokes. Being with him was so easy; there was never anything to explain.

After dinner ended, we headed to the lounge where Rich grabbed us a couch in the corner of the room. He ordered another bottle and I got up to use the ladies' room. A small table sat in front of us, and after all the wine, I wobbled on my high heels as I brushed past Rich. Then I felt a shock through my stomach and down my legs as he pulled me onto his lap.

"Don't you see?" he said into my ear. "Now we can be together." The lounge was dark, and the people around us were just smoky silhouettes. My little black dress had ridden up, exposing my bare thighs. Rich's fingers feathered along them, his touch so delicate and light. I didn't know what this was, but I didn't want it to end. It felt good to be taken care of, it felt good to not be in charge. With reluctance, I got off his lap and walked unsteadily to the bathroom.

As I looked in the mirror, my face came into focus along with his words. We were peers now, and though relationships with junior employees were taboo, relationships with peers weren't. Oh this was crazy, this was bad, this was wrong, and I was drunk and didn't want to do something stupid, but I felt wanted and sexy, and I hadn't felt that in a long time. I checked my phone. It was midnight and Dan had texted "ETA?" an hour ago. I wrote back, "We just got the bill." Then I reapplied my black eyeliner and rose lip gloss and headed back out.

As I approached the couch, Rich looked up, his eyes dancing around my body as he bit his lower lip. He slid down to make room for me, put his arm around me, and pulled me so close that I felt his fast heartbeat. Our eyes locked and he wrapped a wisp of fallen hair around my ear, then he continued to stare. I broke his gaze, but snuggled into him, nestling my head into his neck and breathing in his cologne. I'd never been this close to him, but it felt right as he intertwined his fingers through mine, our bodies wrapped together, sitting in silence. After the server stopped by the fifth time, Rich settled the tab.

"I'll call for a car," I said as I put down my wine glass.

"No, we'll share," he said. "You can drop me off."

His driver was parked out front, and he opened the rear passenger door for us—Rich slid the second-row seat forward and motioned me to the third row. We pulled away as the interior lights dimmed. "You're so beautiful," he said. He lifted my hands and kissed the inside of my wrists; the sensation slithered down my body like syrup. Then we began kissing. The mouth of a man who wasn't Dan felt foreign, but it felt good. The force of our kissing intensified, and Rich lifted me onto his lap and spread my legs open, as the side of my body rested against his chest.

He reached under my dress and put his finger under the thong of my underwear.

"You're amazing," he murmured as he pulled it and released, the snap of the elastic cutting through the tension-filled air. His fingers traced the outline of my underwear until he reached between my legs. He breathed in my ear and kissed my neck as the inside of the car spun around me. My lips felt numb, my mind felt numb, my judgment felt numb. I knew it was wrong and I'd regret it, but I wanted it. His hands slid beneath my underwear and my back arched, and I saw the highway lights as they passed through the window. Rich put a finger inside me, then another, and I moaned as he pushed and pulled them in and out, each time deeper. Then I pulled down my dress and removed my bra as Rich watched. He got on top of me, brushing his nose over my nipples and then sucking them.

I was at the edge of a cliff, and I wanted to jump and fly like a bird free from responsibility, but I was married with three kids and had to stop. I could salvage this and pretend nothing happened, I convinced myself, since we hadn't had sex, and I was in a car, not in a bed. This made sense to me in my drunken stupor, so I pulled away gently as he continued to kiss me, and then the car jolted to a stop. I was relieved to see we were off the highway and a block from his home. As we pulled into his driveway, Rich sat up with a pained look in his eyes while I zipped up my dress.

"You've got to spend the night," he said. Part of me wanted to go but then my phone lit up. It was almost 2 a.m. and Dan had just texted me. He must have been looking for me for hours.

"I can't," I said. "You know I can't."

"Are you sure?" he said, his mouth a full pout.

"Good night."

He left and as I gave Louie my address, my voice seemed to echo in the empty back seat. I grabbed my phone and saw ten missed calls from Dan and double the text messages. I scrolled through them and saw how Dan's tone became more worried with each one. I was a class act, getting fingered by my boss while my husband looked for me. I stared at the back of Louie's head, embarrassed by what he'd witnessed.

Yet, despite all that, my body still buzzed and I wasn't relieved, wasn't complete, wasn't satisfied. My heart raced as I smoothed my sweaty hair down with my fingers.

I walked into the house at 2:30 a.m., kicking off my heels and holding on to the wall to steady myself. I found Dan in the family room pacing back and forth as the TV blared.

"Where the hell were you?" he said. The neck of his blue T-shirt was stretched out and it hung loose around him. His blond hair was wild, and his blue eyes were glassy. I squinted in the room's bright light and the loud TV sliced through my ears. A dozen empty beer bottles covered the rug, the end tables were turned over, and the lamps that once stood on them were in pieces on the floor.

I didn't know what to say or do. We hadn't been getting along, but to cause him this pain was inexcusable. "I'm sorry," I said. "I lost track of time."

"I've been trying to reach you for hours! You always call. I thought you were dead. I was about to call the police." His breath reeked of booze.

"We didn't go to dinner till late," I said. "The service was slow and there was construction on the way home." The lies spilled out so fast and easy, I shocked myself.

"Who were you with, your work husband Pete?" he said. Pete's name jerked me to attention; did he think there was something between us?

"No, I was with Rich. He wanted to celebrate my promotion," I said.

"Oh, I see," Dan said, with a chuckle. "It was Rich. I guess I should've expected that."

My stomach tightened. Did he know what I'd done? Could he see it on my face?

"I was just drinking so much," I said. "I'm sorry."

"What if something happened to the kids?" He looked at me as if the sight of me turned his stomach. Before I could answer, he stormed out of the room, up the stairs, and slammed our bedroom door. I waited with clenched teeth and was grateful the kids didn't wake up.

I went to the bathroom and saw my messy hair and smears of mascara running down my face. Not only did I feel like a whore, I looked like one too. What a cliché I was, making out with my boss in the back of a car. As the room spun around me, I sat on the family room couch and fell asleep.

"Mama? Mama!" The sound stabbed my ears as I felt the pull of my eyelid opening and daylight shooting in like a bullet. I opened my other eye to find Beth over me, her messy curly morning hair covering her face.

"Morning," I said. My head felt like a bowling ball, and I

couldn't remember the last time I was so hungover. The room whirled around me as I stood up and held the wall. Images from the night before flashed through my mind, overwhelming me so much I couldn't breathe.

"I'm hungry," Beth said. "Can you make pancakes?"

I leaned against the kitchen counter. "How about some cereal?"

She puffed out her lower lip. "No! Pancakes!"

I took four ibuprofen with a large glass of water while I made a pot of coffee. Then I started on the pancakes, the smell of the frying batter making my stomach turn. I didn't know how I'd survive this day. By the time I'd finished cooking, Luke called from his crib and Abby had joined us. As I washed the breakfast dishes, Dan came downstairs and poured himself coffee.

"I'm so sorry about last night," I said.

He held out his hand as a signal to stop. "I don't want to talk about it," he said. "Remember, we need to leave by noon for the party."

My head dropped and my hands fell in the soapy water as I remembered the party Dan's sister was hosting for her husband's birthday. I couldn't imagine getting through the next hour, let alone a party with my in-laws who lived two hours away.

"Right," I said. "Can you bring Luke to the girls' swim lessons this morning?" I needed some time alone to try to feel better.

"Sure, whatever," he said.

As soon as they left, I peeled off my clothes and threw them on the floor. Looking at the black dress and the thong made me want to throw up. I took a scalding shower, hoping it would help get the booze out of my system.

I had just crawled into bed when my cell buzzed—a text from

Rich. "Thanks for an amazing evening," it said. I put down my phone. Now was not the time. I dozed off and woke up to my stomach rumbling and churning, and acid crawling up my throat. I ran to the toilet and threw up. I stayed there on the tile floor, grateful for how cold it felt against my skin, and fell asleep. The sounds of the kids returning woke me.

Hours later, we arrived at the party and Dan disappeared with his brothers-in-law. I ran after the kids and took care of them, while I made small talk with Dan's sisters. My phone buzzed with so many calls from Rich that I put my phone in my purse and shoved it in the hall closet.

After dinner, I found Dan, alone in the backyard, at a makeshift tiki bar. My hands trembled as I approached him, which was a strange sensation. Dan was supposed to be my best friend, not someone I was nervous around.

"So, can we talk?"

"You're kidding me," he scoffed. "You think now is a good time to talk?"

"No," I said, "but you've been avoiding me all day."

"Not now," he said and walked away. Deflated, I grabbed my phone to check my work email, but deep-down I wanted to see if Rich had called again . . . and he had, four more times. I went into the bathroom, turned on both faucets for background noise, and called him.

"I've been worried," he said. "You haven't returned any of my texts or calls."

"I'm fine," I said. "It's not a good time to talk."

"Okay," he said, "just know that I'm thinking of you." I hung up and sat on the toilet seat. Rich was thinking of me, and I was thinking of him. As I scrolled through his text messages, shots of excitement went through me followed by pangs of shame. My whole life was out of whack; I wanted to talk to Dan but he refused, and Rich wanted to talk to me but I refused. I knew what I'd done was wrong, but Rich was wedged in my mind so tightly I couldn't get him out.

The party ended late, the kids were asleep by the time we got on the highway, and we drove in silence. When we got home, we put the kids to bed and headed to our room. I didn't know what I wanted to say or what I wanted to hear, but the one thing I knew was that I wanted peace at home.

"Can we please talk now?" I asked. I sat on the edge of our king-size bed and saw Dan's reflection in the mirror. His tie was loose, his blue dress shirt unbuttoned as he looked at me in the reflection.

It was the first eye contact we had all day, and it wasn't even real eye contact. "I have nothing to say," he said. "And your actions have said it all." He dressed for bed, grabbed his pillow, and walked out.

I turned off the lights and got in bed, not knowing what to do.

The truth was I knew what I'd done with Rich was wrong, but I wasn't sure I wanted to stop.

CHAPTER TWELVE

The kitchen was pitch black on Monday when I walked downstairs to get ready for work. Dan normally made coffee for us and worked before the kids got up, but today he was in the guest room.

By the time I arrived at the office, I had decided to try to play it like nothing happened with Rich, even though I knew that was impossible. His hands had been down my pants! Seeing him again wouldn't be normal and I wasn't sure how to handle it since I had meetings all day with him.

I got to my desk where Pete and I chatted about our weekends as usual. I wanted to tell him what happened and get it off my chest. He was like my priest and I needed to go to confession. He was the only one I could tell; I couldn't share it with Dan, and I was too ashamed to share it with my mom. Pete had been my right-hand man since he started working for me seven years before. He understood the world of Goldman Sachs. But I couldn't tell him, at least not yet. A message flashed on my screen from Rich. "Please come to my office."

My head hung down. I knew this had to happen today, but I

wished it wasn't first thing. I wondered if I could pretend that I hadn't seen it, but I knew Rich could see me from his office.

"Have a seat," he instructed, gesturing toward his meeting table. I closed the door and chose the seat farthest away from him.

"I have something to say," he said. I felt like all eyes were on us, in his glass enclosed office at the back of the floor, even though nobody else knew what had happened. Still, a scarlet letter felt stitched to my back. Rich's face was tight and flushed and I held my breath. "I think I'm in love with you," he said.

My eyes widened and my heart pounded. Our flirtation had *meant* something to him. But I wasn't sure what it meant to me. Was I in love with him? And would that mean I wasn't in love with Dan? We hadn't been getting along, but we'd been together for years. Tears welled in my eyes, but I didn't know if they were happy or sad ones.

"Please say something," he said.

I put my elbows on the table and held my head. "I don't know what to say," I said. "I'm married with three kids."

"We'll figure it out," he said. "I'll make you and the kids so happy. Let me take care of you." I closed my eyes and images flashed through my head; Rich, twenty years my senior with two daughters in college, would play the father role all over again; showing me and the kids life in the city, with museums, art galleries, and Broadway shows. Then we'd have our kid-free weekends in his Tribeca apartment, doing *The New York Times* crossword together in bed.

Then I saw Dan and me swap the kids—our kids would have two families and two homes. The girls were in preschool and Luke was a toddler, so they wouldn't remember when their parents were together. And Dan . . . we'd been through so much together, could I walk away from him? And go straight to Rich? And although Rich and I were allowed to be in a relationship since we were both MDs, regardless of title, romantic relationships within a department were not permitted. So one of us would have to find a role somewhere else at the firm or resign. My mind spun, and I felt like I'd throw up. "I can't talk about this now," I said. "I've got to go."

I walked into the bathroom and splashed cold water on my face. This needed to stop, I had to get it together. I was a grown woman, a parent, and I'd just been promoted to managing director. It reminded me of the storylines from the soap operas I used to watch with my grandma, and then tears welled in my eyes at the thought of her, knowing she'd be so disappointed in me.

I returned to my desk and Pete looked at me with narrowed eyes. "You all right?"

"Maybe we can catch up later," I said as casually as I could muster.

I consumed myself with work and avoided Rich, sending Pete to meetings in my stead, because I needed a break to process everything. Dan texted me about the kids instead of calling, which was unusual, but I didn't call him either because I needed a break there, too.

The market closed and Pete suggested we have coffee. We went to the conference room nestled in the back corner of the floor so nobody would see us, and I told him everything.

When I finished, he stared at me across the table, gripping his paper coffee cup. I was so tired—tired of replaying everything, tired of thinking about what it meant to me, tired of thinking about what it meant to others. I was so tired that if I put my head on the table I'd pass out. Pete's face flushed and I was afraid to hear his words, but at the same time I wanted him to slap some sense into me. His eyes were red, and a tear fell down his cheek. The sight released my own tears, bringing with them all the stress, worry, and rumination.

"I'm falling apart," I stuttered.

"It's not you," he said. "It's this place. It's evil. This wouldn't happen in a normal workplace. This environment, the money, the pressure, the hours. It brings the worst out in everyone."

I wiped my eyes with the back of my hand. "You're right. This place is changing me, it's polluting me. This isn't who I am, screwing around with my boss. But I'm drawn to him. I can't help myself, and I'm not sure I can stop."

"You're going to think I'm nuts," he said, "but it's like my smoking." I laughed at the ridiculousness of the comparison. "Hear me out," he continued. "I smoke because it takes my stress away. It gives me a high, a release, and for a moment I don't hate myself or my life. Then it's over and I'm pissed afterward because I know it's bad for me. But I can't stop. Cigarettes are my addiction. Maybe Rich is yours."

I took in his words. This love affair I'd conjured in my mind with Rich, when it came down to it, was an escape. My escape from the stress of the office politics, my escape from the long commute, my escape from the grueling demands of parenthood and no time left to be a wife much less a person. There was no "Jamie time" in my life—there was "Goldman time" and there was "Mommy time." It seemed too simple, but maybe Rich was my fix, maybe that's all it was. Maybe it had nothing to do with Dan or Rich at all. Maybe it had to do with me.

"I never thought about it that way," I ruminated. "Maybe you're right."

"I think I am," he said. "And don't think I'm all high and mighty looking down at you. I'm not in the situation you're in but I'm in bad shape. This place is acid, eating at me every day. I wake up miserable. I leave here miserable. I go to bed miserable. At night, for the hour I see my family, I argue with my wife and I yell at my kids. They don't want to be around me. I don't want to be around me. But I'm stuck, because the only good thing about me is my ability to make a lot of money here." The clock ticked on the wall above us, and I looked out the office door, thankful the hallway was empty.

"I'm on a cycle of misery," he said. "Then there's a week of happiness when I get my bonus, and I feel like I'm worth something. But the other fifty-one weeks of the year, I wonder why I'm even living." His looked despondent. I hadn't realized how much pain he was in, and in that moment, he was a mirror where I saw myself. We both despised Goldman and felt trapped, like prisoners, but we couldn't walk away. Goldman had become more than just a job to me—it was my identity. My entire adult life, half of my total life, I was "Jamie from Goldman." I felt loyal to the firm, I felt like I was part of a family—an abusive family, that made me doubt myself, but a family nonetheless. Yes, being at Goldman was hurting me, but Goldman had also done so much for me, and I felt guilty leaving. I was addicted to all the money I'd made, the prestige of my title, the way I'd made my family proud. I had started as a kid from New Jersey, the loser in the back brace, without knowledge and connections, the kid who couldn't succeed on Wall Street, and became a smart, successful woman. For years Goldman had beat it into us that without its name next to ours, we'd be a worthless nobody, unable to be successful anywhere else. I was petrified to leave.

"Pete, I'm sorry," I said. "I never realized what this place was doing to you. I mean, I knew you were strung out and struggling but—"

"Jamie, we're both dying here, just in different ways," he said. "Our lives and families are at stake. And as amazing as this money is, we can't let this place cost us everything."

➣✦⤚

Dan and I didn't speak for weeks, though he did manage to work in digs about Rich, about how nice it must be to have a bachelor pad in Meatpacking as Rich did, suggesting he knew much more than I realized. We were co-parents and housemates, texting about the kids instead of talking. At night, after I put the kids to bed, I tried to connect, but he'd already be in the guest room behind a closed door. When we were together with the kids, we smiled and were pleasant with each other. We agreed without even needing to discuss that we didn't want the kids to know or sense what was going on. They didn't seem to notice, and I prayed that was true. I'd messed up mine and Dan's life, I didn't want to mess up theirs, too.

On the weekends, Dan started to spend time with his friend, Steve. They'd grown up together and were inseparable until their early twenties. Dan met me while Steve remained a bachelor, a serial dater, each girlfriend younger than the last. He owned his own consulting business, drove a $100,000 Porsche, lived in a penthouse apartment in Hoboken, and loved to party.

Dan and Steve started going out on Saturday nights, after the kids were in bed. The first few times I chalked it up to payback and kept my mouth shut, even when he didn't come home until

3 a.m. But when it became a regular occurrence, I decided to say something.

"Isn't this getting to be a bit much?" I stated. He was getting ready in our bathroom, wearing slim fit khaki trousers and a button-down black shirt. He'd lost some weight and looked good. We never went out on date nights anymore, but when we were out with the kids, he wore T-shirts and jeans. I thought about his evening and the twenty-something-year-old women who would likely be involved. It gave me a headache. Dan's wedding ring sat on the end table next to him. I'd never seen it off his finger, and it felt like a gut punch.

"No," he said, "you have your time out, I need some, too."

I knew that evening with Rich was wrong, but besides that, when I was out late at night, it was for work with clients. Sure, I was at the best restaurants, but I was still working, it wasn't relaxing or fun or with friends. He'd party tonight, while I watched bad Lifetime movies and ate ice cream out of the container at home.

"When can we talk?" I posed. "I want to fix this." His face was expressionless, and I had no clue what he was thinking. I used to know him so well and now he was a stranger. I was tired of having a housemate—I wanted a partner, I wanted a husband, I wanted to go back to the way we used to be.

"There's nothing to talk about," he said.

"What about our marriage and our family and our future?"

"Like I said, there's nothing to talk about." And with that, he walked out of the room.

After he left, I got on the couch and channel surfed. Rich seeped into my mind. Since that day in his office, I'd avoided him. But I wondered what he was doing tonight. He still texted me every day with "Thinking of you," "Hoping you're okay," and "Always here for you." I never responded, but when my phone buzzed, my stomach turned over. There was a man out there who cared about me, he just wasn't my husband.

I pulled up his last text and started to respond, then I dropped the phone like it was on fire. My life was out of control, and I needed to figure out what to do. I wished I could talk to Pete, but I didn't want to bother him on the weekend. During the past weeks I'd thought about confiding in my mom, but I was too ashamed about what I'd done. Before I could talk myself out of it, I called her and asked her to come over.

I poured us coffee and told her everything from the past months. She kept her eyes on me and took in every word, her face giving away nothing. When I was done, we sat in silence. I was afraid of what she would say. She was my mother, she was a devout Catholic, she was a saint in my eyes, always going to mass, praying the rosary, and helping others.

"Marriage is hard," she said. "There are temptations. You're a wonderful mother and provide for your kids. I was that mother, too. Remember, I worked for years in the city. Not your hours, but still." I remembered when she came home wearing a black skirt suit with Reebok high tops, like she walked off the set of *Working Girl*, and I'd stand outside the bathroom door chatting nonstop as she tried to pee. She never had a break, either. I didn't realize until that moment how much she understood where I was, and I wondered how her marriage was with Dad back then.

"Those years were hard," she said. "I went from work to home to work again, never catching my breath. I thought I'd go insane. You need to make time for yourself. Nobody is going to give it to you, so you've got to steal it. If you don't make that time, you'll snap and make poor choices. It's like the oxygen mask on an airplane. You've got to put it on yourself first before you put it on your children. If not, you'll all die."

I'd just told her that I cheated on my husband with my boss, and yet, with her morals and standards, she didn't judge or shame me, she listened and empathized instead. I thought about what Pete had said about escaping. Rich was my escape because I was starved for time, and Steve provided an escape, too, for Dan. He and I were in the same boat—strung out, exhausted, and going insane—but instead of bringing us together, it was separating us. Maybe what I really needed to escape from was Goldman Sachs.

At work, I kept it all business with Rich and made sure never to be alone with him. It was like when I dieted and kept sweets out of the house because I didn't trust myself. If we had a meeting scheduled just the two of us, I'd bring Pete, and Rich's eyes would roll at the sight of him. At larger meetings, I'd leave early or arrive late so he couldn't catch me alone, but the whole meeting he'd stare at me, even when others spoke to him.

One day, as we walked out of a meeting, Pete said, "Dude, it's gotta stop."

"What?"

"The way he looks at you," he said. "He's shameless, like he doesn't care if anyone notices."

I squeezed my notebook to my chest. "Is it that obvious?"

"To me it is," he said. "He looks desperate for you to notice him." Powerful, smart, confident Rich was desperate for me, and that filled some of the void I felt with Dan. Still, I hoped it was only Pete who noticed. Most guys at Goldman assume that women who get promoted either filled a quota or screwed around with someone. I still had the squeaky-clean reputation of "Sister Jamie," so people put me in the "filling the quota" bucket—that was bad enough, I didn't need anyone to suggest I got it for other reasons.

The next Saturday night, Dan stayed at home, and I hoped that after bedtime we could talk. Once the kids were asleep, I went to the guest room. The hall lights were off, and his door was closed, but light streamed out from underneath. I put my ear to the door and couldn't hear a thing. Butterflies fluttered in my stomach as I summoned the courage to knock, then I heard a click, and the guest room light went out.

The next morning while I fixed breakfast, Dan said, "I have a tee time with Steve at two, and then we're grabbing dinner." The kids chased one another around the kitchen, squealing in delight.

"Can you come in the living room?" I said and he followed me, closing the French doors behind us.

"When can we talk?" I said. "I want to make this right."

His blue eyes turned to the floor. "I'm not ready."

I brought my hands to my face and rubbed my eyes again and again, rubbing so hard I hoped that when I opened them, I'd see something different.

"When do you think you'll be ready?" I said. "It's hard to live like this." Desperation lined my words.

"I don't know." I waited and hoped he'd provide some sort of timeline, but all I got was silence.

"Well, I have a presentation tomorrow," I finally said, "and I need time to work on my slides before you go."

"No problem."

I finished up breakfast and although I wanted to go upstairs, crawl into bed with my sadness, and sleep, I couldn't. Instead I retreated to the office. This was a big presentation with Trust Bank, our largest institution, to ask them for exclusive access to one of their new funds. Mike would be there, and since he claimed I was his worst MD, this was my chance to prove him wrong. I worked on the slides for a few more hours, until all that was left was to rehearse my talking points.

Later that night, when the kids were asleep, I went over my slides in front of my dresser mirror, again and again, until I had them memorized. There was one slide that didn't seem right; I wasn't sure how to explain it. I wished I could review it with Pete before the meeting, but we were scheduled first thing. Just then my phone buzzed. A text from Rich: "Good luck tomorrow. Wish I could be there. You'll kill it."

Before I had the chance to talk myself out of it, I dialed his number.

"Hey. I'm happy you called," he said, his tone surprised, which made sense, since it was the first one-on-one conversation we'd had since he'd told me he loved me.

"Thanks for your text," I said. "I'm finishing up my slides. Could you look at them?"

"Of course," he said, "send them over." I emailed him the slides and went over my talking points. He made some corrections and we finalized them, even the slide I was stuck on.

"Thanks," I said. "You saved me."

"It's the least I can do since I won't be there," he said. He was flying out to Boston first thing in the morning. "So, what are you up to?"

"Not much," I said. "Just this presentation. The kids are asleep. Dan left for a two o'clock tee time and I haven't seen him since."

"Ahh. I never knew he was one of those," he said. Rich despised golf, and he couldn't stand the golf guy types and the golf guy culture, another thing that made him a minority as a male at Goldman.

"I'm not sure who Dan is anymore," I said, surprised by my words. I was poking the bear, going against my rules about keeping it all business with Rich, but I was too tired and lonely to care anymore.

"Well, I know who I am," he said. "And I'd never make you a golf widow." My stomach did a somersault.

"Rich," I said, "I just need some time." I couldn't believe how much I sounded like Dan.

"I'm not going anywhere," he reassured me.

The next morning, I dressed for the big meeting, putting on my favorite black pants suit and cream blouse. I also added a chunky gray pearl statement necklace even though I wasn't into accessories. As I backed out of the driveway, I noticed Dan's car wasn't there, so I called him and it went straight to voicemail. Then I texted him and didn't get a response.

I ran back into the house thinking he took a cab home, but when I checked the guest room, it was empty. Even with the way he'd acted the last month, this was out of character, and I worried he'd been in an accident, so I called Steve. But I got his voicemail, too.

I paced back and forth in the kitchen, panic rising with each step. I wondered if I should call the police, but my gut said not to worry, that he was probably sleeping off a hangover in Hoboken.

I couldn't be late to work, though, this was my chance to prove myself, to prove that I wasn't a bottom quartile MD, to prove that I deserved the promotion.

For the next fifteen minutes, I called several times as fear and anger grew inside with each voicemail. My phone finally rang, and I was relieved to see it was Dan. "Are you all right?"

"Yeah," he said, his voice hoarse. "I'm at Steve's. I overslept."

I hung up and wanted to scream. Relief that he was safe was quickly washed away by stress. I was screwed because even if he left for home at that moment, I'd never make it to the meeting on time. I cringed as I called my mom, hating to wake her up so early, but I had no choice.

I headed to work once she arrived, and Dan called when I was on the ferry, but I ignored it. Anger replaced my initial relief over his well-being. This wasn't the time or place to talk to Dan. With my presentation within the hour, I needed all my energy.

My clients from Trust Bank arrived and the presentation went great. My talking points were perfect and at the end, they agreed to give us exclusive access to their newest portfolio of securities. Mike smiled the whole time, and after we walked them to the elevator bank, he asked to meet in his office.

"That presentation was perfection. You crushed it," he said as we walked through his office door. My body felt soft with relief, after all the preparation and the crisis that morning. "And Todd from Trust Bank couldn't speak highly enough of you and your relationship with them."

Thanks." I added with a wink, "I'm just trying to make sure I'm not your fourth quartile MD."

"Oh, don't be ridiculous," he said. "That might be the path for some, but not for you. I know how to pick 'em."

When I got back to my desk, Pete looked up at me with expectant eyes.

"Nailed it!" I rejoiced. We fist bumped, and then I saw a message from Dan asking me to call. I walked into a back conference room as I dialed, realizing I hadn't had a conversation with him on my cell in weeks.

"I'm sorry about this morning," he said. "I thought I'd come home last night but then I decided to crash at Steve's. I forgot to set my alarm." I looked out the floor to ceiling windows as the early morning sun beamed through the skyscrapers in slivers of white. All the fear and frustration from the morning poured out like it was overflowing from a bathtub.

"I deserve you hanging out with Steve," I said. "Doing God knows what with God knows who. That's my penance and I'll swallow it. But today I dragged my mother out of bed to bail your drunk ass out."

"Wait a sec. I was hanging out with my friend, not whoring around like you." His words cut deep, and I held my breath for a few beats.

"You're making a mess of my career and risking my bonus," I said. "You want our marriage to crash and burn to bits, fine, but don't mess with my job that provides for our family." The words spilled out so harshly and quickly, I was out of breath.

"I said sorry. Stop playing the victim," he shot back. "I'm the victim here."

"I've gotta go to work," I cut him off. "I can't deal with you now."

"Okay just walk away and not talk. That's the best way to fix this," he said.

"I'm walking away? You wanna fix this?" My voice got so

loud I thought someone might hear, so I glanced out the door to make sure nobody was around. "You're the one who hasn't been seen or heard from. You're the one who almost cost me my presentation. You're the one going out all the time. You're the one hiding out in the guest room. I've been here. I've been ready to talk. I've been waiting. But you're not making the time. You said there's nothing to talk about." Spit flew out of my mouth.

"You're right," he said. "Maybe it's too late. Maybe I don't have the interest anymore." I hung up and collapsed in the chair next to me. I took off my wedding band and held it, looking at the way the small square diamonds shined under the fluorescent conference room lights. I thought of the day we designed it at the jewelers and the day he put it on my finger. Now, my hand looked strange without it, felt strange without it, and I realized how strange it would be if Dan wasn't my husband. I sat with his words. Maybe it's too late for him, maybe it's too late for me, maybe it's too late for our marriage.

That night one of the lenders threw a party in the Meatpacking district but before I went, I grabbed drinks with the team at a nearby bar. Things at home with Dan were falling apart, but I could at least put my career concerns to bed. All that drama around the presentation made my victory sweeter, and my sense of relief stronger. Despite my conversation with Dan, I was upbeat.

"Jamie! Have a shot with us," Tommy, one of my analysts, said. We were at a small pub on Washington Street and a dozen shot glasses sat in two rows on the shellacked bar, with salt shakers on one side and a bowl of lemon wedges on the other. Tommy stood with the analysts from our group, looking at me with hopeful eyes. Pete, who heard the commotion from across the room, joined us.

"Why not?"

Everyone cheered, while Tommy handed Pete and me the salt shakers, and we all gathered in a circle and took the shot. The glasses slammed on the bar as we clambered for lemons and jammed them in our mouths. Screams and high-fives followed and the analysts' smiling faces made me feel like a feather. I put my marriage on the back burner of my mind, happy for the break.

As the bartender got another round, Pete said, "I'm heading out, so be careful." His eyes shot to Rich, who had just arrived. "Got it," I said as we fist-bumped. I wished I'd told Pete about all that happened with Dan earlier, but it would have to wait for tomorrow. We were so much more than a manager and employee; we had become best friends, which was rare at a cut-throat place like Goldman, where, in my experience, colleagues often threatened one another. It was an atypical situation, but we were different from the others, we had the same values and had gravitated toward each other all those years ago. We were allies, kindred spirits in this crazy world, and we felt like we needed each other to survive.

After he left, I did another round of shots while I chatted with the analysts, and about an hour later, I went to the bathroom to freshen up. When I walked out, everyone had left except for Rich, who sat on a bar stool and looked over the bill. I leaned against the wood paneled wall outside the bathroom and watched him study the receipt and pull out his credit card. If I approached, I'd break my vow of not being alone with him. My mind went to the last time we were alone, the night that had marked the beginning of the disintegration of my marriage. I should walk out and head to the party, or maybe go home, though the kids would be asleep and Dan would be behind the guest room door. Dan's words, "Maybe it's too late," reverberated through my mind and propelled me toward Rich.

"Hey," he said. His hazel eyes sucked the air out of the room.

"Where did everyone go?" I said, trying to sound nonchalant, even though I felt sick to my stomach. I feared being close to him, afraid of what I might do, and yet, not knowing what might happen made me want to be around him even more.

"I guess home or to the party," he said. He swirled his glass of wine as his eyes stayed glued to me. "Sit with me. I've missed you." The room buzzed with the chatter of people around us and the black leather stool next to him was empty. A glass of wine was placed in front of me, and my body pulled onto the stool like a magnet.

He told me about his trip, and I told him about the meeting with Trust Bank. "Wow," he said. "With all that stress you managed to kick ass. You're amazing." My body pulled up straighter. Rich was the one person these days who made me feel good, smart, and competent. Then the bartender came to grab his credit card and bumped his arm, knocking his glass over and spilling red wine over his white dress shirt.

The bartender's eyes went wide. "Oh no," she said. "I'm sorry."

Rich looked at his shirt and surveyed the damage. "I have two dozen of these in my closet," he said, "don't worry about it." The bartender smiled with relief and walked away. Most of the guys at work would've made such a stink over it, and I smiled knowing Rich was different.

"Let's stop at my place so I can change before the party," he said. "It's around the corner." He looked ridiculous, with his white shirt streaked with red, but adorable. It was cute to see him, an impeccable dresser, mussed up. If I went with him, though, I'd be alone in his apartment, after all the drinks I'd had. Alone in a bar was one thing, alone in his apartment was another. I thought back to the back row of the Escalade, but I was sick of thinking, of analyzing and considering options, about what was right and what was wrong. I just wanted to do what felt right, right now.

"Okay."

We walked outside and it had begun to rain, so we stood under the bar's awning. To my left I saw the Hudson River and New Jersey on the horizon, as if calling me to return, but then Rich intertwined my fingers with his.

"It's just a few blocks," he said. "Let's run for it." He pulled me along the sidewalk, and we ran through the cobblestone streets. The cool rain hit my face and I laughed as we darted over puddles. Just following his lead felt freeing, like I was an actor in one of the movies often filmed in this neighborhood. We arrived at his building breathless, and we shook the rain off our bodies as we got on the elevator, standing in silence as he pressed the button for his floor. *This won't take long,* I thought. *He'll just grab his shirt and we'll be on our way.* But I couldn't wait to be alone in his apartment, hidden away from everyone and everything.

"So, here's my place," he said when we got to his door. He fiddled with the key with trembling hands as he pushed it in the lock. I followed him inside and closed the door behind me, then he leaned me against it and kissed me. I dropped my black workbag at my feet and put my arms around him. Water dripped off our heads and down our faces as he continued to kiss my mouth, neck, and ears. I felt dizzy from the day, the tequila, and his touch, and I delighted in the escape.

"You make me so happy," he said. I smiled wide as my body throbbed.

"We're soaked," he stepped back. "Let's get changed." I grabbed my bag as he pulled me into his bedroom. I couldn't believe I was there. I looked around and then admired a photo of Rich and his kids on his nightstand.

"Put these on," he said as he handed me sweats and a T-shirt. "They're not your size, but better than your wet clothes." He motioned toward his bathroom. It was painted pale gray, with a white vanity and a white subway-tiled shower. I looked at my reflection in the oval frameless mirror. My hair was soaked and my makeup ran down my face. I changed into the Brown University T-shirt, where his oldest child attended. I couldn't help but chuckle—my son was in diapers and his daughter was in college.

I found Rich on the couch in his living room in blue jeans and a green T-shirt. The lights were dimmed, and a candle flickered on the coffee table in front of him, alongside two glasses of red wine.

"Come, sit," he said as he tapped the sofa.

"So much for the party," I mused.

"Well, as amazing as you look," he said, "you're not dressed for a party." He smiled and handed me a wineglass and I took a sip and settled into the couch, right into his arms.

"So, how do you like my place?" he asked. He squeezed me into him, and I placed my head on his shoulder and surveyed the apartment. It was one large room with a small open kitchen and the sofa, which faced his TV. Compared to his old house it was tiny, but perfect for him.

"It's great."

"Well, it's a sublet," he said. "I need to buy my own place, and I want you to help me find it." I looked into his eyes, and I realized he was serious. My conversation with Dan earlier felt like the beginning of the end. Was this conversation the beginning of a new beginning? A new relationship and life with Rich, starting over with a new man as a thirty-six-year-old? I felt nervous at the proposition, but I wasn't sure if it was fear or excitement. Pressure began to build inside me, like a tea kettle about to scream out its whistle. I didn't want to respond, I didn't want to think, I didn't want to decide. Instead, I leaned over and kissed him. Thick with intensity, I went after him, wanting to exhaust my body so I wouldn't have to focus on the questions running nonstop in my mind about my marriage, my children, my future. I pulled off his T-shirt and rubbed my hands along his chest, his gray speckled hair tangled between my fingers.

Our clothes came off piece by piece, the removal of each one marking a moment between us, like a step in an intimate ceremony that had only played in our imaginations until now. He pulled off my thong in the final step and we were there, naked, without disguise. I straddled his waist, my arms pushed down against his chest. My phone buzzed and I saw it was Dan and I wondered if he regretted his cruel and rigid words, but it was too late. I let the call go and bent down to kiss Rich again. This was it; it was going to happen, there was no reason for it not to. I was hollowed out and empty, and I wanted to be filled up and whole again. I heard the buzz of my phone again. Dan hadn't called in

weeks and now he called twice in a few minutes, so I sat up and answered, knowing it had to be about the kids.

"Mama, you there?" Beth said in a small voice.

"Honey, hi," I said. "What's going on?" I got off Rich and, looking down at my nakedness, I wrapped my arms around my torso and cradled my phone in my neck.

"My belly hurts," she said. "I want you. When are you coming home?" Rich lay next to me with a confused look on his face. The scene was so unreal, I couldn't believe it was my life. I was a lot of things, but first I was a mother, and those kids were all that mattered—not being a managing director, or a wife, or whatever I was to Rich.

"Oh, sweetheart," I said. "I'm sorry, but I'll be home soon." I grabbed the T-shirt at my feet and pulled it over my head, hard. I couldn't cover up fast enough.

"Is everything okay?" Rich asked.

"Yes," I said. "I've just got to get home." I changed in the bathroom and when I returned, Rich was on the couch, fully dressed.

"My car can bring you home," he said.

"No, I'm fine."

"Okay, I'll walk you downstairs."

"No, that's all right," I said. "See you tomorrow."

I left his building and ran toward the subway, the heavy cold rain pelting my face like a forceful slap; a slap to wake me from my daze, a slap to shake sense into me, a slap to get me back to reality. I never thought I'd be grateful for my children's pain, but Beth's stomachache was the best thing that could have happened. After weeks of indecision, I had my answer.

When I got home, I found Beth and Dan snuggled on the family room couch, and it reminded me of cuddling on Rich's couch, which made me queasy.

"Mama," Beth said in a whisper. Her face was pale, and her eyes were half closed. I put a hand to her forehead, and she was hot. Paired with a tummy ache, I was sure it was strep.

"I gave her some ibuprofen," Dan said. His eyes were fixed on the cartoon that played on the TV. I picked Beth up and she nestled her head in my neck, the same neck that Rich kissed a few hours ago. My stomach sunk at the thought that I smelled like him. This double life weighed me down and I needed to cut one loose.

I put Beth to bed and returned downstairs to lock up for the night. I found Dan still on the couch, beer bottle in hand, his eyes glued to the TV. "Hey," I said. "I didn't think you'd still be down here."

"I want to talk," he said. I sat on the couch and faced him. Maybe he regretted what he'd said earlier, and he'd want to repair our marriage, maybe we'd have a shot at a happy ending.

"So, where were you tonight?" he said, his eyes still on the TV.

"One of the lenders had a party," I said. "I was at a bar in Union Square." I couldn't believe what a liar I'd become. I scarcely recognized myself, how lying came so easy to me now, but I convinced myself it was the last time because I wanted to begin a new life, a new pattern, a new chapter, and I hoped Dan wanted to be a part of it. What I'd done was wrong, but I was so confused, with Dan ignoring me and Rich pursuing me. I'd lost the map to my life, but now I'd found it and knew where I was meant to be. I wanted to start fresh, forget what we'd both done those past months.

Bags sat under Dan's bloodshot eyes, and salt and pepper scruff covered his chin and cheeks. He still looked hungover after his late night out and I realized we'd both made mistakes these last weeks. I was ready to fix it all and move on.

"You lying bitch," he said. "I tracked your phone, and I know where you were."

My eyes went wide, and my mouth hung open. I didn't know that you could track a phone, but he was a tech guy, after all. I felt like a fly trapped in a spider's web and anger at the violation spread over me. I wished I could've done that this morning when I didn't know where he was. At the same time, facing the truth gave me a sense of relief, that I could free myself from all the lies. My balloon of deception had grown so large that it was about to pop. Now we'd address everything; no more hiding behind lies and guest room doors. It would be loud and messy and ugly, but that was better than inscrutable silence. Our building of a marriage was condemned, and we'd have to knock it down and rebuild if we wanted to keep it.

"I'm sorry," I said.

Dan got up from the couch and stood next to the wall, his eyes wild, his hands clenched in fists like he was about to step into the ring. I'd never seen him like this before. It looked like he could kill someone—I started to tremble, so scared of what he'd say or do. Then Dan yelled as he put his fist through the family room wall. I screamed as the sheetrock collapsed and left a gaping hole. The tan wooden studs were visible as dust and chunks of the wall rained on the hardwood floor. I covered my face with my hands and sobbed as I rocked myself, realizing that I'd ruined everything—the wall, my marriage, and my life.

"Enough with your lies," he spat. He looked down at me, his

eyes so bloodshot I couldn't see the blue in them. I felt so small and worthless. I'd lied to Dan, Rich, and myself, telling so many lies I didn't know what was real or fake anymore. "If you don't stop it with him," he said, "I'm leaving. For good." He walked out of the room and stormed up the stairs.

I curled up in a ball on the couch and tucked my knees in my chest so hard that my stomach hurt. I closed my eyes and sobbed. He'd leave. I'd never thought about that ending before. Me running off with Rich and leaving Dan, yes—but Dan moving on and leaving me, it hadn't crossed my mind. Why hadn't that crossed my mind? He'd leave and take the children. I couldn't take care of them and work. I could lose everything, and I hadn't considered it. I held my head and dug my nails into my hair as visions of all I'd built with Dan—our marriage, our family, our home—became a mirage just out of my grasp. I'd lose them all, I told myself, as my fingers dug deeper and deeper. I grabbed my phone and saw my bloodied fingertips as I emailed my assistant to tell her I was taking the next day off.

I emptied my workbag on the floor, fished for my bottle of Xanax, and swallowed two dry. I crawled on the couch and watched the happy cartoon characters singing cheerful songs on TV. If only life were that simple, if only I'd been a better person, if only I'd been strong enough to keep everything together. I cried and waited for the Xanax to kick in so I could pass out, fading my horror show life to black.

I woke up before dawn, in a ball on the couch, the TV still blaring cartoons. Crust lined my puffy eyes and I felt gross, like my disgusting morals seeped in my skin and polluted my body. I tiptoed upstairs to shower, the water scalding my skin as I washed my body, Rich's scent, and my old life away, the dirty nasty water swirling down the drain. I wasn't sure what would happen, but today I was different, renewed and recommitted to my children and husband, if he would let me be.

I was making pancakes when my phone buzzed from Rich's texts. "Is everything okay?" "Did you get home all right?" I could only think that it was time to cut him off as I heard the kids' footsteps coming down the stairs.

"Mama, you're home!" Abby said and hugged me. Beth trailed behind her and Dan followed with Luke.

"How come you're home?" he asked as he put Luke in his highchair.

"Well, it's Friday and with Beth sick I thought I'd make it a long weekend so I could help out," I said. "And maybe we could talk."

"Sure," he said.

Later that morning, Dan was at the kitchen table with his laptop, and I joined him. "It's over with him," I said. The sun shined though the sliding glass door. Its rays burned my eyes, and my head throbbed from last night's wine and tears, but Dan looked better, clean shaven, with bright eyes. "I want to be a family again," I said. "I've screwed up everything and I'm sorry." Dan looked at me, and his silence bored a hole in my chest.

"I'm crumbling," I said. "All my waking hours are at Goldman. I'm strung out, not thinking straight, and making bad choices. Rich was a bad choice, a huge mistake. Please give me a chance, I want to fix this."

We sat side by side at the table we bought when we were newlyweds. The once bright white painted chairs were chipped, and the table's surface was dented.

"I want to fix it, too," he agreed.

I closed my eyes and let the words wash over me. Even though we had a lot of work to do, at least I had the chance.

"I hate Goldman, too," he said. He pressed his hand on his chest, like he was trying to tame his emotions. "I hate being a dad alone, and that I sacrificed my career. We used to have a life together. Now you have another life, and I don't have one at all. I'm medicating myself with alcohol and Steve to forget it all. I hate what Goldman has done to us. It's not worth the money."

I grabbed his hand. He was doing what I wanted, raising the kids, but he wasn't happy either. We were both sacrificing and although Dan had never walked into Goldman's doors, it was killing him, too.

"Things need to change, though," he said. "No more Rich and no more late nights with Steve. And I think we should see a counselor."

"Yes," I said. "Definitely. I'm sorry I didn't know you were going through any of this."

"I think there's a lot about each other that we don't know anymore," he said.

"And Dan," I said. My heart was in my throat and tears filled my eyes. "Despite everything, you've always been my best friend, and I want to return to what we used to be, not just for the kids, but for us."

"I want that, too," he said. I smiled and got up from the table to check on the kids.

"Hey, Jamie," he said. I turned around and he pulled me in, and we wrapped our arms around each other. I closed my eyes and rested my head on his chest, his heartbeat echoing in my ear as I breathed in his scent—soap and mint mixed with coffee, the scent of home.

❈

Later that weekend, I had coffee with my best friend Lily at her house. She'd been telling me to leave Goldman for years, and after I'd told her what had been going on with work and Dan, she was even more forceful with her opinions.

"Now will you leave?" she demanded. "Do you finally see that you have to get out of there?" We were sitting around her kitchen table, a plate of chocolate chip cookies between us. I held my head in my hands and massaged my temples with my fingers.

"I know I have to go," I said. "It's just not that simple." I hated making excuses for myself, but I was so confused.

"Goldman has been your abusive boyfriend for years," she exclaimed. "The guy who treats you like crap and then takes you out to a fancy dinner." I knew she was right on some level, but it wasn't like I had bruises, and it wasn't that bad considering what they'd given me: the status, the prestige, the money. I knew I had to leave, but now that I was walking away from Rich and recommitting to Dan, I could take time to figure everything out. I didn't have to leave immediately, I reasoned with myself, that seemed rash and foolish.

"But you don't see it all," I pleaded. "It's like a glacier, where you only see the top, but most of it is underwater. I've been there my whole adult life. For years, they've drilled it into us that I'll fail if I leave, that I'm nothing without them, that I'll never be able to work again. I'm so afraid they're right." My voice trailed off and I couldn't believe how pathetic I sounded. I wish I could see what she saw, but for me, this was more than just a job, it was who I had become, it represented everything I'd done for my family, proving that the nobody kid in the back brace from New Jersey could be somebody. And no matter what my rational brain said, there was a part of me that believed Mike and his promise that I was nothing without Goldman.

"My God, Jamie," Lily gasped. "They've really done a number on you." She shook her head, looking at me with a mix of shock, pity, and sadness.

"Leave her alone, Mom," Emma, her thirteen-year-old daughter interrupted. I hadn't noticed that she'd been standing behind me. "You know Aunt Jamie will never leave Goldman Sachs."

I looked at Emma, her blue eyes laced with sympathy, and my stomach lurched. Here was this young girl, on the brink of womanhood, watching as I made excuses for the awful way I was being treated. Is this the role model I wanted to be for her and my girls?

I was so confused, constantly fighting myself. A small voice in my head whispered louder that I should walk out, that I deserved better, but the booming voice of Mike kept beating her into silence.

CHAPTER THIRTEEN

The following Monday I wanted to talk to Rich as soon as possible, so I went straight to his office, my pulse quickening with each step. He saw me through the glass wall and opened the door.

"We need to talk," I said, and walked to the other side of the room.

"Okay," he said. "I've got to tell you something, too." We looked at each other, the pressure building by the second.

"You go first," he said. We stood on opposite sides of his conference table, surrounded by empty chairs. I smelled my perfume as it mixed with the sweat that collected on my neck. Rich's face was expectant, and a tentative smile curled his lips.

"This has to end," I said.

His face fell. Clearly, that wasn't the response he'd been expecting. He dropped into a chair. "I don't understand," he exclaimed. "We make each other happy." His eyebrows pulled together, and his mouth turned down.

"It's not about us," I said, sitting down opposite him. "It's about my family. I need to fix my marriage, for them, and for me." His eyes were wet, and I looked out the glass office wall because I couldn't see him like this, I couldn't stand what I'd done to him, I couldn't stand myself.

"Please, don't do this," he said. "Think this through." I looked into his eyes, a color that I couldn't describe—they reminded me of cinnamon and honey. Deep lines framed them, etchings of his knowledge and confidence. I didn't know if I loved him, but I loved who I was when I was with him—just me, a woman, not bound by obligations to anyone or anything. My mind tried to focus on Dan and the kids, not on Rich's crestfallen face.

"I've thought this through for months," my voice cracked, "and we need to be over."

He folded his hands and rested his mouth on his fingers. I wanted to leave and put this behind me, but I was glued to my seat.

Rich cleared his throat. "Today's my last day at Goldman," he declared. I took a sharp breath in. I knew him so well and we shared so much, yet I didn't know this. Still, he didn't have to say what had happened; I knew. The "one in, one out" rule I'd heard about for years proved true—the firm was managing the number of MDs and, to make room for me, Mike had to fire an existing one. "And here I thought your promotion would make it easier for us to be together," he said with a faint chuckle.

I felt like human poison. I ruined everything I touched—marriages, careers, and relationships. After working for years in this awful environment, I'd become just as toxic as Goldman Sachs. And the most despicable thing of all was that his words brought me relief. Now I'd be free of temptation and sin, now I could be with my family, without the reminder of my mistakes in my face.

"I'm so sorry," I said.

"I'm leaving soon and don't want any attention," Rich explained. "Mike will announce it later, so don't tell anyone."

I nodded.

"Well then," he said. "I guess this is goodbye."

He smiled and then turned toward his desk while I stared at him from behind, watching the back of his head, the hairline along his neck, and his wide shoulders. Then I walked back to my desk, my body trembling.

I dialed into a conference call while my thoughts were on Rich's office behind me, but I willed myself not to look. When the call was over, I turned around and saw his door was open, but his desk was empty. No coffee mug, no workbag, no coat.

"Team meeting at the back of the floor," Mike said from his office. Everyone popped out of their seats. Some exchanged concerned glances, others laughed and joked around as we gathered in the open space behind the trading desk.

"I have an announcement," he said. "Rich has left the firm." Gasps erupted, then Pete looked at me wide-eyed, and I mouthed, "Later."

"Justin Lansing will be returning from Los Angeles in a month to run the desk," he said. "I'll be running the day to day in the interim." Mike looked over us for a beat and went back to his office. He never took questions. Everyone lingered and chatted, as we walked back to our desks, digesting the news.

When I started at Goldman, Justin Lansing was just a junior guy. A native New Yorker, he'd worked for Mike in various offices across the United States over the last decade. He was an MD and also good friends with Mike, since they were both Duke alums. When he was in New York on business, they'd hang out a lot. Whenever there were big management changes at Goldman, there was always a hidden story. Rumor had it that Justin wanted to return to New York and this move was Mike's way of thanking Justin for living away for so long; now he was able to return home for a larger role, maybe make partner and take over for Mike someday.

There was an unofficial limit of MDs who could work for Mike, in order to keep the role exclusive and elite at the firm. Rich was gone now that I was a new MD, so Mike's overall numbers remained unchanged. Justin was already an MD under Mike, so relocating him from Los Angeles to New York was an acceptable move and didn't put any other MDs in jeopardy.

That afternoon, Pete and I grabbed coffee and headed to the back conference room.

"What. The. Hell," he said.

In hushed tones, looking out the glass wall to make sure nobody was nearby, I gave him the download, from Dan's partying and oversleeping, to Rich's apartment and my awkward, screwed-up goodbye to him.

"I shouldn't have left you at the bar," he said. "I knew this would happen." He ran his hands through his thick silver hair.

"I'm not your responsibility," I said. "And it's over. Dan and I will be okay." As I said the words, I knew deep in my core that they were true.

⭤

"Higgins?" a woman asked. She was beautiful, with high cheekbones and perfect makeup. Dan and I followed her and sat on a gray microfiber sofa, while she sat in an oversize red chair across from us. She looked older than us, but had a youthful energy, like she had life experience, but was young enough to relate to us—just what we needed in a marriage counselor.

"Welcome," she said. "What brings you here today?" She held a clipboard and pen in her hand, and although I knew how to answer her question, I wanted to hide under the couch instead. Water from the stone fountain next to me trickled and I swallowed the lump of shame in my throat.

"I cheated on my husband," I said.

She nodded with a small smile that indicated she had heard this story before. Hearing my admission to a stranger made it real. Dan grabbed my hand and squeezed, and I couldn't believe he wanted to touch me. I was so grateful for him and so disgusted in myself.

We walked out an hour later, and while I was exhausted from the tears and regret, I felt optimistic that we'd taken the first steps to repair our marriage. That night, after the kids were asleep, there was a knock on the bedroom door. Dan stood in his blue sweatpants and yellow T-shirt. His pillow was under his arm and an expectant smile played on his lips. After months of sleeping apart he was really, actually there, and my stomach flipped as he walked in.

CHAPTER FOURTEEN

A few weeks later, Justin took over Rich's office, and through the floor-to-ceiling glass wall, I could see he'd made it his own. Framed photos of country club greens covered the once bare walls, signed baseballs and footballs sat on the bookshelf, and a large Jets green foam finger was perched on his desk.

"Jamie, our little analyst," Justin said as he saw me at his door. "We cross paths again."

"Yes," I said. "Welcome back." We shook hands and I sat down at his meeting table, placing two copies of my business plan in front of me.

"So, Mike tells me you're my go-to," he said, "and I've gotta say, I'm surprised." His blue eyes gleamed, his thinning strawberry blond hair was cut short, and freckles covered his pale face. In his hands he held a mini Jets football. "I didn't think Sister Jamie could hang with the big boys."

"I can hang with anyone," I smiled, even though I wanted to punch him in the face. I hadn't heard "Sister Jamie" in years.

"Let's hope so," he smiled back, revealing a set of oversize white teeth. "Because there's a new sheriff in town."

"Okay," I said, not sure how to respond. In that moment, it felt like all my years at the firm were erased and I was back at my first interview. I waited for him to speak, but he just looked at me as silence filled the room. "Well," I finally continued, "I'd love to share my business plan with you."

"Have at it," he said. "I'm all ears." I placed a presentation in front of him and began, while he reclined in his chair, stared at the white ceiling tiles, and tossed his Jets ball in the air, again and again. He didn't react to a word I said, he didn't ask a question, he didn't even act like I was in the room. It was just him, the ceiling, and the ball.

After the meeting, I sat in front of my computer and stared at the screensaver, which blurred as tears filled my eyes.

"So, how'd it go?" Pete asked, leaning toward me.

"Well, the good news for you is he likes football," I said, "so you'll have that in common." It was already apparent that would be about all they had in common.

The next day, I stood at the end of the trading row in front of the printer, waiting for a document, when I heard Justin across the floor.

"I've got to find me an assistant," he said. "Nobody too old, too ugly, too flabby. You know what I mean? I want 'em young, high, and tight!" He faced Jerry and Vito and cupped his hands over his chest as if he had breasts. Jerry and Vito looked at him with bright eyes, like they'd found their long-lost leader, then they high-fived and fist bumped as they laughed. I looked straight ahead and focused on the beige wall sconce on the other side of the floor. In my periphery, I saw their jovial back slaps and impromptu game of toss with the mini football. I clenched my jaw so tight I felt it in my temples. When my papers came out of the printer, I headed to my desk as fast as I could without running.

On my way back to my seat, my assistant Katie flagged me down. She supported many of the managers on the floor, but not Justin. Her desk was my safe haven where I could get a dose of a "real" person. We'd swap stories about our kids, talk about the latest parenting hacks, and complain about how exhausted we were.

"I just heard what Justin said," she whispered. "He's disgusting." I nodded in agreement as I heard Justin's laughter over my shoulder. "I don't know how you survive here as an MD," she continued. "You aren't like any of them. It must be lonely." Just then Jerry walked by and dropped off a thick envelope of travel receipts for her to process without acknowledging her.

"It is," I agreed as I watched Jerry walk away. "But at least I'm like you." We smiled at each other and high-fived before I returned to my desk.

The next day, Sandra, a female vice president whom I had mentored for years, asked to meet with me. "So Justin's invited all the guys in the department to go to a gentleman's club for scotch tasting and God knows what else," she said. "It's all they talk about. How are the women on the desk supposed to get to know him? Go to a strip club? Or does Justin not care about knowing us?"

I looked at her big brown eyes on her young face. Of course Justin would take the guys to a gentleman's club. My mind churned and I tried to produce an acceptable excuse—I hated my role as the lone senior woman in the department, covering up for the bad behavior of men.

"He just got here," I explained. "Give it time, maybe he has something different planned for the women." I tried to believe my words, but I knew better.

The fact is that the majority of people on Wall Street were men, both at Goldman and our clients. So many of the "extra-curricular activities," both with clients and colleagues, were tailored to the assumed interests of cis white men: golf, cigars, scotch, strip clubs, and shaves.

Although I met with clients at the office and at dinner during the week, guys like Justin would bond with them over golf weekends to Ireland, skiing in Vail, and romps in Vegas, where women would never be invited. There was no way I could build the same relationships with them. The same went for interoffice networking events. Women who worked for Justin would never be invited to a gentleman's club, where the "bro" type guys would smoke cigars and bond for hours. There was an intentionality behind this madness: to keep the strongest relationships with management and the largest clients, and therefore the influence, with these types of men. It maintained the old boys' club and solidified its power.

That next evening, our biggest client, National Trust, was in town from Chicago. I'd planned a dinner with them weeks ago, before Justin took over, so this was an opportunity to show him the great relationship Pete and I had with them. We had reservations at a steak house in Midtown and Justin ran late so Pete and I went ahead of him.

"I'm not optimistic about this guy," Pete muttered as he closed the door to our town car. "I'm nervous for us."

"Why?" I asked, even though I was nervous too.

"I'm saying this as a guy here," he said. "Justin's a man's man, a scotch drinking, cigar smoking dude. You and I don't fit into that brand. And I'm hearing he's asked some of the guys to go out scotch tasting. I didn't make that list. With a wife and kids at home, that's no surprise."

"I've heard all about it." The buildings on the West Side Highway whizzed by, rock music playing from the car's radio. "Let's just focus on dinner and show Justin how good our relationship is with Cameron and Curt," I attempted to reassure us both, referring to the guys from National Trust.

Justin arrived just as we sat down for dinner. "Justin, good to see you, my man!" Cameron said. He jumped out of his chair and gave Justin a big bear hug. I flinched and looked at Pete. The announcement of Justin's new role had just happened, and I hadn't had a chance to tell Cameron myself.

"So, you guys go back?" Pete said as they sat down.

"Oh yeah, we've known each other for years," Cameron said. "Remember that crazy conference in Hong Kong?"

"Yeah, I'm surprised we weren't jailed for half the stuff we did," Justin said, and then let out a big laugh.

"Well, we probably would've been if we were in the States," Cameron laughed, then they high-fived across the table.

Pete and I looked at each other with muted smiles. It took everything in me not to roll my eyes. We settled into our meal and talked about business, and I was grateful that Cameron said nice things about Pete and me, but it was clear I'd never have the type of relationship with Cameron that Justin had.

The next afternoon, Curt called me once he'd returned to Chicago. "Oh man," he said, "that Justin knows how to party."

"Really?" I said. "I didn't think it was *that* crazy of a night."

"Well, you weren't at the after party," he said.

"Oh," I said. "What happened?"

"After you and Pete left, Justin called Jerry and Vito," he said. "Then we headed to this go-go bar in Times Square." I saw Justin across the room fiddling with the stupid Jets ball, surrounded by Vito and Jerry. Jerry and Vito both wanted to make MD and I guessed they thought Justin would make that happen.

"Wow," I said. "Sounds like quite a night."

"Yeah, sure was," he said. "Justin's a good guy."

A good guy. To whom? Not to women older than thirty who needed a job as a receptionist, not to the women on the team who wanted to know their new boss, not to me who—as a mother with young kids at home—couldn't stay out until 2 a.m. drinking and ogling women . . . and wouldn't want to even if I had the time. As the only managing female MD, I felt responsible for advocating for the women on the desk, but as my family's primary breadwinner, I needed to protect my career. It felt impossible to do both.

A few weeks later we traveled to Chicago to visit National Trust, and since we'd just done the big steak dinner, we opted for something more fun—pool and karaoke. I hoped that since Jerry and Vito weren't around, there wouldn't be any after parties.

"We might miss our flight," Pete said under his breath as we waited for Justin at the office.

"I know, but God forbid he doesn't have the slides," I said. "He'd be naked without them." Justin sat at his desk and reviewed the presentation that I'd worked on all week.

"I hope he has time to memorize your work," Pete said. Justin slipped on his black trench coat, grabbed his overnight bag, and walked past us.

"No time to spare, guys," he said as his coat ballooned behind him. We got in a town car and I sat wedged between the two in the back seat. I heard Justin's whispers as he reviewed my presentation, and I felt cheated hearing my words come out of his mouth. It was a managing style I wasn't used to. Rich was confident enough in himself that he gave others opportunities to present to clients and be the face of Goldman Sachs.

When we got to National's office, Cameron greeted us in the lobby. "Justin, buddy," he said as they embraced and exchanged back slaps.

We proceeded to their cream conference room and sat at the round wooden table, where mini water bottles adorned each seat. Justin recited my presentation from memory, getting all the credit for my work. I sat ready to answer questions about daily operations, but there weren't any because everyone wanted the meeting to be over with so they could go out and party.

Afterward, all twenty guys from National Trust and the three of us went to Kings Billiards, a high-end pool hall that served top-shelf liquor, venison sliders, and ham and brie sandwiches. The flat screen TVs above our tables displayed "National Trust welcomes Goldman Sachs."

We played several games as we drank martinis and ate shrimp cocktail, and after a few hours we moved to the karaoke bar next to the pool hall. Some of the National Trust guys left, including Curt, so drunk they stumbled into their corporate cars. I was tired, but there was a rule at Goldman: you always outlasted the last client, so I had to stay. Justin had done tequila shots with Cameron all night, his eyes bloodshot, and he hooted and hollered as he hobbled into the karaoke bar. Everyone already seated at tables looked up at him, and I couldn't help but roll my eyes when he and Cameron went to the bar for another round. A stage stood next to the bar, and a man who worked the karaoke stand sat on a wooden stool in front. He was Black and looked young, in his early twenties, and wore a white tee and blue jeans.

Justin and Cameron finished their shots, their glasses coming down with a loud bang, and then Justin headed to the karaoke table and almost tripped. The man grimaced as Justin slurred out his song selection and then burped.

"Why don't you take a break?" the man suggested. "Drink some water and come back later."

Justin's fair face turned blotchy and it was like his freckles came to life—I watched a crimson wave travel from his ears down his neck. I'd heard of his temper but had never seen it yet. It was like watching a car accident in slow motion, and I sat frozen, unable to stop it.

"Who the fuck do you think you are?" he shouted. The room, once loud with conversation, fell quiet. The spotlight for the karaoke stage was on Justin and his eyes were opened wide, so bloodshot that the whites were pink. "You're a faggot, a homo, a dumb [racial epithet]. Do you know who I am? I work at fucking Goldman Sachs," he said as spit flew out of his mouth. "I can fucking sing what I want, when I want."

Cameron grabbed Justin's arms and pulled him backward, and the bartender ran out and grabbed the man, who looked like he was about to punch Justin in the face. I wished he would. It was like ringside at a boxing match, as the managers pulled the fighters back after a round. Pete and I stood next to Justin, looking at each other with wide eyes and gaped mouths. Then

Cameron pulled Justin out of the bar and the bartender released the man. They talked in hushed tones.

The seriousness of the situation overwhelmed me. I'd cleaned up plenty of other people's messes over the years: I'd lied to HR about Lizzie's lawsuit, which cleared Jerry and Vito; I kept my mouth shut when Eric assaulted me; and I'd made light of Justin's behavior on the desk. I'd spent years talking brightly to young women entering the firm, feeling like a flight attendant telling passengers that everything was okay while the pilot nose-dived the plane. I'd never encountered a mess like this, though, and I didn't know what to do.

Pete stood at my side as I approached the man. "I am appalled, embarrassed, and so sorry," I told him. "There is no excuse for the disgusting behavior of my colleague."

"You're from Goldman Sachs, right?" the man said. "I'm sure they'd want to know how racist and homophobic their employees are."

He walked away and I felt so dirty being a part of this, like I needed a shower to wash away the experience. Everyone else had left, so Pete and I settled the tab and gave a large tip, which felt gross, like I tried to pay them off.

"I can't believe this," I said once we were in a taxi. "I'd heard of Justin's temper, but that was crazy. He crossed a line. Do you think that man will say something?"

"Who knows?" Pete said. "Maybe he sees this all the time, just another close-minded prick who rules the world at Goldman."

The next morning, I felt a lead weight in my stomach, and I was relieved Justin missed our flight back to New York. Pete and I spent the entire journey in silence. I wanted to talk to him and get his advice, but I didn't want to get him involved. If I reported this it would be a huge deal, and I didn't even want him as a confidante. My heart told me to report it, but my head knew it might get me in trouble.

That afternoon Justin returned, and I heard laughter as he talked with Vito and Jerry.

"You wouldn't believe this guy," Justin said. "So I told him off. Nobody talks to me like that." I saw the back of Justin's head over my screen as he threw his football to Vito across the desk, like it was a normal day. It shredded my stomach that he actually seemed *proud* about what happened. Vito and Jerry gave him high-fives.

Oh, hell no. This was not okay.

I wouldn't be able to stay silent this time. I was tired of looking the other way, lying to the women on the desk, and lying to myself. I had witnessed terrible behavior at Goldman over the years, but this was different, this was outside the family, this was in public. No longer the dirty laundry kept inside the house of Mike's *family*, now our nasty knickers were hanging out for everyone to see. And from that perspective, in that moment, I saw everything with renewed clarity—like the glasses I wore, coated with the Goldman tint of tolerating bad behavior, were replaced by crystal clear lenses.

I turned those lenses on myself and realized how much I had changed, how I walked in all those years ago so innocent, with the values and morals I was raised with, by my grandmother and my parents, and how, over time, my life at Goldman morphed them and changed me into someone I wasn't proud of. I wanted to return to the old Jamie, and this was a start. I knew there was a lot at stake with my career, I knew I was taking a risk by being a whistleblower, but not to say anything was a bigger risk for my character.

I couldn't take this up with Mike. He'd do anything to protect Justin, including ignoring bad behavior. As long as nobody knew about it outside our department, Mike could keep up the squeaky-clean façade to senior management. Mike wasn't alone in his protectiveness; it was a common practice at Goldman. It's why they created a department that handled sensitive situations, called Employee Relations. Their motto was "if you see something, say something" and they even had a hotline to leave anonymous messages of concern.

I knew an attorney in that group named Art, whom I'd worked with a bunch over the years, mainly when we had to fire people. He vetted all the terminations to protect Goldman from any future litigation, and he'd make sure our decisions were airtight and within Goldman's rights as an employer. He was the consummate professional and I trusted him. Yes, he and his department protected Goldman, but they also protected Goldman employees. Art's main goal was to ensure things were done appropriately and that our Employee Handbook was followed. I needed to call him, but I didn't want anyone in my department to know. There was a vacant floor under construction a few floors up, but the conference rooms were available, which would be the perfect place to make the call. I took the elevator up and walked down the deserted hall, looking behind me every few steps, paranoid I was being followed. As I saw a free conference room at the end of the hall, my heart clobbered in my chest. I walked into the room and sat down at the oval wooden table, then rocked back and forth in my chair like I was calming one of my kids. My left hand shook as I grabbed the phone and I tightened my grip to steady it, then I dialed Art's extension and squeezed my eyes shut.

"Hi, I need to tell you about something that happened in Chicago," I said, "but before I begin, you need to promise that I'll be protected. My name can never be mentioned."

"Of course," he said. "I couldn't do my job any other way."

"This is unacceptable," he said after I told him everything. "I know you're in an awkward position, but you did the right thing. Your name will not be associated with this."

"Thank you," I said. "I'm relieved to hear you say that again." I hung up and felt a hundred pounds lighter.

The next day Mike called me to his office, and I figured it was for our weekly update, so I brought copies of my latest profit-ability report.

"Close the door," he said as I walked in.

"I have my weekly report to review," I said.

"Won't be needing that," he said. He leaned so far back in his desk chair, with his arms folded above his head, that the buttons on his white shirt struggled to stay closed. "So, I heard from my friends in Employee Relations today," he said. "They said you made a complaint against Justin."

I started to sweat, the fabric around my armpits dampening. I bit my lower lip so hard that I broke skin, and the taste of metallic blood coated my tongue.

"Oh Jamie," he said as he leaned forward. His shirt cuffs were rolled to his elbows, and he rested his forearms, covered with black hair, on the table. His face and neck were so red they looked like they were on fire. "It seems you need a reminder. We're one big family in this department. I've taken care of you like a daughter. You are supposed to treat me like your father. With this complaint you've gone against the family, *my* family. I don't put up with that. If you have a problem with someone in *my* family, you come to *me*. You *don't* call Employee Relations, you *don't* call compliance, you *don't* call anyone else. We solve family problems within the *family*. Got it?" His voice was like a hammer, and I felt like I'd been nailed into the tan office carpet.

The pages of my report were in my hand, still warm from the printer. What a fool I'd been. Mike's brown eyes were wide, and I willed myself not to cry.

"I'm sorry, Mike," I said. "I understand."

"Good, I'm glad we're clear," he said. "This will never happen again, got it?"

I nodded, and he turned his chair back to his computer. "Leave the door open," he said.

As I walked out, Justin stood at his desk flanked by Vito and Jerry. They stared at me with their arms folded over their chests, their eyes following me as I walked back to my seat.

"Is everything okay?" Pete said as I sat down. I stared at my screen, grateful I hadn't told him about my call to Art because I would've been paranoid that he'd betrayed me.

In the end, I wasn't sure who sold me out, but Employee Relations was a cost center business where money was spent, not a profit center business like ours where money was made. I figured either Art or someone else in his group was jonesing for a role on the "money side" and there was no better way to get into our business than to get in good with Mike. Mike was an information whore—any nugget of intel that would make him seem smarter, any gem that would give him a leg up amongst the firm's partners, any tidbit that would keep him one step out of trouble, would be rewarded. The fact that someone in HR viewed this as an opportunity to further their career, and that Mike was more upset by me going "outside the family" rather than the hateful words that Justin had used, wasn't lost on me.

I'd tell Pete what happened at some point, but not today. "Yes," I said. "Everything is okay."

My body trembled, and I grabbed a Xanax from my purse and washed it down with coffee. I was not okay. With that one phone call, I knew my career at Goldman Sachs had changed forever.

A few weeks later, the firm's annual review process started. It was called a 360-degree review, because not only did your manager review you, but so did your peers and those more junior. Many thought it was meaningless since people picked their friends to review them, and pre-negotiated "9 clubs" so they'd get perfect scores. But other than Pete, I didn't have any friends, so I just played by the rules and picked a cross section of people.

I always scored close to 9, the highest score, and year after year I was in the top 25 percent of my peer group. The review process seemed to work because even though I wasn't a good old boy, my performance was recognized. Not long after I submitted my review list, I got an email notification that Justin added more people to it. That had never happened in all my years at Goldman.

I looked over my computer and saw Justin's back as he stood at his desk and held court with Vito and Jerry. They were in a circle, doubled over with laughter. As I walked over, they saw me, and their smiles melted from their faces, like I was a cop breaking up a college frat party. Vito and Jerry scurried to their desks and Justin faced me.

"Hey, I got an email that you changed my reviewer list," I said. "That's never happened before, so I wanted to ask about it."

Justin folded his arms across his body. "This is your first MD review," he said, "so you need to get broader feedback from more people."

It seemed a reasonable enough argument, so I took it at face value.

When I had to fill out my reviews for others, Justin's was the hardest. After my meeting with Mike, I knew I could only write positive things, so I lied my way through it because I couldn't risk another issue with either of them. Once the reviews were submitted, it took a month to calculate scores and rankings and to produce the summary performance reports, then everyone met with their managers to review the results.

"Well, Jamie," Justin said when we went over mine. "It's your first managing director review and we have lots to discuss." He looked at the piece of paper in his hand, then handed it to me. I searched the bottom for my review score and ranking. The score was 6.5 and the ranking was the bottom 50 percent. I squinted at the paper and bit my lower lip as I looked for a name, because it couldn't be my review, it had to be a mistake. My mouth went dry as I read *Jamie Fiore Higgins* across the top. "This can't be right," I said. "I've been here more than fifteen years, and I've never scored less than an 8.75."

"Nope, no mistake," he said. "Looks like this just isn't your year." I swear I saw the slightest smile cross his face. I looked back at the sheet, my mind churning as I crunched numbers in my head, trying to figure out how this happened, how my score and the perception of my performance changed so much.

"Can I ask about the scorers?" I said. "Were there a few people who scored me low to bring down the average or was it more across the board?" I could hear the panic in my voice.

"I can't say," he said, "except that people just don't think much of you anymore." I heard laughter from the trading floor, and I looked at the serene golf greens on the walls while my mind was in chaos. It was like Justin had just changed the rules of the game I'd played well for years. I'd been a rock star within these walls, and now I felt like an outsider kicked out on the street.

"You've got lots of digging out to do," he said. "I'm not sure you can make it here as an MD. I need a commercial killer, Jamie, not a class mom. Take your desk, for starters. It looks like a daycare center, with the photos of your kids and their drawings. That's not the desk of a Goldman MD."

My eyes burned as tears threatened to push through. Those pictures and drawings were the only things at work that made me happy, they were my lifeline to home. All day long I'd stare at my kids, and they'd get me through. Here I was assigned another role as a woman, "Mom Barbie," and it seemed there was no room for her within Goldman's walls.

"Let's just review the report," he said. "Then you can see what your issues are." My ears filled with buzzing, and Justin's mouth moved but I didn't hear a thing, I just smiled and nodded and stared at the paper, my eyes glued to the score. Something didn't add up, and Justin seemed so pleased.

"So, give me your action plan in a few weeks," he said. His

words woke me out of my panicked daze. I looked at Justin through my black-rimmed glasses and hoped they disguised the heaviness in my eyes. The large Jets foam finger sat right behind him and I wished I could shove it up his ass.

"Yes," I said. "Thanks for your time." As I walked out, I felt clammy and nauseous.

When I got back to my seat, I put all my pictures and the kids' artwork in my desk. The frames rattled as they hit the metal drawer, their sweet little faces stared up at me as I closed it shut. I wanted to go in there and join them.

Pete looked over. "What are you doing?"

"Following Justin's directions," I said. "He says my desk looks like a daycare center." Pete's eyes went wide, and his mouth dropped.

Justin walked by my desk soon after. "Wow, Jamie," he said, "cleaned and streamlined. Now that's an MD's desk!" His toothy smile was wide, and I wanted to cry. My desk was now empty, the reminders of why I endured this job were gone. Justin walked to his desk where a golf trophy, pictures of him on the eighteenth hole, and multiple Jets mini footballs were displayed. If my desk looked like a daycare center, then his looked like an aisle at Dick's Sporting Goods.

I thought Mike and Justin were out to get me; it was obvious to me. Ever since the day Mike chastised me for going against "the family," I thought I would experience some retaliation. But I thought it would be light stuff, like not inviting me out with clients, not my review, which affected my bonus.

I wanted to know for sure, though. What if I was just being paranoid? What if I'd lost objectivity, and my performance really had gone down that much? Then I got an idea. I went to a conference room, picked up the phone, and asked the operator to dial Nicole Rodriguez. She worked in the human resources department and focused on the firm's review process. We'd started at the firm together and had kept in touch throughout the years, and she answered my call on the first ring.

"Nicole, I need a favor," I said. "It's a big ask and I won't mention anything you tell me to anyone. I got an alert at the beginning of review season that my manager added people to my reviewer list. Could you tell me who he added?"

"Oh, I can't do that," Nicole said. "That's confidential."

"I understand but I'd be so grateful for your help," I said. "I promise I won't share it with anyone, I just need to know for myself. I'm in a tough situation and desperate to know. Please help me." My tone was sad and pathetic, and I held my breath and heard the clicks of Nicole's keyboard.

"Okay," she said. "But you did not hear this from me, do you understand?"

"Yes, I got it," I said.

"Two people were added to your reviewer list by Justin Lansing. Someone named Vito and someone named Jerry. Does that help?" she said. I stared out the window at the other office buildings in Tribeca, wishing I worked somewhere else.

"Yes," I said, "thank you so much." I hung up the phone and massaged my temples with my fingers. What could I do at this point? Call and report it to Employee Relations? Look where that got me the last time. That group seemed like another sham of Goldman, a farce, something that looks wonderful on paper, but doesn't exist in reality. In my world of Goldman, the bullies were in charge. It was like I was a kid back at school, and instead of the mean girls mocking me and my back brace, grown men were spreading lies.

I wasn't safe at Goldman anymore. I had nobody to protect me, and there was nothing I could do about it. It was official: My career and reputation were being sabotaged.

CHAPTER FIFTEEN

O ur couples' therapist had recommended that we spend some time alone together, so a few weeks later, Dan surprised me with a night away—a trip to New Hope, Pennsylvania, a little town forty minutes away on the Delaware River. We stayed at Phillips' Mill, our favorite restaurant and inn in the area. I took in the rustic gray stone building covered with lush green ivy, the bright blue front door. The air smelled so fresh and crisp, like the trip was giving us a clean slate.

The innkeeper took our bags while the dinner hostess showed us to a private room in their glass enclosed porch. A vase of pink roses sat at the center of our table next to a short votive candle. Strands of white lights draped along the walls, and it was magical, like we were outside under the stars.

"I took care of everything," Dan said, "and called ahead and ordered our favorites. Tonight is about us and enjoying ourselves."

I smiled. Most men wouldn't have forgiven me after what I'd done. Thoughts from that dinner at Nobu when Rich took care of everything circled my mind. That night was an escape from

my life, it was hiding out, running away. Tonight was a celebration of my life, tonight was enjoying time with the person I
created it with, tonight was good for me and for my family. As
the hours went on, we had more and more fun. Dan started a
game, where we had to retell a funny story that had happened
to us since we'd been together, and try to make the other person
laugh. As we'd known each other for fifteen years, there was a
lot of material—I reminded Dan of the time when he trimmed
our hedges and disturbed a beehive, and had to jump in the pool,
fully clothed, to escape them. Dan recounted the time when I
claimed to have "scratched" my car door when I grazed a pole in
my Jersey City parking lot, when instead, it needed to be totally
replaced. We were in stitches.

After dinner, we walked up to our room, giddy and tipsy.
Dan shut off the lights and lit the candle on the bedside table as
I dropped into bed. He joined me and we lay down in silence,
Dan's arms wrapped around my waist, my head on his chest.
Although we had shared the same bedroom since the night Dan
had appeared at the door with his pillow, we still hadn't been
intimate. We were taking our time to rebuild trust first.

I looked up into his eyes and he kissed me, the first a small
and tentative peck, like a first kiss, coated with uncertainty and
insecurity. These were familiar waters, but ones that hadn't been
traveled in a long time. Then came another kiss, and then another,
each one was a little harder and lasted a bit longer, until Dan's
tongue parted my lips, and then we were unstoppable.

We pulled off each other's tops and pushed down our pants,
until were naked, our clothes tangled at our feet at the bottom of
our sheets. Then we went after each other with our hands and our

mouths, as we explored each other's bodies with the excitement of the first time but with the knowledge of old lovers.

I couldn't remember when I'd wanted him so much, wanted him to touch me, wanted him inside me. The sensation sent a shower of pleasure down my body, my toes stretched out in satisfaction. We were in sync and wet with sweat as we reached a crescendo together, without a care about how thin the walls might be. Then we collapsed, satisfied, and I kissed him and looked into his blue eyes.

"I'm so happy, Dan." After months of uncertainty, my personal life had come together, the gaping wound I had slashed into my marriage was sutured and stitched and had started to heal.

Dan smiled wide. "Me, too."

❧❀❧

I'd told Dan everything about Justin since he started, his obnoxious comments, the after parties to go-go bars, the scotches, the night in Chicago, and my terrible review. Dan was so fired up about everything that a few weeks later, he scheduled a meeting with an employment attorney. I thought back to Lizzie. Suing the firm had worked for her; I'd heard years after she'd settled out of court for a decent sum, so maybe it could work for me. He found an attorney named Charlie Newton, who had a reputation for getting great settlements, and we had a meeting where I recounted everything that had happened with Justin.

"Here's the deal," Charlie said. "I've represented dozens of Goldman employees over the years." He removed his glasses and tossed them on his desk. "Goldman's lawyers are the best. I mean *the best*. You have a case here and you'd get a settlement, but we have to crunch numbers."

"What do you mean?"

"You're an MD," he stated, "so you're in the seven figures pay scale, right?" I closed my eyes and nodded. Even after all these years, my compensation filled me with a mixture of pride and shame, and it also warped my thinking, making me delusional about the amount of money I truly needed. "And then there are other perks," he went on, "like paid vacation, 401(k) matching, and health insurance, right?" I nodded, reminded of the fringe benefits that I received on top of my salary and bonus. "What about moving to another department at Goldman, or another firm?" he asked. I smiled and shook my head; to others it seemed so easy.

"Well, it will be hard to move as a managing director internally, especially with my recent low review score," I explained. "And I have such a senior role, there aren't many similar ones available at other firms." He nodded and bit his lower lip.

"And there's no reason to believe that they're looking to terminate you, correct?" he clarified. "I read in your file that they got you a coach because they want you to be successful." I nodded; the prior week human resources called me and said that my poor review score flagged me as a low performing MD and I now qualified for a personal career coach.

"Well, that's how they want it to appear," I stammered, "but they want me to fail."

"Well, appearances are everything. Whatever settlement you'd get from Goldman, I'd take 30 percent of it. I could probably get you one to one and a half million dollars, which means you'd walk away with between $700,000 and $1,000,000. It'll be stressful to work there while you sue them though, because even though Goldman should treat the case as confidential, they'll spread the word about you. That will not only make working there a living nightmare, but also would hinder your ability to get employment at another firm. If I were you, I'd put up and shut up for another year or two, and then get the hell out with your reputation intact. You'd be crazy to leave now. I'd stay and bank the next two bonuses, instead of suing."

My shoulders slumped. I needed to stay. Those large bonuses year after year distorted my view of what a lot of money was and what I was willing to put up with to earn it. Jamie Fiore on her first day of work would have thought a million-dollar bonus one time would be enough to set her up for life. She would've been able to walk away. But "Jamie from Goldman," after seeing that money year after year, didn't see it the same way. I was convinced I couldn't make money anywhere else, and the more I made, the more I thought I needed, even though I didn't spend it frivolously. In fact, I hardly spent my money at all, still saving most of it like my grandma had taught me. My relationship with money was just as distorted as my relationship with Goldman.

Charlie saw my crestfallen expression and shook his head. "I'm so sorry," he said, "but you'll never beat Goldman Sachs."

On the way home from our meeting with Charlie, I called my brother, Tony. He was also a lawyer, and I wanted to get his take on Charlie's advice to stick it out for two more bonuses.

"Run with the baton as far as you can," he said. "You've pushed through and succeeded your whole life. From your scoliosis, to landing the Goldman job, to becoming an MD.

That's your MO, you suck it up, dig deep, and prevail. You can do it one more time."

I listened: Suck it up, push through the pain . . . it was my family's anthem. Strength was paramount, as was endurance and survival, even though it hurt.

"I know I can," I said, "but it's another year and a half." I could hear the fatigue in my voice.

"What's another eighteen months after all these years?" he asked.

What was eighteen months? I didn't realize until after I left Goldman that even though I wasn't frivolous with how I spent my money, I was with my time. Money trumped happiness when it came to time, and as long as I was making money, it didn't matter that I spent years unhappy. I treated my time like I had an unlimited supply. It wasn't until after I extracted myself from Goldman's world that I treated my time as a valuable resource. But at this point, my head for numbers kicked in, and if it were just eighteen months out of eighteen years, well that would mean I was 90 percent done. I'd never quit a race before, so I couldn't quit one when the finish line was so close. I didn't appreciate then that I had the power to end the race whenever I wanted.

"Jamie, you're the rock star of the family," he continued. "Look at what you've accomplished. For Grandpa Fiore, his attempt to break through immigrant poverty into success broke him. Janine and I moved the ball forward, but you, you've raised the bar. You've shown what's possible for the next generation. You have elevated the family."

I felt my shoulders square with pride, and I was reminded again that I wasn't just doing this for me and my nuclear family, but for my entire family and the generations that came before me. Here I was the baby of my generation, running with a baton, and I didn't want to let them down. But I also realized in that moment that I didn't want to pass it on to anyone else. Carrying it was too big of a responsibility. The race would finish with me.

That night, Dan asked to sit down with me after the kids were asleep, to have a glass of wine.

"We've got to get you out of there," he said. His face looked pained and pale, and I had to remember this took a toll on him, too.

"I know," I said, as I took a large gulp of wine. "I can't take it anymore."

"Look at this," he said and handed me a sheet of paper. "I've been looking at the 'Spreadsheet of Freedom.' It's time to walk away. Look at what you've done for our family, you should be proud."

Numbers filled the page, balances in our savings accounts, 401(k)s, and 529s—the total was circled at the bottom in red marker. It was a big number for a couple in their late thirties. All those years I'd saved and never splurged—my suits were still from Marshalls, my shoes from Payless—added up. I didn't have the fancy jewelry like Genevieve, I still drove a used car, and we never spent on big trips, going to the Jersey Shore instead. I even brought my lunch to work every day. My grandma would've been proud. My body sat up straighter. I'd felt like such a loser at work lately, but this paper showed what I'd gained.

"Give yourself permission to leave," Dan said softly. He smiled, dimples forming on his cheeks. "I'll go back to work full time. I'll work three jobs if I have to. We'll be fine. Let's stop talking about you leaving and let's pick a day. We don't need more money, we need more you."

I took in all he said, wiped my eyes, and looked carefully at the sheet of paper. Analyzing spreadsheets was part of my job, and I reviewed each line item, calculating them in my head.

"Let's take Charlie's suggestion," I said. "Two more bonuses, a year and a half." It came out with such clarity and certainty that I knew it was the right call. I wasn't mentally ready to break up with Goldman overnight, I couldn't quit cold turkey. This would give me time to prepare emotionally to walk away, and I needed to feel comfortable financially to do that. This would be enough time to fill up the 529s and 401(k)s, and save extra money to support us as Dan built his business. We'd be okay, even if we had to buy our own health insurance, and we'd even be okay if one of our kids needed expensive surgery like I had, something that was always at the back of my mind. I'd sucked it up for all those years—eighteen months was nothing. For the first time in a long time, I felt lucky. I was still young enough to leave to do something different.

"To our exit plan," I said. We clinked our glasses, and a triumphant smile slid over my face as I pictured the day I'd leave Goldman Sachs for good.

The next day I met Pete first thing for coffee in the back conference room to tell him my plan. "All I do is bitch about this place," I said, "and wonder when I'll leave. I'm tired of talking about it. I'm doing it!"

His eyes opened wide. "So, what are you saying? Are you leaving?" His voice sounded an octave higher.

"Not yet," I explained, "but I've made a decision. Two more bonuses and I'm out." My body relaxed. Telling Pete made it real. It wasn't a joke, or a dream; it was a reality, and I couldn't wait.

"Wow," he gasped, and stared at the wall behind me, panic covering his face.

"You can do it too," I encouraged. "Crunch your numbers, figure out what you need, and set a date. Then you can finally be a guidance counselor. Imagine if we resigned together!"

Pete's face softened, and he looked down into his coffee.

"Can you go over my numbers with me?" he asked. "Help me figure out how much more I need? I need to resurrect my plan, because I don't think I can survive this place without you." While Pete had initially made that "Spreadsheet of Freedom" all those years ago, he hadn't managed it as closely as I had. I'd encouraged him over the years, to have something to work toward, but he felt he had to stay longer than I did, since he was younger, so he put it on the back burner.

"Of course." I reached across the table and grabbed his hand. "Let's do this together."

That afternoon I got a call from Dennis Shaw, the personal career coach sent by human resources. I was assured by him that Goldman wanted to support me, and after I hung up, I couldn't help but chuckle. This was Goldman's smoke and mirrors at its best. Mike most definitely did not want to support me, and I knew, no matter what I did for this Dennis guy, he wouldn't be able to save me. Regardless, I had to see this charade through, and I met with him the next week.

"So, I'm here to identify your weaknesses," Dennis instructed, "and develop a plan to address them." He smiled, showing off a mouth full of crooked yellow teeth. "I met with your reviewers," he said, "and you only have a few naysayers, but they have strong opinions. That you aren't serious about your business and are too focused on your family. Now don't get me wrong, family is important, but you work at Goldman, so while you're here you need to be focused on your work first." I felt my jaw clench as I thought about my "few naysayers"—Justin, Jerry, and Vito.

"What would you recommend I do?" I asked. "I already had my kids, and I'm unable to return them."

His fidgeted in his chair and coughed, and I loved how uncomfortable he looked. "Oh, of course not!" he said. "We just want to change perception."

"So what do you suggest?"

"Well, for example, I'd stop talking about your kids during the day," he said. "One person said that you're too motherly, so just take your kids out of the equation at work. Don't talk about them to anyone. And no calls to your family from your desk. If you need to talk to them, call them from a conference room or from your cellphone in the bathroom."

I looked at Dennis and studied the contrast between his long shaggy beard and bald head. Pretending I didn't have kids and making clandestine calls to home in bathroom stalls were crazy, and I wondered if he realized how outrageous his advice was. I wanted to tell him off, but I didn't, and instead just smiled and nodded.

We continued to meet, and after a few more sessions, we finished our allotted time together. I'd written a kick ass personal development plan and completed all my deliverables; my relationships with our customers were strong, the size of my book of business and its profit margins had grown, and I was on track to deliver my best end of year performance yet.

On the personal front, I'd peeled away my layers of motherhood. The photos were gone, the artwork was gone, the phone calls were gone. I'd check in with Dan from a bathroom stall in the ladies' room and talked to the kids in muted whispers as instructed. Except for my conversations with Pete, my family didn't exist within Goldman's walls. I was focused, I was all business, I was the commercial killer they wanted. I addressed every comment from my initial feedback meeting with Dennis and implemented every suggestion for change. And it was all showcased in a thick document that I secured in a white plastic three-ring binder to present to Justin at a meeting the three of us had to close out my coaching.

"I've coached a lot of people at Goldman, but Jamie's been the best," Dennis said. "She really embraced the feedback and made meaningful changes. I have no doubt you will agree."

Justin pushed the binder to the center of the table. "I'm not impressed. She checked things off a list," he said, "but that doesn't mean her performance changed."

Dennis's mouth dropped open while Justin sat back in his chair and a faint smile danced across his face. Deep down I had expected this, but part of me still hoped this binder would be an olive branch, and I'd be welcomed back into the family and resurrect my career.

After the meeting, I walked Dennis out to the elevator bank. He pressed the call button and then looked around to confirm we were alone. He came up close to me and I smelled cigarettes and mint. "Jamie, I'm sorry," he said. "I don't know what to tell you. You've done everything you could." He turned and scanned for people again. "Off the record: This is not about you but about Justin. You've done all you can but you're in a bad situation here and I don't think his view of you is going to change. Remember, you can fight City Hall, but you can't beat City Hall." He gave me a feeble smile, then the elevator dinged and he entered. Although his words gave me some vindication, I felt crushed.

I watched him disappear as the elevator closed. That was my career, a closed door. I'd listened to the feedback, I'd made the changes, I'd done everything that Goldman asked, but it didn't matter. The family had disowned me, they'd locked the door to my career, and thrown away the key.

CHAPTER SIXTEEN

"Welcome to the Mixology Mixer," the receptionist greeted me as she opened the doors to the rooftop patio at the top of the Goldman tower. Adjacent to the executive offices, I'd never been there in all my years at the company, but that night the Goldman Sachs' Women's Network had taken it over for a cocktail party.

On this clear, warm evening in early summer, the patio offered impressive views of the city and beyond, the Empire State Building in one direction, Brooklyn in another, and New Jersey from still another angle. But the views on the patio itself were also good, a who's who of Goldman women: partners, managing directors, and a handful of high-performing vice presidents. Few men were there, but it was quality over quantity, with division heads and C-suite executives scattered among the crowd. The women looked like they walked out of a glossy advertisement in a fashion magazine: Christian Louboutins on their feet, diamonds around their necks, and Prada hanging off their shoulders.

Part of me felt a bit frumpy in their presence, but I knew I had something these women didn't—freedom. They were Goldman lifers, and their lifestyle, with their clothes, cars, and handbags, would require them to prostrate themselves at the altar of Goldman Sachs forever. They were addicted to wealth and status, as I was, and Goldman was our dealer. I had let my addiction get out of hand, but I'd finally recognized it, and with this new clarity was committing to detoxing from this world, weaning myself off the hold Goldman had over me.

I went to the bar and grabbed a glass of the signature drink called the Goldman, a bright yellow pineapple flavored concoction with a sugar rim, while I watched groups of women crowd around the token men. Here we were, supposed to be empowering one another as women, and instead, we competed for airtime with the few men in the room.

Of all the competition at Goldman, the harshest was often amongst the women. You'd think that we'd all band together, pledge solidarity, and be a force to be reckoned with. In this room, we were the majority—which never happened at Goldman—and we should've been setting the tone. Conspiring to *blast through that glass ceiling* the way Genevieve said we could in what I'd come to think of as her "Battle Cry at Bryn Mawr." But despite the Women's Network mantra of "Bringing up another woman with you," that rarely happened. The company culture seemed to foster a scarcity mindset, as if women knew there were few spots for them, that they were a token to fill some quota in the boys' club. So once in the club, if they brought another woman in, everyone might like her better, and then someone would get kicked out. It was a zero-sum game mentality, where in order for one woman to win, another had to lose, which was ironic because the men were winning together.

I wished I had someone to talk to there, share what was really going on with my career and utilize this network. But there was nobody. The women partners focused on getting larger leadership roles, the managing directors gunned for partner, and the high-performing VPs wanted to make MD. All on a fast management track, they didn't have time to pull over to attend to my broken-down career. I couldn't blame them, I had been one of those women, too. I'd done the same to Lizzie. I was concerned, but when it came down to it, I was so focused on making MD that I didn't stop to really help her. Don't get me wrong, I'd gotten to know some women over the years, especially my mentees, so I knew I wasn't alone. I'd heard their horror stories before they hightailed it out of Goldman, like the associate who left because her boss always creeped her out, the way he'd create busy work for her so she'd have to stay late, then linger at her desk, while he rubbed her shoulders and eyed her breasts. Or Jackie, the senior VP I knew, whose boss started having an affair with her kids' nanny, and the firm did nothing, which put her in an uncomfortable position at work. It had started off innocent enough, where Jackie's boss would make small talk with her nanny when she'd call in, then it morphed to flirting, next cell numbers were exchanged, and a relationship ensued. After, when the nanny would call Jackie's desk, Jackie would panic that something was wrong with the kids, only to find that the nanny was just calling to talk to her boyfriend. Then the boss and nanny would go on vacation together at the last minute, which was a double whammy for Jackie, since she'd have to find alternate childcare for the kids, and was expected to cover her boss in his absence. And anytime Jackie wanted to reprimand the nanny for the liberties she was taking, she couldn't, because she'd face the wrath of her boss. She ended up leaving the firm, while her boss ended up marrying the nanny. Or the woman who had been the head of this women's network one year who told me that her boss ironically advised her to stop helping so many women because it wasn't good for her career. She left Goldman a few years later.

As for me, despite being a smart, strong, and competent woman who wanted to succeed and help other women as well, I'd been complicit in Goldman's war against the "other." After living within these walls for so many years, I discovered that in order to be successful, I had to break through the stereotypes they built for me and become Mike's enforcer and adopt his good ol' boys' values. If I hadn't, I would've never been successful and instead would've been forced out. I hated who I became because of it, and I would soon leave. Despite what the firm proclaimed from the executive office, about bringing up more women, BIPOC, and LGBTQ+ candidates, in my experience that's the opposite of what they wanted or what their environment engendered.

As I nursed my drink, Sarah, another managing director mother in the division, found me at the bar. I couldn't help but cringe inside because, despite our shared rank, we had little else in common.

We made small talk, and I mentioned that I was out of the office the next day because it was Parents' Day at Beth and Abby's school. She rolled her eyes and her Hermes scarf, wrapped around her neck, lifted in the breeze. "Why would you burn your vacation time on that?" she said as she took a sip of Goldman. "That's what nannies are for."

I should've expected that kind of answer. As a managing director, I got a lot of vacation days, and not only were we discouraged from using them (guys frequently bragged about how many roll-over days they'd accumulated over their careers), but there were also preconceived ideas of *how* you should use them. While most of my peers used theirs for golf outings in Ireland and boondoggles in Vegas, I used mine for my kids, and I always got crap for it. I'd never forget how Sarah had judged me when I told her I was taking off to watch the girls' Halloween parade.

"You got guts to do that, Jamie," she said. "Do you think the Goldman MD dads take off for Halloween?"

The fact was, the senior men *didn't* take off for Halloween—or for any school-related thing—so the senior women didn't either. Justin once bragged that he wasn't sure he knew where his kid's school was, and the guys on the desk gave him high-fives.

I hated that the expectation was to aspire to be a Goldman MD guy, when I wasn't one, and that we were all different people, with different sensibilities—or at least I was different from the typical Goldman MD. I felt sorry for the dads, too, who were like me—like Pete, who wished he could see his kids more, and Nick, whose bonus was slashed for leaving early to see his kids. Even Eric, who was demoted for coaching his kids' little league. I wished Goldman would celebrate all our differences, both in interests and perspectives; but it seemed to me that individuality and diversity weren't embraced, conformity and assimilation were. And the company got it completely wrong to flag employees who wanted to be active parents, because being a mom didn't make me worse at my job, it made me better. I was more efficient, organized, and focused, because I understood that every minute counted, and I made the most of each one while I was on Goldman's time, for the firm's benefit.

I was relieved when our division's head approached the bar alone and Sarah ditched me for him because suddenly I wasn't feeling well. A wave of nausea came over me and my stomach gurgled, so I headed to the bathroom, and I barely made it there before I threw up.

I wondered if the cocktail had upset my stomach, but I'd only had a few sips; nobody in the family was sick either. Sometimes PMS gave me stomach problems, so I logged in to my period app and my eyes grew wide as I realized I was five days late. I chalked it up to all the stress at work. I couldn't be pregnant—I was thirty-eight and we'd needed major fertility help to have our kids. I headed home, but when I passed the Duane Reade on the corner, I went inside because, although I knew I wasn't pregnant, I might as well confirm it with a test. When I got home, the kids were already asleep and I told Dan I was five days late. After an initial moment of shock, a huge smile lifted his face.

"I'm sure it's just stress," I cautioned, "but I picked up a test just in case."

I went into the bathroom and hovered over the toilet while my trembling hands held the stick, then I placed the test face down on the counter while Dan started a timer. I paced the hallway and Dan leaned against the wall, his eyes closed. The timer buzzed and Dan looked at me. "I can't do it," I said. "You have to."

He grabbed the stick and examined it, then he looked up at me, his eyes wet with tears. "We're pregnant," he exclaimed.

"Are you serious?" I gasped. He handed me the test, and I saw the two lines. "I can't believe it." I stared at it dumbfounded, afraid that if I looked away the result would change.

"I know," Dan smiled. "How do you feel?"

"I'm happy but I'm scared," I said. "Scared about something going wrong with the pregnancy and wondering how this changes our plan. Babies cost money, you know."

Dan faced me and grabbed my shoulders. "Listen to me," he said. "The plan doesn't change, do you understand? No matter what, you're not staying a day more at that place." He wrapped me in a tight hug, and my body relaxed. He was right, I had to leave, and this baby wouldn't change that. I smiled as I realized that I'd have a chance to be more present in the life of this baby. I could witness its first steps and first words, an opportunity I'd never had before.

"Look where we are compared to six months ago," Dan said. "This baby represents something for us, Jamie, it was meant to happen."

It was kind of poetic. This pregnancy, this future baby, was the result of our healed marriage, a prize after an exhausting journey. I went to bed and propped up the test on my nightstand, and as my hands cupped my stomach, I stared at it until I fell asleep.

The next week I scheduled my first ultrasound. The day before, I had pulled Pete aside to tell him. The appointment was on a Friday, and summer Fridays were always short staffed between vacation days and golf events.

"So, I've got news," I said as we took our usual seats in the back conference room.

"You're pregnant," he declared, and my mouth dropped open.

"Jamie, we're together all the time," he commented. "You seem different, and you've been rubbing your stomach a lot." I laughed, not realizing my new habit and knowing I'd have to stop, at least until I was out of the first trimester.

"I have an ultrasound tomorrow," I confided. "I got their first appointment. I know we're short staffed, but I need to make sure everything is okay. I'll be in by market open."

"Don't think twice about it," he said. "I'll make sure everything is fine."

The next morning Dan and I went to the doctor's office and went straight to an exam room. I felt so sick, and I wasn't sure if it was the pregnancy or worries about the ultrasound. As we waited, my phone started dinging and, when I checked it, my body went cold. Two guys from my team had called in sick, and Justin would have a field day with me out, so I called Pete.

"I'm so sorry," I said. "I'm literally on the exam table waiting for the doctor. I can't leave."

"Relax," he said. "We're fine. Text me when you're done and good luck."

I didn't have time to stress about it because Dr. Drake walked in. She reminded me of those Disney fairies that Beth loved. She was tiny and thin, with blonde hair cropped in a short, spiked pixie cut.

"Good morning!" she said, grabbing blue rubber gloves from the wall dispenser. "So, you know the drill. Scoot yourself down and put your feet on the stirrups." Dan grabbed my hand and I shimmied down the table.

"Ready?" She held the wand up and I nodded.

"So here's the sac," she explained and pointed at the oval of blackness surrounded by white static. "And in it, is your little baby," she said. I squinted to see and found it at the bottom of the black oval, two little white balls joined together. I smiled.

"Let's see what we hear," she said. She turned up the volume and my face tensed as I strained to hear. The rush of white noise filled the room and my stomach felt sick as I heard the unchanging sound, but then I picked up a rhythm. "Now that's a strong little heartbeat," she said. Dan kissed my forehead as I teared up.

She left and I jumped off the table into Dan's arms for a hug, then I got dressed and texted Pete that I was on my way. I walked into the office around nine and sat at my desk.

Pete smiled and we fist bumped. "Things have been running great," he reported.

Relieved about the pregnancy and work, I settled into my day. An hour later I got an instant message from Justin to go to his office.

"There were loads of complaints this morning about how short staffed your team was," he said. "You didn't show up till 9. Where the hell were you?"

My stomach tightened—Pete said everything went fine and I'd been back for an hour. If something had gone wrong, I would've heard about it already. I couldn't tell Justin about the ultrasound because I was barely pregnant.

"I had an appointment," I said. "I didn't know about the sick calls until I was there, and I couldn't leave. Pete said things were fine. Who complained?"

Justin looked at me, his face blushed, and his freckles looked like red hots.

"It doesn't matter who complained," he said. "It matters that someone did. Get yourself together, Jamie. Commercial killer, not class mom, remember?" He got up and left.

I stared at him as he walked back to the trading desk, and I wished my eyes were lethal lasers so he'd drop dead. My hands shook as I texted Pete, "Back conference room please."

"It's a total lie," Pete said when I told him what had happened. "I paid attention, Jamie. Nobody said anything. He's just trying to screw you." The volume of his voice raised, and I hushed him as I looked out the door.

"I believe you," I said. "I just need to be careful. He's going to undercut me any chance he gets, and I have no room for error. Head back to the desk and I'll wait a minute. I don't want them to suspect we've been meeting."

He left and I sat at the table, my head in my hands. My stomach rumbled and I raced to the bathroom, where I vomited up my breakfast.

As I cleaned up, I looked at my face in the mirror; dark circles lined my eyes, and splotchy red broken blood vessels covered my face. If this was any indication of how the pregnancy would be, it would be a hard one, and working at Goldman with three kids was hard enough. I couldn't keep up with work if I was constantly feeling like hell. I realized I might need to forget about the eighteen-month exit plan, because I didn't know how I'd survive the next nine.

Over the next weeks, I became obsessed with the contents of my underwear. The last time I'd gotten pregnant on my own, I'd had a miscarriage, so every twinge made me wonder if something was wrong. I became paranoid, drinking tons of water, so I'd need to pee more often and be able to go see if something awful had happened.

I was twelve weeks along when I saw blood in my underwear. It wasn't a lot, but the sight sucked the air out of me. My mind went to an ugly place, but I knew I couldn't trust my thoughts because the hormones that raged through me cooked up a buffet of catastrophic scenarios. I'd been to the doctor the day before for a checkup and everything was fine, but I called them anyway and they told me to come in.

I called Dan. "I'm bleeding, and I'm scared," I said. "The doctor wants me to come in." My voice was hoarse and cracked.

"Relax," he reassured me. "It's probably nothing. I'll get you at the ferry in Jersey City."

It was 4 p.m., late enough to sneak out, so I grabbed my stuff, as Jerry and Vito watched me and exchanged snickers. The only person who knew about the pregnancy was Pete, and I refused to announce it until I was out of the first trimester. But I'd begun to show weeks before, so I knew many suspected it.

As I walked to the elevator, a tightness grew in my stomach. It gurgled and constricted, and I felt pressure. I headed to the bathroom, and as I opened the door, I felt a gush in my under-wear, like a gallon of fluid escaped my body. I ran to the handicap stall and pulled down my pants with the door still open. Blood was everywhere, in my underwear, down my legs, and on the floor. I'd never seen so much blood and I thought I'd pass out. The wave of tightness passed, my lower abdomen relaxed, and the blood stopped. The whole thing reminded me of a contraction.

"No, no," I whispered. This wasn't normal and I took a breath and held on to the wall to steady myself. I had nobody to call for help. Pete had left earlier for a client meeting, so I just had to get to Dan. I grabbed the end of the thin industrial toilet paper from the dispenser and rolled it around my wrist until it was the size of a boxing glove, then I stuffed it down my pants. I washed down my legs as best as I could. Maybe it wasn't a contraction, maybe it wasn't a miscarriage, maybe everything was okay.

I looked at myself in the full-length mirror. Blood saturated my skirt, but it was black so it didn't show. I walked out of the stall leaving a pool of blood on the floor, but I couldn't do anything about it. Darcy, our cleaning woman, would find it and I felt awful. She was a single mom from Queens with three kids, and we'd often chat. She always looked pale and haggard, but she always smiled. I'd have to get her a gift to apologize.

I walked out as fast as I could, afraid that running would cause another episode, as the tacky blood glued my skirt between my legs. I thought of calling Dan and having him come into the city, but with the Holland Tunnel traffic, the fastest way to get to him was the ferry. I headed down Vesey Street, passed the outdoor bars where folks enjoyed happy hour under colorful umbrellas. Once at the dock, I felt the urge again—my lower stomach churned as pressure built and I ran into a bathroom stall at the ferry terminal; another wave of blood came out, but now there were clumps of clots too. It was all over the blue and cream tile floor, all over my hands, all over the walls. I cried out and felt lightheaded, and I heard people scurry out of the bathroom, no voices, just subdued shuffling as they left. The wave of pressure passed, and a bloody mess covered the toilet and the floor. I started to mop it up with paper towels, but all I did was spread it more. The tile was now shaded hot pink.

The crackly overhead speaker announced that my ferry had just docked, and I had to catch it. As I walked out of the stall and looked over my shoulder, it looked like the opening scene from a *Law & Order* episode—it just needed the neon yellow tape and swarms of cops and crime scene investigators.

I stood in the line for the ferry, surrounded by a bunch of Wall Street workers. Most looked down, buried in their phones.

Drops of blood rolled down my legs and collected at my ankle, turning the edge of my white socks maroon.

I boarded the ferry and an anchor of pressure sat between my legs. I wanted to sit down, but the seats were covered in cream fabric, and I'd surely stain them. Everything spun around me, and my mouth tasted sour and dry. I was scared, scared about losing the baby, scared about what had happened, and scared about what might come next.

The ferry pushed off and started its seven-minute trip to New Jersey. I rested my head against the dark paneled wall, closed my eyes, and prayed the litany of memorized prayers from my Catholic childhood; again and again they came out in whispers from my chapped lips.

Halfway through the ride, one of the deck hands, a man with golden blond hair, approached me. He looked like he was twenty years old and wore a crisp blue NY Waterway button-down, short white shorts, and tan boat shoes.

"Ma'am," he said. "Your legs are bleeding." He pointed to the drips of blood that rolled down my kneecaps.

"It's not my legs," I said, my face slack with exhaustion. "I'm having a miscarriage." He nodded and walked away.

I was the first one off the ferry. The air was thick, and my black workbag felt stuffed with bricks. I knew I'd lost a lot of blood and I was scared. This pregnancy was over, and I wondered if I was next.

I got to the corner and sat down cross-legged on a patch of grass, too tired to walk farther. Blood poured out of me as I called Dan, and he picked up before I heard it ring.

"Where are you?" I whispered.

"A few blocks away," he said. "Are you okay? Are you still

spotting?" He had no idea that the symbol of the rebirth of our marriage was gone. I wanted to tell him, but the words disintegrated on my tongue.

"Yes," I said. "I'm on the corner of Hudson and Grand." I lay down and curled up in a ball and faced the street. The sun beat on my face and the blood grew sticky between my legs. I smelled the exhaust from the Jeep before I saw it and Dan jumped out of the car and ran toward me. His eyes were wide, as he hoisted me in one motion to my feet, and with one arm behind my back and one under my legs he put me in the car.

"Traffic is clear," he said. "We can get to the office in thirty."

"I can't make it," I said. "We need to go to the hospital here." We pulled away and I winced as we drove through the pothole-scarred streets; we arrived at Jersey City Medical Center in minutes.

I walked into the ER as Dan parked the car and stood at the registration desk where a woman sat behind a bulletproof glass window. She wore blue scrubs and glasses that hung from a beaded chain.

"Why are you here?" she said, her eyes facing down.

"I'm having a miscarriage," I said. Her one eyebrow raised as she looked at my face, then my stomach, then my face again. I guessed I wasn't convincing enough.

"Take a seat," she said, and pointed to the adjacent waiting room. I sat down and rested my butt on the edge of a seat so I wouldn't get it dirty. An old woman sat next to me, in a pink velour tracksuit. Her gray hair covered her face as her fingers massaged the black shiny rosary beads nestled in her hands. Hushed prayers came from her lips as she went from bead to bead; I thought of my grandma and wished she could pray for me now. The old woman scanned my body, starting at my legs, then my stomach, then my face.

"How far along," she said, her face so wrinkled that she looked like a raisin.

"Twelve weeks," I said.

"Don't be afraid," she said. "God is with you."

I nodded and wished she was right, but I wasn't sure. Blood flowed out of me, and droplets hit the floor as they fell from my skirt, forming a bright red puddle under me. Dan entered the waiting room as a nurse with a long blonde ponytail came out and saw me. "I need a wheelchair now!" she said.

Within seconds I was in the ER with Dan by my side. The nurse pushed me down the narrow halls of the emergency room, so many colors and shapes passed by so fast I felt dizzy. The nurse hammered me with questions, and I tried my best to answer them, but the last hour was a blur.

"The ultrasound tech will come to scan you," she said. "Then I'll come back." She wheeled me into the room and Dan helped me onto the exam table. The room was silent and desolate, the blue painted walls were cracked and circular brown stains covered the drop ceiling. A wave of pain and tightness came over me and I curled into a ball.

"Oh God!" I cried. I grabbed my stomach—it was as hard as concrete. "Danny, help!" I begged. He stood next to me, his face was white, and I could see blue veins under his eyes. He lifted me up and placed me on my feet as I hunched over and lurched toward the adjacent bathroom.

I sat on the toilet and felt the release as my muscles went slack, and a hailstorm of blood clots pummeled the toilet water. I waited for it to pass. It lessened in intensity and stopped.

Dan stood next to me, his body framed by the light of the exam room, his hands covering his mouth. "It was just spotting until now, right?" he said. I just stared at him, too tired to form words.

The nurse ran in, and she and Dan got me onto the table. She hooked me up to an IV. Another wave came, then another. They were fast and furious, as sweat rolled down my face. I screamed through them and felt more wetness between my legs.

"I'm giving you morphine for the pain," the nurse said. She adjusted bags of fluid on the metal rack next to me and I nodded.

"No," Dan said. "That can't be good for the baby."

The nurse looked at me, her blue eyes heavy. I wanted it to be over, I wanted the pain to stop, I wanted relief.

Dan's shirt was wrinkled, his arms folded over his chest. The look of hope lingered in his sad eyes.

"Oh Danny," I sighed. "There isn't a baby anymore."

CHAPTER SEVENTEEN

"Hey, what's going on?" Pete said when I called him later. I needed him to tell Justin I wouldn't be in the next day, a Friday. My voice was robbed from my throat, all I could muster was a faint cracking stutter. He was sympathetic and reassuring, and I took a deep breath and told him the whole story.

"I don't know what I'm going to do," I said. "I've ruined everything. This is my punishment for all I've done. I wanted this baby so much. I don't know if I can come back from this and go back to that office again, to that ferry, to those bathrooms." I heard my heartbeat speed up on the monitor.

"Relax," he said. "Don't think ahead. I'll tell Justin tomorrow that you're out sick. Try to rest and I'll call you over the weekend."

The next morning, we went straight from the hospital to see Dr. Drake. "You're very anemic," she said. "I'm surprised they didn't transfuse you. You'll need two weeks to recover."

Two weeks off, in the middle of the summer when everyone was on vacation. Justin was already on my case about staffing and my career was on thin ice, it wouldn't survive this.

"Are you sure I can't go back to work on Monday?"

"No way," she said. "Severe anemia puts pressure on your heart and extra stress could lead to cardiac arrest. The only job you have the next two weeks is to rest."

The weekend passed in a blur, and on Sunday I realized I needed to tell Justin I'd be out for two weeks. Before this, I'd dreaded telling him I was pregnant; now the idea of telling him I needed the time off was worse. I was punishing myself for this miscarriage, and now Justin would punish me, too.

I shuffled to the bathroom and splashed cold water on my face while I rehearsed what I'd say. Then I called him.

"Last Thursday I had a miscarriage and was in the hospital," I said. "I wasn't far enough along to tell you, but I lost a lot of blood and my doctor said I need two weeks off." I sat on the couch, relieved I remembered all my lines.

"Sorry about that," he said. "But I'm confused. You were hardly pregnant, and it's been three days already. Two weeks sounds like a lot. When my wife had a miscarriage, she was fine after a few days."

I'd memorized my lines, but I hadn't anticipated questions. I felt like I was in high school debate club. Did he want me to go into details and talk about the blood? Talk about the shape of the clots? Talk about the bathrooms I'd ruined?

"The doctor told me I lost a lot of blood, and that I can't work," I said. "Do you need a note from her?"

Justin cleared his throat. "No," he said, "but it's summer and we're short staffed. This just isn't a good time."

I smiled and shook my head and wondered when a good time would be to have a fetus die in your stomach and fall out of you.

"I'll try to come back sooner," I said.

After, I called Pete and told him about my conversation. "What a dick," he said.

"So, can you keep an eye on things for me?" I asked.

"My vacation starts tomorrow, remember?" he said. My stomach twinged because I'd forgotten, and without Pete there, Justin, Jerry, and Vito would have a field day picking apart my business.

"I'm sorry," Pete said. "I already paid for the house rental and it's too late to cancel."

"Don't worry about it," I said. "Have a great time."

My shoulders slumped as I trudged into bed. Everything was such a mess I didn't know what problem to tackle first. Overwhelming depression devoured me, and I wanted to hide and run away, so I took two pain pills and went to sleep.

My mom had taken the kids for the weekend, and the sounds of their return as they barreled up the stairs woke me. The girls ran into my room and jumped on my bed and my mom carried Luke in her arms.

"Honey," my mom said, "how are you feeling?" The sight of her flooded my eyes with tears. I'd give anything to crawl on her lap and have her rub my back and kiss my head. I didn't say a word to her, though. If I talked, my bottle of sadness would uncork and spill all over the bed. She kissed me on the forehead, and I took Luke from her.

"Mama, let's watch a show," Beth said. I put on one of their favorite cartoons and the three of them surrounded me.

"I missed you so much, Mama," Abby said.

I looked at them, at Abby's missing front teeth, at Beth's wild curly hair, at Luke's pouty full lips. Even though I'd miscarried, I was still alive, I was still loved, I was still a mother. My career was in shambles, but they reminded me to count the blessings I had, even though my heart ached for the one I lost. "I missed you all so much too," I said.

I was home for the next few days, and it was nice to spend so much time with the kids. I loved being there when they got up, I loved reading them stories in the afternoon, and I loved cutting up their food at dinner. It made me look forward to when I could do it more.

Each day my body felt stronger, but worries about work filled my mind. Justin had it in for me, and my unexpected absence put kerosene on the dumpster fire of my career. I feared he was going to make my life even more miserable if I didn't try to return. There was still a tiny bit of me that wanted him to accept me and think I could hang out with the big boys like he said at our first meeting. I'd enjoyed so much success up until his arrival, I wanted to leave the firm on a good note, with my reputation intact. I'd worked so hard and sacrificed so much up until that point, I didn't want these last months to cast a shadow over the years I'd been there. I still wanted "Jamie from Goldman" to be the Golden Goldman child.

"I need to go back to work tomorrow," I said to Dan as he cleaned the dinner dishes.

"No way," he said. "Tomorrow's only Wednesday. It hasn't even been a week."

"I know," I said. "But I'm feeling better, and every day I'm away from work I'm getting more stressed."

Dan looked up, his hands covered in soapy water. "I don't think you should go," he said. "This is your health we're talking about."

"Trust me," I said. "If I felt I was putting myself in danger, I wouldn't suggest it." I thought back to Dr. Drake's advice, but

I felt I was weighing the stress on my heart and my body versus the stress on my career, and with my warped Goldman glasses on, attending to my career trumped taking care of myself.

Dan's five o'clock shadow covered his face. This loss had taken a toll on me, but it'd been hard on him, too, and now worry lines creased his forehead. He knew there was no negotiating with me. When it came to my career, I had the firm belief that I was the expert and knew best and nothing he could say would change my mind.

"Okay, but I'm driving you in," he said. "Right to your building." I was happy he wasn't fighting me and relieved he'd drive me to the office. It was bad enough to face work again, but I couldn't face the ferry and the terminal.

The next morning, I put on black maternity pants and surveyed myself in the mirror. My stomach filled the waist's stretchy panel. I pulled on a white maternity blouse, grateful it was baggy. My mom came to watch the kids so Dan could drive me in.

"I wish you'd stay home," she said, her arms crossed, her lips pressed into a thin line.

"I know," I said, "but they're going to kill me for taking so much time off. I've got to try."

"Your health is the most important," she said. "Not your career." I gave her a weak nod and walked away. Her tune toward Goldman had changed over the years, but I was so emmeshed in Goldman's world, I couldn't see what she saw.

We got in the car just as the sun started to rise, and as we drove down our street, a gray blue light covered the houses and trees.

"Take a nap," he said. "I'll wake you when we get close." I reclined the passenger seat and closed my eyes and was asleep before we hit the highway.

Dan nudged me awake. Darkness wrapped the car, and my cheek was wet with drool. The lights in the Holland Tunnel flashed through the window. We'd be at the office in a few minutes. I grabbed my makeup bag and inspected myself in the mirror on my visor. I looked so gray, and none of the makeup I applied seemed to make it better. Soon, Dan pulled up to the side of the building.

"This is it," I announced. I saw the constant flow of people on the way to their offices. My head felt airy and woozy and I didn't know if it was my nerves or the anemia. "I'm scared of what Justin will say to me," I confessed.

"Relax," he soothed me. "Anticipation is worse than reality. Just take it minute by minute. When you're ready to come home, just call and I'll come get you." He pecked my cheek and I walked toward the building. It had only been a few days, but it seemed like a month. I looked around the lobby and admired the colorful abstract mural on the tall walls, not sure if it was always this bright or if it was touched up while I was gone. I smiled at the security guard as I swiped my ID and when I got to my floor, I turned my head away as I walked past the bathroom.

I opened the door to the trading floor, and even though it wasn't even 7 a.m., the sound of ringing phones filled the room. The floor was empty, just a few people sat across the different trading rows, and I made a beeline to my desk while I looked at my feet. When people passed my desk as they walked onto the floor, they slowed down and gawked at me, like I was a traffic accident. Pete told me that everyone knew what had happened. Justin emailed me that he wanted to see me, and my head dropped. I wasn't ready to face his wrath, but I got up and headed to his office as my heart raced. He was at his meeting table looking over papers when I came to his door, and he signaled me in.

"Welcome back," he said as his eyes stayed on the papers.

"Thanks," I said. Then he leaned back in his chair and stared at me as he tapped the table with his pen. With each beat of the pen, my temperature rose a few degrees, and I started to sweat, then he tossed the pen on the table and leaned forward toward me.

"So, I'm just going to get to it," he announced. "This thing that happened to you. The timing couldn't be worse. I talked to you about staffing your team and being a leader, but with what's going on I'm not seeing it."

My hands shook and I clasped them together and squeezed.

"I'm sorry, Justin," I said. "I don't know what to say. I wish it never happened either."

"Well, you're back now," he said, "and I expect you to be 100 percent focused on your work."

He picked up his pen and looked down at his papers, my signal to leave. I walked out of the office and my chest squeezed tight. My breaths were fast and shallow. I walked past my assistant Katie's desk as I headed toward mine, and she got up and approached me.

"Jamie, are you okay?" she said. She placed her arms on my shoulders and my body buckled.

"Just a little tired and dizzy," I said through squinted eyes.

"Come with me," she said, moving me toward the elevator bank. "We're going to the health center."

She put her arm around me. "You're pale, you're sweating, and you're shaking. You shouldn't be here. You haven't had enough time to recover. You're about to pass out," she said, and when she pressed the elevator button, I did.

I woke up in an exam room in the health center. A woman with curly black shoulder length hair and large blue eyes stood over me. Her nametag said "Anna Lewis, MD, Medical Center Director." She asked me a ton of questions, and I told her about my miscarriage and my anemia.

"Did your doctor advise you to come back so soon?" she asked.

"Well," I said, "no, but it's the middle of the summer, and we're so short staffed, and I need to manage my team, and I need to run my business, and I need to be a leader." I thought the words came out fast but as I heard them they sounded slow and blurry.

"I need your OB's name and number," Dr. Lewis said, so I found her contact in my phone and showed her. She jotted it down and then pulled out her stethoscope and listened to my heartbeat.

"I'll be right back," she said, and after she left, I curled up in a ball on the exam table and fell asleep. I woke up to her returning.

"I just talked to Dr. Drake," she said. "And you were told to not come back to work for two weeks. Are you being pressured to return to work before your doctor approved it?"

I stared at her, my face slack.

"It's just so busy," I started. "And I missed so much work already, and I worked with a coach, and I need to do better." My voice trailed off and I forgot what the original question was.

"Dr. Drake said you are seeing her Friday," she said. "After that she'll tell me her recommendation, and then we'll discuss next steps."

"What about my manager? And my team?"

"From now on, I'll talk to your manager about your medical leave," she said. "That's my job. Your job is to rest."

My shoulders slumped. I did it again, talked to someone who wasn't in our department, got an outsider involved in our business, went against the family.

"Please, let me handle it," I said. "Let them hear it from me." Panic covered my words.

"Jamie, you're not well," she said. "You need to go home and not to think about this anymore. I will handle it."

My head dropped into my hands. It was too late, the damage was done. I called Dan and told him to come get me, and I fell asleep on the exam table while I waited.

"Hey, how are you feeling?" Dan said when he got to the medical center. I couldn't tell him about Dr. Lewis and Justin's meeting. I was just so tired.

"Okay," I said. "I just want to go home."

A week and a half later, I returned to work. I felt stronger during the drive, but I weakened as I exited the highway into Jersey City and passed the landmarks of my miscarriage; the hospital, the street corner where Dan found me, and the ferry terminals. Fear and mourning rose inside me like the resurrected dead, and I trembled as I walked onto the trading floor. The sight of Pete, back from vacation, was the only thing that brought a smile to my face.

"I've missed you so much," he said as he hugged me tightly like he was afraid to let go. I heard him sniffle, which caught me off guard, so I pulled away, not wanting to cry.

"I'm so glad you're back, let's catch up," I said, and we walked to the back conference room.

"So how are you doing," Pete said. "For real?" A look of pity covered his face.

"Okay," I said. "I'm still tired and feel like I'm in a huge hole here. But I just want to focus on my plan and get out."

"Good," he said. "And during my vacation I made a decision." I braced myself, I couldn't handle any more surprises. "I just signed up for my guidance counselor certification. I need to stay longer than you, but time's flying and it'll be here before I know it."

"Yes!" It was the most positive thing I'd heard in weeks. "We'll get through it together."

"I'm counting on it."

Justin never acknowledged my miscarriage or Dr. Lewis. I imagined her calling and scaring Justin into actually following the firm's rules. Looking back, I know Dr. Lewis had seen more than a few cases of employees being pressured to return to work prematurely. The firm might have advertised "unlimited sick occurrences" in the employee handbook, but in my opinion, they weren't as generous as they seemed. A few times over the years, some of my reports had health issues that required longer recuperation than just a sick day. Whenever I let Mike know, the requests were met with eye rolls and disgust instead of sympathy.

"We pay people to work," he scoffed, "not to lounge around at home." I had just told him one of the guys on the desk needed emergency surgery due to a biking accident. "So let's make sure he doesn't take advantage."

Dr. Lewis had never gotten involved in any of my team's situations, and I wondered if it was because I'd smoothed things over for them with Mike. Now, without a manager to advocate for me, I felt fortunate that I had Dr. Lewis on my side. She seemed to know exactly what needed to be done.

The months flew by. I signed on new clients and structured new trades, and my team's profits were the highest yet, but it wouldn't matter. I was being punished by Mike and Justin, and they'd make my life miserable until the day I left. But I was determined to stay and reach my goal, as the voices of the Goldman "you'll nevers" reverberated in my head. I'd proved those naysayers wrong with my math proof, with my lack of connections, with my promotion to MD. I was going to suck it up and push through, and leave when I said it was time, no matter what they threw at me.

I knew what was coming for me, though, because I'd seen them wage war on people before, like two people on the desk, Krissy and Paul. Once successful traders, they had both been managers. At one point Krissy had been the most senior woman on the desk. But both had gotten on Mike and Justin's bad side, for stupid things: Krissy made fun of their suits one day and Paul made fun of the town Mike's wife had come from. That's all it took, they were blackballed. It happened slowly, over time. First, their responsibilities were changed, until they ended up doing grunt work meant for analysts, not the seasoned VPs they were. Even the section where Krissy and Paul were moved to was called "Death Row." Then, rumor had it they were paid down year after year, but they never left, which only fueled Mike's conviction that they were grossly overpaid.

You would have thought that Mike and Justin would have just fired them by now, put them out of their misery, but that would be too merciful a death and not nearly as entertaining. No, it was much more fun for Mike to sit and watch them suffer a slow, agonizing demise. Plus, they would save the firm from having to give them expensive termination packages.

Now I was playing the game of beat the clock, and I hoped they wouldn't do too much damage to me in the time I had left. Of course, I didn't want to get paid down, but it was more that I wanted to hold on to my reputation that I worked so hard to build. I wanted to leave on my terms before they had a chance to ruin me. Upon reflection, I see how that environment made me so insecure that my entire identity and self-worth was tied to Goldman and their opinion of me. I should've recognized that my success came from me and not them and that I deserved better, but at the time, I truly believed I was nothing without them. I didn't fully see until I was gone the power they had over me.

Although I tried my best to stay afloat, I was drowning. My bloated body still fit in nothing but maternity clothes, and I was in a constant state of fatigue. Coffee didn't exist that was strong enough to pep me up. I was living life, but I only felt alive at home. At work, I was just existing. Justin would never forgive me for the miscarriage. I was a marked woman.

A new year was starting, though, and I was determined that 2015 would be the year of a New Jamie. I couldn't change Justin's perception of me, but I could change the perception of myself. This moment was the start of a shift that continued until years after I left, where I began to see myself as an individual. I wanted to eat better, exercise more, and pull myself out of the doldrums I was stuck in. My New Year's resolution started with a physical—after work, on the first Monday in January, I walked into Dr. Drake's waiting room. Four women were there, sprinkled around beige-colored chairs along the perimeter, all in different stages of pregnancy. My eyes were drawn like a laser to the one in the corner. Her full stomach stretched the fitted red cable-knit sweater she wore, and I figured she was due when I'd been.

Dr. Drake's assistant called me in right away for my urine sample and bloodwork, and I was grateful not to be stuck in the waiting room next to that juicy ripe belly. I wanted to grab it and run away with it.

"Hi there," Dr. Drake breezed in. "How have you been?"

I sat cross-legged on the exam table; my shoulders slouched toward my knees. "I've been better," I said. "I don't think I ever recovered from my miscarriage. I've eaten my way through it, so I've gained weight and I have no energy." She pouted in sympathy, and I sat up straighter.

"But I'm going to turn things around," I affirmed. "I'm going to lose weight, exercise, and get my life back."

She nodded and smiled and looked at the clipboard in her hand. "Give me a moment," she said, and opened the door. I heard her muffled conversation with a nurse, and then she returned, rolling a blue metal stool next to me and sat on it.

"So, I wanted to check the results of your urine test," she said, "because it's been flagged." I leaned in toward her. *Flagged?* I wondered if something was wrong: I'd wallowed in self-pity these past months, and now, I might have a real reason to be unhappy. Maybe I was sick and dying, and my mind flashed to my kids.

"Is something wrong?" I heard the panic in my voice, and she smiled. How could she give me bad news with a smile?

"You're fine," she confirmed. "But the urine test shows you're pregnant." I cocked my head and scrunched my nose. That couldn't be true. I looked at Dr. Drake's glasses, and the right lens had a fingerprint smudge on it.

"No," I said. "That's old info you have. I was pregnant, but I lost the baby."

"No, this was from today," she said. "When was your last period?" The calendar in my mind flipped through in a white blur.

"I'm not sure," I said. "At my last appointment you said it would take time to return to normal, so I haven't kept track."

"Have you been sexually active?" she said, and I bit my lower lip because although my career was dying, my relationship with Dan was alive and well.

"Yes," I said. I looked at the wall calendar that hung on the door with a pushpin, and my mind clicked loose pieces together— the fatigue and bloating, an inability to lose weight.

"Could I really be pregnant?" I wondered aloud.

"Yes," she said, "but let's do an ultrasound to confirm."

I looked at my watch. It was 3:30 p.m., and Dan was in the thick of school pick-up and homework, but he had to be here.

"Can I call my husband?" I said.

"Of course," she said as she got up to leave. "We'll do the scan when he arrives."

When I called Dan and told him to come, he was as shocked as I was.

I lay back on the exam table. As I waited for him, my left hand rubbed my belly while my right hand fingered the gold cross around my neck.

"Hey," Dan said when he got there twenty minutes later. I jumped off the table and into his arms. He gave me a tight hug. "I can't believe this," I whispered, afraid if I said it louder it wouldn't be real.

"I know," he said.

Dr. Drake followed him in. "So let's see what's going on," she said. She went to the ultrasound machine and took out the abdominal paddle, which was only used later in the pregnancy. "Aren't you going to use the wand?" I said.

She smiled. "Let's see if we can pick something up this way."

I lay down and lifted my shirt as she applied gel to the paddle. As she pushed it down and moved it, I craned my neck, and Dan stretched over me to look at the screen as he held my hand. There was no small circle to search for, no flicker to find—the infant profile was as clear as day, the forehead, the turned-up nose, the chin.

"Oh my God," my voice crackled as Dan squeezed my hand.

Dr. Drake smiled again. "Let's listen," she said, turning the dial. *Bah bum, bah bum, bah bum* filled the room and I savored the sound.

"Let's take some measurements," she instructed. She clicked on the screen with the mouse as I lifted my head and watched the numbers at the bottom, and I smiled as I saw the result.

"We're sixteen weeks pregnant," I said.

"Yes," she said. "Well into the second trimester."

Dan stood over me and held my hand and smiled. As the cool gel slid down the sides of my round stomach, I began to cry.

CHAPTER EIGHTEEN
Seven Months Later

My phone buzzed in the back pocket of my jean shorts. It was August 2015, and I was on maternity leave. I'd just dropped off Abby and Beth at camp and was now on the family room sofa reading to Luke while Hannah, two months old, slept in my arms. I handed Luke the book and fished out my phone.

"This is the third call today," I said. "It's called maternity *leave* not maternity *work*." I laughed as I said it. I didn't want to sound too harsh. I was happy to pick up his call, I'd do anything to help Pete in my absence.

"I know, I'm sorry," Pete said. "But I'm drowning."

Justin asked Pete to be the interim manager during my leave, a great sign that they'd give him my job after I left. But he'd never managed before.

"What's going on?" I asked as I rocked Hannah.

"Justin asked me for that monthly presentation," he said, "and I'm not sure I can do it."

I felt sick for him; we'd gone over it once before I had Hannah and two more times since I'd been on leave. He knew the presentation cold, he just wasn't used to this kind of pressure, he had to be struggling if he still needed help. I didn't mind his daily calls, but it gave me pause. I knew he'd depended on me, but I hadn't realized the extent of our codependence until then. A small worry rose about how he'd manage once I left.

"Okay," I said. "I'll resend it."

"Not much longer till you're back," he said in a sing-song voice.

"Don't rush it," I said.

"Aww come on, Jamie," he said. "Once you're back, you're on borrowed time."

I was close to the finish line where I'd leave Goldman for good, but first I'd have to leave the kids for four months to get my last bonus. After all these years, I could do anything for four months. Plus, nobody ever leaves a Wall Street firm mid-year, before bonuses, unless they get fired or hired somewhere else. The vast majority of an employee's total compensation is in their year-end bonus. My bonus was around 70 percent of my total compensation, and after all that had happened, I was not going to leave that kind of money behind. I was going to get through the year. The only thing left in my career that I could control was picking the date of my departure. The thought of missing the kids, though, vise-gripped my chest.

"I know," I said, "and then maybe you'll get my job once I resign."

"Being you sucks," he said. "Justin's always on my case. I don't know how you've dealt with him all this time. And everyone on the team wants something from me constantly, and it's never as good as you would've done it."

His words gave me some validation: that my job wasn't easy

and that my contribution to Goldman Sachs was valued, by someone, at least.

"Well," I said, "I'll be back before you know it." I looked at Hannah as she slept. Her rosebud lips were full and shiny, and her tiny earlobes peeked out of her pink infant cap. She looked just like Dan and smelled that delicious new baby scent. Being Jamie at home was much easier and enjoyable than being Jamie at Goldman.

My maternity leave passed like a blur and just like that my return date was two weeks away. I didn't want to go—working there with four kids seemed impossible, with their homework, and school pick-ups, and activities, but it was just four months. Dan and I would keep it all together, the kids would survive, my marriage would survive, and I'd survive—at least that's what I told myself.

Knowing I had such a limited time left, I decided to do it differently when I returned—I was breastfeeding Hannah. Goldman had robbed me of that opportunity for our other kids, and she was my last chance. I found the pumping supplies I had bought earlier covered in dust in our basement, and I was washed over with delight that I'd be able to use them finally. The Goldman lactation consultant advised me to pump early on to build up my supply, and our freezer overflowed with liquid gold.

The week before my return, HR mailed me a pamphlet called "Your Return-to-Work Playbook" and even though I'd received it before, this time I read it. "No travel or evening work commitments for the first month you are back," the first page promised. I circled the sentence because, this time, I was determined that the rules would apply to me. That I'd finally hold Goldman accountable for what they preached and put in fancy brochures but never played out in my experience.

Later, as I cleaned out my work email, I saw a meeting request from Justin for breakfast a few days before my return. My shoulders slumped. I didn't want to burn one of my last days on him, but I didn't have a choice.

I got to the restaurant and took a seat at the square table set for two in the back. Floor to ceiling windows surrounded me, and I watched the New York Waterway boats shuttle passengers to and from Jersey City. I sat up straight in my chair, pulled up by confidence, proud I'd made it there early.

Justin arrived in his black suit, white shirt, and red tie and I looked down at my outfit and wondered if my skirt and blouse were formal enough. We shook hands and sat down, getting to business almost immediately.

"So about your first day back," Justin jumped in. His strawberry blond hair was cropped short and he looked thinner than I remembered. His tie was turned backward to avoid getting stained, so the Hermes label faced me. "You'll need to fly to Miami for the conference and stay the week."

The noise of the restaurant's chatter buzzed in my head and the sun glared in my eyes. The playbook said I didn't have to travel. Everyone at home had gotten so used to me being there, that I wondered how Dan would deal with the kids on his own. Hannah barely slept through the night, and Abby had a spelling test I said I'd help her with. Beth was so anxious about me returning to work that she cried every night, and Luke, although he hadn't shed a tear, had started wetting the bed. I wondered if breast pumps were allowed on planes and if I could save the milk, or maybe I should just walk away and screw the last bonus. Damn it, damn it, damn it. After all these years, I wanted to walk away on my terms, and leave when I said it was time to leave. I didn't want to give up my last big payday, but I knew they'd make me work the hardest for it.

Justin smiled and his freckles lit up with delight as I took a gulp of water and swallowed.

"Okay," I said. "I'll be there."

I wanted to yell and scream and shove the pamphlet in his face, but he would've just ripped it up. And I knew, from experience, that going to Employee Relations was futile. Once again, I saw the disconnection between the executive office and the day-to-day businesses. And while I talked a good game in my head, I knew better. If I put up a fight and refused to go to Florida, he'd show me his disappointment by slashing my bonus. Telling Justin off, although it would feel so good, would only cost me money, and that's the only reason I was there at this point.

As soon as I was away from Justin, I called Dan. "I haven't even started," I said, "and he's screwing me already. It never ends. He knows I'm just back for the bonus."

"Relax," Dan said. "We have our four-month plan, it's going to be fine. Goldman has screwed with us for years and we've weathered it all."

"But what about the sleep training, the homework, the bed wetting?" I said. "You can't do it all." Dan still got some help from my mom, but he carried the brunt of the childcare while trying to maintain some of his IT business.

"It's just a week," he said. "I'll make it work. Traveling will be hard enough, you've got to leave the home stuff to me. Soon it'll be yours. Maybe you'll miss Goldman when you're knee-deep in homework and bed wetting."

I sat in my car, in the dark corner of the Jersey City garage, my face wet with tears. "No, Dan," I said. "There's never going to be a day when I miss this."

On my first day back at work, I got up at 3 a.m., delirious with exhaustion because apprehension and worry kept me awake all night. I had to hurry because my car service was due within the hour, and I was grateful I didn't have time to think.

Hannah slept in the crib next to me and I leaned over the railing and heard her breathe, her body a black silhouette in the dark room. A lump formed in my throat. We'd been together every day of her life, and I missed her already.

In the darkness I put on jeans, a T-shirt, and a hoodie, grateful I didn't have to wear a suit since I was traveling alone. It was too early to nurse before I left, so I crept downstairs, skipping the last step that creaked. Dan was in the kitchen, in Homer Simpson pajama pants and a blue T-shirt, and he handed me a travel coffee cup and smiled. I hoped he would go back to sleep after I left because he'd need the rest.

"I can't believe you're up," I said.

"Come on," he said, "it's your first day back." As I looked at him, I thought about all we'd been through, how he was a sturdy lighthouse in my crazy sea of life, and I wished I could put him in my pocket and take him with me to Florida. "Here we go again," I said.

"Yes, but this time it's different. We have a plan," he said. "Come here, I have something to show you." He took my hand, led me into the playroom, and turned on the light. Ride-on toys, dolls, and oversize Legos covered the floor, the kids' artwork hung on the yellow walls with tape and thumb tacks. A chain of construction paper links was draped along the ceiling, featuring alternating colors of red, blue, green, and yellow. They varied in size and their edges were jagged. "There's one for each day you have left," Dan said. "The kids and I made it. Once you're back you can rip off five."

Tears welled in my eyes, and I fell into Dan's arms. We had a plan, this was the last stretch of my marathon, and my family was at the finish line, cheering and calling my name.

"I love it," I said. "This chapter is almost over."

I got to the airport with enough time to pump before take-off, so I headed to a handicap bathroom. I wouldn't save the milk, I just wanted to keep my supply up while I was gone. As I turned on the bright fluorescent lights, the smell of urine smacked me in the face. Pieces of toilet paper were scattered on the floor and crumpled up paper towels surrounded the overflowing metal garbage can. I found an outlet right above the white pedestal sink and I balanced the pump on its edge, then removed my hoodie, shirt, and bra and hung them on the metal hook on the wall. As I looked in the mirror, I saw the rolls of wrinkled fat that covered my stomach, the result of four kids and a poor postpartum diet. I'd lose the weight once I stopped working, I thought. I grabbed both falanges with one hand and held them against my breasts as I turned the power knob with the other. The motor from the pump hummed. "You're winning!" "You're winning!" That's what my pump said as we worked together. I closed my eyes and appreciated the relief of my breasts emptying. I was winning! It would be okay, and I'd be home in no time, but I couldn't see the pump's vibration shift it little by little off the side of the sink.

The falanges ripped off my chest mid-pump, blistering my nipples with pain. The machine crashed to the floor and sat on its side as the bottles bounced to the ground, and milk poured onto the floor. "No!" I said, my voice echoed in the tiled room as the machine continued to pump and a puddle of milk rolled toward my feet. "No, no!" I scrambled to grab paper towels and dropped to the floor, my nipples burning as the cool air hit them. I wiped up the milk on my chest, the tears off my face, and the mess on the floor.

When I arrived at the hotel in Miami, I changed and headed to brunch with my client, Evan, and his new boss, Harry.

"So how's Sandy doing?" I asked. Sandy was Evan's colleague, who'd had a baby a few months before I did.

"She resigned to stay home with her daughter," Evan said. "I miss her."

"Her choice made perfect sense to me," Harry said. "Mothers shouldn't work. They need to be home with their children."

I gritted my teeth as I smiled, and Evan looked at me wide-eyed.

"So, Jamie," Harry said, "tell me about yourself." I took a long draw of my mimosa, its bubbles burning as they went down. "I've been at Goldman close to twenty years," I said. "I've managed the institutional desk for a decade, and today is my first day back from maternity leave. I just had my fourth child."

Harry's bushy eyebrows raised so high that they disappeared under his bangs. "Wow, a real working mom," he said. "That's got to be hard, to be pressured to provide while you miss out on your kids. I don't know how you do it, it seems unnatural to me."

He took a sip of his Bloody Mary and dribbled some of it on his yellow golf shirt. I was overwhelmed by a desire to punch him in the face. But he was a client, so I couldn't react. Instead I squeezed my chilled champagne glass hard, its condensation dampening my fingers.

After brunch I FaceTimed with Dan and the kids before my next meeting.

His silver blond hair sat upright on his head and salt and pepper scruff covered his cheeks. "We miss you," he said.

I heard, "Mama! Mama!" in the background, then the girls crowded around him and screamed in his ear, Abby grabbing the phone first. "I miss you, Mama, when are you coming back?" she said in a high-pitched whine. "Daddy can't help with my spelling like you can." Then Beth ripped the phone out of her hands. "Mama?" she said. "Will you be home to snuggle me tonight?" My gut wrenched.

"Oh sweetie, I wish I could," I said, "but I'll be home soon." Beth's lower lip puffed out, then Dan offered the phone to Luke, who refused, while Hannah just cooed as she bumped on Dan's knee. I waved goodbye, hung up, and threw the phone on my bed. I did all this for my kids and the only one who wasn't upset at me was the one who was clueless.

I was overflowing with frustration, and I wanted to scream at the top of my lungs. Instead I found the fridge next to the dresser and poured a small bottle of vodka into my mouth. I had another meeting soon, but screw it. Everyone would be drinking there, too. As I swallowed its cold bitterness, I saw my reflection in the mirror above the dresser. My face was flushed and dark circles drooped under my eyes. This would be a long ass week.

The conference was a cycle of meals, golf, handshakes, meetings, and cocktails. I didn't care about the business plans, trading strategies, and market predictions. Like a bad case of senioritis in high school, I wanted to coast and wait this week—and the next four months—out, until it was over.

I continued to FaceTime Dan and he'd smile and say all the right things, but he deteriorated with each day. By the third day, his five o'clock shadow morphed into a full beard and the bags under his eyes had ballooned. Everything was unraveling: Hannah was off her schedule, her cries in the middle of the night woke up the others, then Luke wet the bed the first two nights, so Dan put him back in pull-ups. Dan wasn't sleeping, instead he played musical beds, and went from one bedroom to another to console each kid.

I got home on Friday afternoon. The house was quiet, and I stepped over the Hula-Hoops and board books that covered the floor. I knew Beth and Abby were still at school, but I found Dan on the family room carpet, Hannah on his chest and Luke at his side. They were all sound asleep. I peeked into the playroom, and in the daylight the chain looked so long, the five rings I just earned wouldn't make a dent in it.

I got off the ferry dock Monday and looked up at the Goldman tower in the distance. Relief flooded my body as I realized that soon I'd leave Goldman for good.

As I walked down Vesey Street, I noticed a new café that had popped up during my leave. Overall, everything looked the same, but I felt like a stranger. I was different, no longer a Goldman lifer. Instead, I was finally on borrowed time.

I swiped my ID and entered the lobby, which echoed with the clicks of footfalls as people rushed in from different entrances toward the elevator banks in the center. I didn't follow them. Instead, with my black workbag on my left shoulder, and my new green bag of pump supplies on my right, I went to the fire stairwell behind the elevators and pushed open the heavy gray metal door that led to the lactation suite. I walked down the dark wood-paneled corridor lined with pump rooms. All was silent, save for the faint buzz of the fluorescent lights. At the end was a large open space with floor-to-ceiling windows on one end, a wall of wooden lockers on the other, and in the center, a small kitchenette. I transferred the milk from my morning car pump into a storage bag, labeled it, and put it in the fridge, then washed my pump accessories and put them in my locker. I smiled with satisfaction. Everything had worked like I'd planned.

Then I headed to the trading floor, and when I opened the door, I stopped to take it all in. Chatter and ringing phones filled the room, people walked up and down the rows, and I had to admit it, there was a small piece of me that had missed the symphony of Wall Street. But I knew I'd happily trade it all for my family.

"I'm so relieved you're back," Pete sighed when we caught up later. "How're you doing?"

"Seventy-five more workdays," I said. "But who's counting?" I laughed, but Pete didn't. He leaned back in his chair, his large belly hanging over his blue pants. His face was rounder than I remembered.

"I'm dreading life once you're gone," he admitted and then looked up at the tiled ceiling. "The last four months were hell."

I felt a pang of guilt that I'd be leaving him behind. After seeing how much he needed me during my leave, I wasn't sure how he'd fare at Goldman on his own.

"That explains the smoking," I said. He looked down; his round cheeks tinged with pink. "I smelled it when we hugged earlier. You've got to stop, Pete, it's so bad for you."

"I know," he said, "but it's been my crutch. It's been so tough with you gone. Now that you're back, I'll stop. But I've got to rethink my plan. I don't think I can work here without you." Pete and I had worked on his "Spreadsheet of Freedom," but since he was four years younger, he wanted to put in a little more time.

"Yes, you can," I said. "Look how fast my maternity leave went. And if you take over for me, you'll be making more money and will get to your finish line before you know it. And I'll always be a phone call away."

He rolled his eyes at me. "You'll move on with your life," he said, "and forget about me and Goldman."

This surprised me. After all we'd been through, I wondered why he thought I wouldn't help. I sat back in my chair and my eyes narrowed. "You're one of my best friends," I said. "I'd never forget you."

He shrugged his shoulders. "Yeah, thanks," he said, and looked out the windows. I noticed the photo on the ID that hung from his neck. It was taken his first day at Goldman, when his hair was jet black and he was fifty pounds lighter.

"So, I know you're leaving in a few months," he said, "but can we not talk about it? I know I'm going to have to face it, so I'd rather not relive it daily."

I nodded and my face pulled down with guilt. I felt like a convict who got early parole and was leaving her cellmate behind. Looking back, it was a prison in my mind, but it was a prison nonetheless. Even though I was slowly beginning to pull away from Goldman's hold on me, I didn't feel right preaching to Pete. He had to get there his own way.

"Last thing," I said. "I'll be off the desk a few times a day to pump. I'll give you a nod when I go. There's a phone there so you can reach me."

"Got it," he said. I got up to leave, but he remained in his seat. "I've got to get back," I said, and he nodded. I walked down the hallway and before I turned the corner, I looked back and saw Pete resting his head on the table. He didn't return to his desk for a half hour.

About an hour later my meeting reminder went off for my first pump session. It went great, and I even dialed into a call and participated like normal. Goldman provided hospital-grade machines and all the supplies that I brought worked with them. Everything was as the lactation consultant promised.

When I stowed away my stuff in my locker, I noticed they were all empty but one other. I recalled my decision with our other kids and guessed that most women who worked here made the same call, experiencing the same pressure I had.

When I returned to my desk, I saw a small container of milk next to my keyboard and my body went cold. "What's this?" I said to Pete as I pointed to it.

"I don't know," he said, "it's the first I've seen it." I scanned the room and didn't pick up a set of eyes on me. I tossed it in the trash.

A few hours later, I got up for my afternoon pump and as I

headed toward the door, I heard a sound coming from the other side of the floor. It sounded like muffled moaning at first, but then it was clearer. "Mooooo. Mooooo," it said. Jerry leaned back in his chair, his hands cupped on either side of his face as he called out in a deep voice, while Vito sat next to him and gestured like he was squeezing breasts.

My face got hot as I scanned the floor. Justin was in his office in the back and no other managers were around. Across the trading desk, everyone's heads were down. They either were avoiding the situation or were too engrossed with their work to notice. Pete looked up from his computer and we locked eyes. "Just go," he mouthed.

Jerry and Vito laughed, their faces turning red as they doubled over in hysterics. As I walked out, I heard their cackling laughter as the door closed. Once I got to the lactation room, I called Pete. "Can you believe this crap?" I said.

"I know," he said. "Don't let them get to you. They want to get a rise out of you. If you don't react, they'll stop." I sat in a stuffed leather chair; the room smelled like hand sanitizer and spa music played overhead.

"I know you're right," I said. "I just forgot how awful this place is."

At the end of the day, after my last pump, I stopped by my desk to grab my workbag, and I found a pink gift bag filled with yellow tissue paper. The attached card said "Welcome Back." I looked around the floor, and there wasn't a person in sight. I reached through the tissue paper and felt something soft and fuzzy, then pulled it out to reveal a stuffed cow. I squeezed it in frustration and a canned "moo" escaped from it, then I threw it on the floor so hard it bounced down the aisle.

A gift from the dynamic duo, Jerry and Vito. They were forever Justin's boys, forever gunning for me, forever making my life miserable. I thought about Pete's advice as I saw the stuffed cow on the floor, and I grabbed it, fluffed up its hair, and balanced it on top of my monitor in full view. Then I walked out the door.

CHAPTER NINETEEN

"Are you ready?" Dan said on a Monday morning in late January. The alarm had just gone off and we were still in bed. Only one link remained on the paper chain. We'd made it through four months of me working with four kids, and my bonus had just landed in our bank account. Today I'd resign from Goldman Sachs.

"I think so," I said. I felt pinned down by exhaustion. I'd tossed and turned all night with nightmares about Goldman. My dreams were a "greatest hits" of the last two decades: first Tom White kicked me out of an Open Meeting, then Eric choked me and pinned me against the wall, Mike screamed at me for going against the family, Justin sabotaged my review, and Jerry and Vito mooed and mocked me.

I got up, my body trembling, my hands clammy. I couldn't believe I was so nervous. Here *I* was the one about to quit, and on my terms. But I was scared. Goldman still had a bizarre but powerful hold over me. There were no more people to impress though, no bonus to wait for, no reason to stay. I could only put my petrification down to muscle memory. But when I really thought about it, it made sense. This hold over me was two decades in the making, I couldn't expect it to go away in one day.

"It's funny," I told Dan. "I've never known an MD who left for their family. Fired, yes; went to a competitor, yes; but never just left."

"It makes sense," Dan commented, "because you never fit their mold." It was true. I still hadn't come across a managing director who I'd connected with or found another mother of four.

I looked into his blue eyes and thought back over the last two decades. I'd sacrificed almost half my life so far in the name of Goldman Sachs . . . but I'd also sacrificed some of my morals, and it had almost cost me everything.

On my drive to work, my hands gripped the steering wheel as my resignation speech played in a loop in my head. I'd resign to Justin, but first I'd tell Pete. He knew it was coming, but I wanted to let him know that it would happen today. He'd be upset. He dreaded my departure and still refused to talk about it, even when I tried to bring it up the past few weeks.

I got on the ferry, relieved I didn't recognize anyone. I couldn't make small talk and pretend it was another Monday morning, not with what I was about to do. I looked out the window and noticed the Statue of Liberty covered in snow flurries. I realized this would be one of the last ferry rides I'd ever take.

When I got off, the harsh wind downtown whipped around me, so cold my skin felt like it could crack, yet underneath my puffer coat, my armpits dripped sweat. As I swiped my ID and entered the building, it was as if my mind escaped from my body, like they were two separate entities. My mind watched my body do its normal routine, the routine of the last two decades. This was the last time I'd do it as a Goldman employee.

Everything slowed down, the faces of the security guards, the crowds of employees, the high ceilings of the lobby, the colorful geometric murals on the walls.

My hands quivered as I pressed the elevator button, so I clutched them into balls and shoved them into the pockets of my black down parka. I was the first one on the floor and couldn't wait to get everything over with. Once Pete arrived and got settled, I asked him for coffee in our usual conference room.

This room was our haven: We'd laughed in here, cried in here, complained in here, and dreamed of different futures for us, and now, after ten years, this would probably be our last meeting.

"What's going on?" Pete quipped. "Some post–bonus drama?"

"Nothing like that," I looked down at my coffee. Then I took a breath and faced him. "Pete, I can't believe it, but I'm ready."

"Ready for what?" he said with a small smile and a cocked brow. My brows knitted in confusion. He knew this was coming.

"To leave," I said. My words were breathy, like they were scared to come out. "I crossed my finish line. It's time for me to walk away and be with my kids." He stared at me, his face stone, as I waited for my hug and congratulations.

"So, you've decided this," he said. "It's over?" He chewed on each word like it was tough meat and his face and neck turned red.

"Pete," I begged. "We've talked about this for a year and a half. You know I can't stay. I'm terrified, but I'm going through with my plan." He looked at me through squinted eyes, and I could see a bulge form in his neck.

"I can't believe you're doing this without me," he said, his volume building into a loud crescendo. "You selfish bitch!" His fist banged the table, and the vibration made my coffee spill out of its cup. "This affects my family, too. We should've done this together."

I was dumbfounded. My mouth dropped open, and confusion scattered my thoughts.

"Pete," I said. "I was always going to leave before you. I don't understand." I looked down into my coffee and tried to read it like tea leaves, to see if it would help my brain process his reaction and make sense of this craziness.

"I don't have to resign today," I said. My voice was splintered and desperate. "I'll wait, so you can think about it. You're one of my best friends. I'd never want to hurt you."

His nostrils flared and foam collected around the corners of his mouth.

"Do whatever you want, whenever you want," he yelled. "You're dead to me." Drops of his spit sprayed the table, and when he got up, his chair flew behind him and bounced against the windows.

"Pete, please," I pleaded in desperation. "Let's talk about it. This is an amazing opportunity. You'll get my job and make more money with me gone. If you just put in some more time, you can walk away too!"

His face was so red, I'd never seen anything like it. I worried it would explode, or that he would kill someone. "I never want to talk to you again," he screamed.

My faced crinkled in confusion. "Please," I almost whispered. "I don't understand. It can't end this way."

He walked out and the door slammed hard, its vibration reverberating in the room and causing the furniture along the glass wall to shake. Questions rushed through my head: What did I do wrong? Why was he so angry? Did he forget the years of us talking about leaving? Maybe he was in denial, or thought I was too scared to leave. After all, I'd complained for years and never had.

I looked around the room and thought of all the hours we'd spent there. We'd always been on the same page. Pete was the one person here who understood me, but today we spoke different languages. My fingers shook as I grabbed my cell and called Dan.

"Dan," I choked, my voice strangled with tears. "I told Pete and he went ballistic." I recanted the whole meeting between us as I cried.

"Are you still there?" I said when I finished. The only thing I heard was the tick of the wall clock.

"Yes," he said. "I'm just shocked. He knew this was coming. I'm just so confused."

"I feel guilty," I cried, "like I did something wrong."

"Are you kidding me?" he raised his voice. "You've done everything for him. Sang his praises to the higher-ups. Talked to him every day of your maternity leave. That can't be it."

Dan's words soothed me a bit, but I didn't feel much better so on the way back to my desk I went to the bathroom to decompress. I headed into the handicap stall—my miscarriage stall. I shared a bond with that space, we'd been through a lot. I looked in the mirror. My eyes were so bloodshot that even the whites were pink, and blotchy red marks covered my cheeks. I took off my glasses, sitting on top of my head, and put them on, grateful the thick black rims covered up some of the damage. It felt like the end of the day, and when I looked at my watch, it was only 7:17 a.m.

When I got back to my desk, Pete was smiling and laughing

along with a bunch of coworkers and I marveled at how he turned off his hatred for me like a kitchen faucet and was happy-go-lucky to everyone else. He hated those people, and always complained about them, but he seemed so stable and normal when he'd just ripped me to shreds. I couldn't help but think about his days acting in high school, and how he'd always talk about the musicals he'd starred in. Maybe he was just a supreme actor, and everything I'd known about him the past decade was just a character that he'd played.

As I looked at my email, tears blurred the contents of my inbox. I grabbed a tissue as Pete's laughter cackled in my ear. After a while I felt better, and I leaned over to him.

"Hey," I said in a soft tone, "we need to talk." He looked straight at his screen. "Pete, it can't end this way," I said louder. Our faces were less than twenty-four inches apart, but he was miles away. He stared at his screen and typed as if I weren't there and my stomach ached. I'd never been so confused. It was like I needed a translator to tell me what I'd done. I responded to emails and typed fast, which helped busy my trembling hands, but I couldn't get a deep breath in my lungs. It was like my windpipe stopped at my throat. I was dying for a Xanax, but with breastfeeding, I couldn't.

All morning, people approached me, asking me questions about workflow, strategy, and budget. I gave them answers and directions, having no idea what I was saying. After Pete's reaction, I felt like a bumbling idiot, and I needed to get it together because I had one more thing to do: resign to Justin.

It was late morning when Justin arrived, and I let him get settled before I approached him.

"Got a second to chat?" I asked as casually as I could.

Our eyes met and his widened, as if he knew what was coming. I walked toward his office and he followed. I sat at his table and faced outward to the trading desk while he faced me and the office wall. I knew that everyone's eyes were on me and this meeting; in the days that followed bonuses, everyone's eyes were on everyone else's, and I wanted to control the narrative. I didn't want anyone to see Justin's expression, only mine.

Justin wore his signature smiling smirk. "What's up?" he said.

"I have two jobs in my life," I started, "my family and Goldman Sachs. It's come to a point where I don't feel I have the time needed to excel at both. So, I'm leaving Goldman to be with my family." My body relaxed. I'd had the guts to say the words.

Justin smiled so wide that I thought I could count all his teeth. This was all he'd wanted for years.

"Wow," he said. "Are you sure?"

I looked out the glass wall onto the trading floor, and I heard the phones ring and the shouts of my colleagues. Jerry and Vito laughed at their desks, and the stuffed cow was perched on top of my monitor.

"Yes," I confirmed with certainty.

"Were you planning on leaving today?" Justin asked. "Can you give me a little time?" I sat back in my chair and saw the large Jets foam finger on his desk. After all he'd done to me, I didn't want to give him another second, I wanted to walk out for good, but I knew that wasn't the right thing to do. After close to twenty years of building this career, I was going to leave the right way.

"I don't want to hang around too long," I explained, "but I'll stay the week." Justin nodded and I walked out. A huge weight lifted off my shoulders, soon replaced by the weight of everyone's stares and whispers.

I tried to get Pete's attention again and again throughout the day, but he treated me like I was invisible. In all the years I'd known him, we'd had some disagreements, but he'd never acted this way toward me. I wondered if he deemed me worthless because I was no longer useful to him—I couldn't help him with projects, or fight for his career and compensation, or cover for him when he wanted to leave the office early to see his kids. Is that what our relationship was about for him? For me, our relationship had been about so much more, and I felt like an idiot.

Commuting home that night was strange because I'd usually hear from Pete. Most nights we'd talk during our drives home. I called and he didn't answer. I texted and he didn't respond. I was numb, hurt like a middle schooler just dumped by her best friend, but I was also worried about him. His reaction was so strange: he wasn't himself, and I hoped he wouldn't do something rash.

The next morning at 4 a.m. I got a text from him. "I'm resigning today," it said. I read it a few times as I wiped the crust from my eyes.

"Let's talk first," I texted back. I tried to call him, but it went straight to voicemail.

I wanted to beat him to the office to try to talk to him before he resigned, so I caught an early ferry and ran the second I got off the dock. When I reached my desk, breathless and sweaty, I found Pete's workbag on his chair and saw him in Justin's office. I was too late.

Ten minutes later, Pete returned to his desk and, without a word, he grabbed his workbag and walked out the door. The guy who was supposed to stay a few years after me ended up leaving a few days before. For the past decade we'd survived that place together, like two captives in an underground bunker.

We'd clung to each other for support, helped each other survive, and dreamed of a different future. And then just like that, he was gone, and I never saw or talked to him again.

I wish I could say that we met up years later, after the intensity had passed, and he came clean. That he realized he had deep ambivalence about leaving Goldman, and how he'd channeled it into our friendship. Or that he realized he'd been afraid of taking my job once I left but couldn't admit it to himself. But that never happened. Voicemails, emails, and holiday cards went unanswered.

Even though Pete was a cis white man, the Goldman culture seemed to negatively impact him because he didn't fit the mold. Although the glass offices were filled with people who looked like him, that didn't cement his success there, because he didn't have their values and interests. And from my experience, achieving success at Goldman was more about assimilation with those in power rather than one's intelligence and work ethic. Perhaps, without my presence and support, Pete didn't feel like he could make it. I couldn't blame him, I was worried about his future at Goldman without me there. I know I wouldn't have wanted to be at Goldman without him either.

I Googled him not long ago and learned he's a guidance counselor in Indiana. I'm happy for him, but I still wonder, and probably always will, why I lost my best friend so suddenly that day.

CHAPTER TWENTY

"Did I really do it?" I exclaimed. "Did I really walk away?" It was before dawn, on the Monday after my last day at Goldman, the first day of my new career as a stay-at-home mom. Instead of running out the door to catch the ferry, Dan and I sat at the kitchen table having coffee.

"Yup," Dan smiled, "you did." His blue eyes shined and he looked so proud. I still couldn't believe it—after all the years of talking about it, I'd finally had the guts to leave Goldman Sachs. I started to understand just how much power it had held over me, as I started to feel released from its vise grip.

It was a gray cold day in February, and I was equal parts excited and scared to start my new job. I'd decided to spend this first week organizing myself and figuring out what this new gig would look like, but my family had other plans.

"Mama," Luke called from upstairs. "Mama!"

I looked at Dan and he chuckled. "Good luck on your first day," he said.

I headed upstairs and followed the sound of Luke's voice into the bathroom, where the smell of diarrhea hit me in the face.

"Mama, my butt's on fire," he cried. "My butt's on fire!" He was on the toilet, his Spiderman fleece pajama bottoms were on the floor at his feet, his Teenage Mutant Ninja Turtle briefs sitting on top of them. He looked so small and helpless, and I thought he'd fall in. As I went to him, I saw that although some of the diarrhea made it into the toilet, most of it was in his underwear, down his legs, and on the toilet seat.

"It burns, Mama," he wailed, "it burns." He pushed his lower lip out and thrashed his legs, spraying diarrhea in the air, while he held his arms out to me.

"Oh baby, I'm sorry," I said as I turned on the shower. "Mama's going to help." After I cleaned him up and settled him in front of the TV, I went to the kitchen to make more coffee, and Beth came downstairs. "I don't feel so good," she said.

She stood in the middle of the kitchen, her curly brown hair wild on top of her head, her face a greenish gray hue. She burped and then a gush of vomit flew from her mouth and splattered across the room. It was on the floor, the cabinets, the walls, and me. I watched it, wide-eyed. I'd never seen anything like it—it reminded me of that scene from *The Exorcist*. After she was done, she looked at me in stunned silence, her eyes in disbelief about what her body had done, and then she howled at the top of her lungs.

Dan rushed down the stairs and covered his mouth with his hands when he entered the kitchen. "What happened?" he said. I was barefoot in the middle of the sea of vomit. It smelled like acid and last night's tacos, and I tried to keep from gagging. As I held Beth in my arms, I felt some of the vomit roll down my neck.

"Vomit!" I cried.

"I'll cancel my meetings," he said. Dan had a day of back-to-back meetings scheduled. He'd lined them up to jump-start his business, now that he was going back full-time.

I closed my eyes and reminded myself that this is what I'd wanted. "No, Dan, go," I reassured him. "This is mine to deal with now. I've got this."

I showered Beth and brought her downstairs, then checked in on Abby and Hannah, who were both still asleep. Abby felt warm, so nobody was going to school, and for the next few hours I cleaned the kitchen floor and the bathroom upstairs.

Later in the morning, everyone was up watching a movie in the family room while Hannah crawled around them and chewed on her plastic toy keys. I was in the kitchen making soup for lunch when I heard coughing and choking.

Abby, sprawled on the floor under her Hello Kitty blanket, had thrown up, and the vomit covered the new cream family room carpet as well as Hannah, who was at her side. It was in her fine blonde baby hair, her yellow polka dotted onesie, and the folds of her neck. She cooed at Abby and crawled away, tracking vomit all over the family room floor, while Abby burst into tears.

This went on for days. Something was always coming out of someone's hole—vomit, diarrhea, or urine. There were wet beds, gag-inducing smells, and clogged toilets; there were filled bowls of vomit and soiled pairs of underwear; there were high fevers and temper tantrums; there were too many loads of laundry to count. I was a captain on a sinking ship, and I tried to patch up one hole before another cracked open, all while the hull flooded with water. I wondered if I'd made the right decision; yes, working at Goldman had been hell, but at least there, people shit all over me metaphorically. I spent most of the week on my hands and knees as I wiped up dried diarrhea off toilets, vomit from the floor, and fever-ridden foreheads.

One afternoon, while everyone napped, I smelled onions, which reminded me to start dinner. Then I took another whiff and realized it came from my pink fleece pajama top. I couldn't remember the last time I'd showered. I loved my kids and was glad to be out of Goldman, but this was suburban misery.

I curled up in a ball on the kitchen floor. My head rested on the hardwood, next to the garbage can. Nobody was there to bring me coffee, our old cleaning person—who used to come weekly before I stopped working—wasn't there to clean the kitchen and fold the laundry. I was alone now, and although I'd always prided myself on being independent, I hadn't realized how much I'd come to rely on the support and company of other adults. I was exhausted and lost. *I used to be a somebody*, I thought, a managing director at Goldman Sachs. I used to run a billion-dollar book of business, and now I was on my dirty kitchen floor, in pajamas I'd worn for days, my greasy hair piled on top of my head. "What have I done?" I said in a whisper, afraid to hear the words come out of my mouth. *I left Goldman*, I thought. *You can only do that once.* Was this what I'd worked so hard for? I wondered if I made a terrible mistake, that maybe the corporate me was the real me all along, and I had no business being at home.

I was petrified, yearning for the life of my past, which I knew was so bad for me, and afraid of my future. I realized that the transition into my new life wasn't just about changing my job and environment. I needed to give myself more time to make the most important change, the change of my mindset. I couldn't expect that to happen overnight.

The illness passed, recovery came, and peace and control in

the home was restored. Moment by moment, day by day, the veil was slowly lifted. I was so programmed by the Goldman machine, so beat into submission, that it took time to recover. As I decompressed and detoxed from the world of Goldman Sachs, I saw my time there with clarity. I was the perfect candidate for their warped world: Coming in without connections, feeling the pressure to be successful for my entire family—for my grandfather who died, for my parents who'd sacrificed. And with the cloak of defectiveness I always wore from my childhood health issues, I was determined to prove any "you'll never" that I came across, that I was just as whole as the next person. I lived in their virtual reality, where I was indoctrinated to their values and taught that I was nothing without them. I'd believed their lies and I found that with each dollar they paid me, I was more beholden to them, to believing that I deserved to be treated worse.

In the months that followed, as I pulled away from their grasp, I realized that my success there had been because of me, not them; it was because of my innate skills, not solely because of their name like they led me to believe. Looking back, I knew that I didn't need to stay there all those years so I could save more money. It wasn't just about the money, and I know we would've been fine if I had left years before. With my modest background and our lean living, I knew I didn't need to make a million a year to have a good life. Like a former hostage with a case of Stockholm syndrome, all I needed was time to deprogram myself from the notion that I couldn't survive without Goldman, that I was nothing without their name, and that I was nothing without their money.

Days turned into weeks, and the mild spring winds came carrying promise and optimism, then the hot sun of early summer burned away the last of my winter whispers of sadness and regret. I'd settled into my new routine: I loved watching Hannah grow up from infancy and experiencing her milestones. I loved being the first face the kids saw when they came home from school. I loved being on the frontline of their childhood battles: mean kids on the playground, difficult spelling tests, or lunchroom table drama.

And although I'd always made it a point to go to the kids' school events before, I'd usually have to lie to be there, saying that I had a client meeting so I could duck out of the office for a bit. I would check my messages surreptitiously the whole time—with one eye on my phone and one eye on the kids, fearing that I'd been caught as "mom Jamie," or that some sort of shenanigans had gone down in my absence. I'd attended the kids' musical performances while logged into meetings, but with my phone on mute, worrying that a colleague, or another parent in the audience, would figure out what I was doing. Now, I didn't need to have my phone with me at all. I could just be present, soaking in the ups and downs of the elementary school set. I could be more than just a stressed-out body taking up space in a crowded auditorium, trying to be in two places at once. I was finally free to be myself, and I knew that I'd made the right decision.

I decided to clean out my home office one afternoon in the summer, and my first task was to empty the three banker boxes that I'd brought back from Goldman on my last day. They'd sat there for months, since the day I left, relics from a different life, and I feared them as much as I revered them. I'd gotten into my new groove at home so well that sometimes I even wondered if my time at Goldman had ever happened. Since the day I'd left I hadn't put on a suit or heel, I hadn't worn a stitch of makeup, I hadn't followed the markets, and I hadn't talked to anyone from the office.

Stacked next to my desk, the boxes sat closed. I couldn't face them. As much as I wanted to leave Goldman, I knew I still had some regret and pain—regret over the loss of Pete, regret over how my career ended—and I didn't want those boxes to resurrect the hurt and loss I'd buried the day I left. But it was time.

Beth and Abby, who were seven years old, wanted to help, as Luke (now four) and Hannah (eleven months), napped. We each took a box and I unwrapped plaques, commemorative paper-weights, and glass awards with my name etched in them alongside the Goldman Sachs logo. Beth pulled out nametags, finance books, and boxes of business cards. Abby opened her box, filled with hardbound black leather books, and she lifted one out.

"What are these, Mommy?" she asked, holding up a book. It looked so large in her tiny hands, with my name engraved on the cover in gold ink beneath the firm's logo.

"Those are my journals, sweetheart," I explained. "I used to write about work, my ideas, and what happened. Things I liked and didn't like. I always kept one, and once I'd filled it, I'd put it in my desk and start another."

Abby examined the book and turned it over in her hands, while Beth grabbed another one from the box.

"So, these make up a story about your life at work?" Beth observed.

I peered into the box at the stack of the other journals and smiled. "Yeah, that's what they are," I said. "The story of when I worked at Goldman Sachs."

EPILOGUE

I left Goldman Sachs in 2016, before the "Me Too" movement, Black Lives Matter, and other progress we've made in society. Some readers might consider that an eternity ago, and say, "Well that was then, and this is now." But that would be naïve. While cases of misogyny and racism and inequality might not be as overt as they used to be, I'm sure the underlying culture has not changed much. I'd like to think, for example, that my assault wouldn't be tolerated today. But that doesn't mean Goldman has really changed—just that people are more careful and better at keeping the dark side under wraps. PR talking points, fancy perks, company-mandated sensitivity trainings, and more can't cover up the outdated values that in my experience set the tone for the environment, and employees can see through the hypocrisy.

The culture I helped to abet, even though I didn't believe in it, needs to end. It's time for Goldman and corporate America to change, to live up to the principles they are touting but not living.

During my career on Wall Street, nobody wanted to hear about problems unless you had a potential solution. And now that we've identified the problems in these pages, here are my solutions for how to fix a broken system—not just at Goldman, but also at other powerful organizations. These issues need to be addressed in concrete and tactical ways where quantifiable goals are set and results are monitored.

First, a message to the powers-that-be at Goldman and other large companies: Bridge the divide between executives and the people running the day-to-day business. Currently, it's like a bad game of telephone where few people know the original message. And this information is powerful and ultimately shapes the culture of your organization. Don't just take the company's ideals and create a list of business principles or best practices, or stick them as chapters in an employee handbook. Instead make them permeate the offices and be modeled by everyone in senior management. If day-to-day managers don't embody the talking points coming from the CEO's office and help put those ideals into action, they are worthless. Don't let middle or upper management's personal values shellac over the ideals of the company; rather, make them responsible for abiding by the standards you have set forth. Hold managers and above accountable for their character and the culture on their teams as strongly as they are held accountable for their profit-and-loss statements—because it is just as important. Don't compensate them or promote them just because of their profits or their market share, but also because of the kind of work environment they engender. Show that you care about both equally.

Reputation is so damn important to Fortune 500 companies, and especially to Goldman. That business principle is driven into employees' minds from day one. So enforce a no-tolerance policy for poor character and discrimination. Hire culture officers to enforce anti-discrimination policies on the desk as fervently as compliance officers police for insider trading and unethical business practices. Hold managing partners accountable for discrimination on their watch, regardless of how profitable their business is. Don't give them brooms to sweep the problems under the rug; give them walking papers. Manage out bad actors, no matter how much money they make for the firm or how good their golf handicap. Make the human resources and employee relations departments truly independent, or take those roles out of house. Know that they cannot possibly protect employees and be simultaneously pushed around by the power of their senior leaders.

To the Goldman C-suite: You know that Wall Street is driven by metrics, and you're making strides. That's why at the World Economic Forum in 2020, you announced that Goldman would only underwrite IPOs in the United States and Europe of private companies that had at least one board member who was not a white heterosexual male. The firm has stated "aspirations" of hiring 50 percent women, 11 percent Black, and 14 percent Hispanic/Latino at the junior entry level. That's a great start, but those metrics need to be continued beyond the hiring class. Make those representation goals the same at the managing director and partner levels. If you are so concerned about having women, BIPOC, and LGBTQ+ among your ranks, shepherd them as their careers advance, making sure they have the support they need to be successful, instead of just hiring them and letting them fend for themselves. They aren't invited to the scotch tastings and rounds of golf where the cis-white guys find their "Godfathers," so create a "Guardian Angel" program for women, BIPOC, and LGBTQ+ hires, where these Angels have a sincere interest in their mentees' success, from new hire all the way up to managing partner. You know that Goldman strategists come up with analytics to slice and dice everything, from market trends to customer behavior. Strategists even track keywords on resumes to predict applicants' future success at the firm. So track the careers of diverse candidates with the same fervor—note big swings in review scores and large P&L dips. Really look into them. Ask "why did this happen?" And care about the real answer.

Look, Goldman: You have some of the best and the brightest people in the world working for you. You strive to be number-one in everything. You want to be the first ones to arrive with the best ideas. Strive to retain and promote women, BIPOC, and LGBTQ+ hires with the same cutthroat competitive enthusiasm. The world is filled with sharp, thoughtful people who would be an asset to you, or any of these large organizations. You don't have to choose between character and intelligence when it comes to employees. You can have both. And don't just pursue it because it's good for your reputation—do it because it's also good for your business. Multiple studies have shown that "diverse companies are more likely to outperform less diverse peers on profitability," and "non homogenous teams are smarter . . . challenging brains to overcome stale thinking and sharpen performance." Workplaces that are inclusive and supportive of all employees, regardless of their background and interests, are good for everyone.

To the new hire, I say this: Despite the fact that the glass offices are filled with white cis men, you belong there. Learn from my mistakes. Your unique voice is worthy and shouldn't be silenced. Rip off your muzzle and change the firm for the better. Demand to be recognized for your ideas and your content, not for how much you have in common with your partner or are pressured to conform to outdated ways.

I know everyone you talked to at Goldman said all the right things when you were recruited. Hell, when I was hired the tagline was "Minds. Wide. Open." and that couldn't have been further from the truth. I'm not surprised that once you got there you felt like you were sold a false bill of goods. Do what you would do in any other similar transaction: Point out the discrepancy and demand they fix it. What you were promised when you interviewed should be what you experience once you've been hired, period.

Here's what not to do: Don't break through *their* Glass Ceiling. You don't want to join the ranks of the Boys Club and morph into who they are. You don't want a space with walls penning you in.

You want a big sky of possibilities.

Don't settle for anything less.

To my readers—these situations don't just happen in Fortune 500 companies, but across all work organizations: large and small, public, private, or nonprofit. But the tide is turning, because people are saying "enough." Mindsets and behaviors are changing, and while we are seeing progress, more needs to be done. We are all responsible and have a role to play. We need to step up and collectively make our workplaces more inclusive for everyone. Large transformations aren't possible without individual change.

NOTES

116 *In fact, in 2019, after I'd left, Goldman set a goal that*: Goldman Sachs. "Goldman Sachs Press Releases." Accessed February 16, 2022. https://www.goldmansachs .com/media-relations/press-releases/archived/2019 /announcement-18-march-2019.html.

116 *The same went for the LGBTQ+ community*: Ibid.

118 *Although . . . 50 percent of the firm's new hires*: finews .com. "Goldman Sachs Wants More Women MDs," March 19, 2019. https://www.finews.com/news/english -news/35770-goldman-sachs-women-md-pay-promotion -gender-diversity. Goldman Sachs. "Goldman Sachs Press Releases—Goldman Sachs Announces Partner Class of 2020." Accessed February 16, 2022. https://www.gold mansachs.com/media-relations/press-releases/current /gs-partner-class-2020.html.

295 *That's why at the World Economic Forum*: https://www .bloomberg.com/news/articles/2020-01-24/goldman-rule -adds-to-death-knell-of-the-all-white-male-board.

295   *The firm has stated "aspirations" of*: *Washington Post*. "Analysis | Goldman Sachs Says It Wants Half of Its Entry-Level Recruits to Be Women." Accessed February 1, 2022. https://www.washingtonpost.com/business/2019/03/18/goldman-sachs-says-it-wants-half-its-entry-level-recruits-be-women.

296   *Multiple studies have shown that:* How Diversity, Equity, and Inclusion (DE&I) Matter. McKinsey. Accessed February 15, 2022. https://www.mckinsey.com/featured-insights/diversity-and-inclusion/diversity-wins-how-inclusion-matters.

296   *and "non homogenous teams are smarter . . ."*: Rock, David, and Heidi Grant. *Harvard Business Review*, "Why Diverse Teams Are Smarter." November 2016. https://hbr.org/2016/11/why-diverse-teams-are-smarter.

ACKNOWLEDGMENTS

There are so many to thank, and not enough of a word count to do it! Writing a book can be an isolating experience, and yet I had a wonderful group by my side.

To Robin Finn, who first showed me that I am a writer and have a story to tell. Thank you for convincing me to finish my book instead of enrolling in law school.

To my writing teacher, Jules Swales, who taught me how to be open and generous not only on the page but in life. Thank you for showing me how to be a better storyteller. You have been more than just a teacher, and I'm proud to call you my friend.

To JB Hollows and Ria Iliffe-Wood, I can't believe we still haven't met in real life, but our bond is so strong we don't need that. Here's to 2022 being the year of our books!

To my Book Bunny crew, Sandra Koenig and Jhanna Dawson, thank you for the encouragement and the laughs!

To Ivy Kaller, your fearless approach to the blank page has inspired me to take more risks as a writer.

To Gabi Wagner Mann and Linda Condrillo, you not only

provided valuable feedback but also have been such enthusiastic champions since day one.

To my friends: Mitchell Bakst, Jennifer Cantelmo, Barbara Geary, Danielle Holmes, Pina Hornyak, Lisa Karbiner, Karen McLaughlin, Maggie Morris, Laura Pavlosky, Trish Pavlosky, and Elizabeth Vinhal. You have supported me in so many ways, from encouraging me to keep on writing when I faltered, to reading early drafts, to reading them again, to giving excellent feedback, to strategizing marketing, to helping me select my author photos. I'm so grateful to each of you!

To my California friends: Sarah Redmond, the bestest friend whom I never met. Thanks for being the most enthusiastic cheerleader from across the country. To Allison McGuire, for the constant support when I wanted to give up.

To Marie Poliseno: meeting you at Goldman was a gift that keeps giving today. I'll gladly still pay the nickel to get advice from my dear Lucy anytime.

To my "Co Mom" EJ Pagani, you have not only been supportive with my writing, and every aspect of the book, but have been there to help with my kids. I'm grateful to be parenting with you!

To Stacey Harvestine, for your unextinguishable enthusiasm. Thank you for having my back, with everything.

To Courtney Fox, the best thing to come out of Bryn Mawr besides the diploma. I finally left, Courts! You were there when it all started and are still here today. Thank you!

To Wendy Behary, for being by my side through it all, and helping me become a better person because of it.

To Jesse Kornbluth, for your honest feedback and generosity in sharing your experiences and contacts. To Carol Fitzgerald and the Book Reporter team, thank you for demystifying the crazy world of publishing! To the DEY team: Rimjhim Dey and Andrew DeSio. Thank you for all the last-minute meetings, guiding me through the publishing process, and helping *Bully Market* have the greatest impact.

To Jenna Land Free, my friend, my Yoda. *Bully Market* is here because of you. Knowing you has been a gift! Thank you for seeing me and hearing me and challenging me. You've been there for all the moments, big and small, and always pick up my "phone a friend" calls! I'm forever grateful.

To my agent, Gail Ross. I could not have a stronger, more intelligent, and fierce woman by my side. Thank you for believing in me and for your tireless advocacy and support! You were right, we Jersey Girls have a certain something!

To the fantastic team at Simon & Schuster: Emily Simonson, Cat Boyd, Elizabeth Venere, and Kate Lapin. Thank you for your assistance and enthusiasm. To my editor, Stephanie Frerich. From the moment we met, I knew you understood everything. Thank you for taking a chance on me, believing in me, and challenging me. We make quite the dynamic duo, and I couldn't have asked for a better teammate in this process.

To the next generation of fierce Fiore women, my nieces Sydney, Lyndsey, and Casey. I hope this book inspires you to break down your own barriers.

To my dearest friend, Linda Benzi, my soul sister, who has been there for me from the start. From the day I met you in 1998 to last night on the phone. From drying my tears to lending me sewing kits, I couldn't have done this or be here without you!

To the other members of the original Fiore Five and my first teachers: Mom, Dad, Tony, and Janine. Thank you for loving me, supporting me, and advising me. To Grandma, you have been gone half my life, but I think about you each day. I pray that I've made you proud.

To my children: Abby, Beth, Luke, and Hannah. Thank you for your excitement, understanding, and patience as *Bully Market* has become a bigger part of our lives. I hope I've made you proud, and that this work helps improve the workplaces you will eventually find yourselves in.

To Dan: you are my everything, and this is all for you.

ABOUT THE AUTHOR

JAMIE FIORE HIGGINS worked as a managing director at Goldman Sachs. One of just 8 percent of Goldman employees to earn the managing director title, she was the highest-ranking woman in her department. Fiore Higgins managed top equity clients and $100 billion in stock while also running the trainee and internship programs and recruiting. Now she is a trained professional coach, working with teens and college graduates on leadership skills and with professionals as they navigate the workforce. She lives in New Jersey with her husband and four children.